PERCEPTION, OPPORTUNITY, AND PROFIT

PERCEPTION, OPPORTUNITY, AND PROFIT

Studies in the Theory of Entrepreneurship

Israel M. Kirzner

THE UNIVERSITY OF CHICAGO PRESS
Chicago and London

ISRAEL M. KIRZNER is professor of economics at New York University. He is the author of *The Economic Point of View, Market Theory and the Price System,* and *An Essay on Capital,* in addition to *Competition and Entrepreneurship,* which is published by the University of Chicago Press.

THE UNIVERSITY OF CHICAGO PRESS, CHICAGO 60637
THE UNIVERSITY OF CHICAGO PRESS, LTD., LONDON

Printed in the United States of America
83 82 81 80 79   5 4 3 2 1

Library of Congress Cataloging in Publication Data

Kirzner, Israel M
    Perception, opportunity, and profit.

    Includes bibliographical references and index.
    1. Entrepreneur.   2. Austrian school of economists.
I. Title.
HB98.K57   338.5'2'01   79-11765
ISBN 0-226-43773-6

B'EZRAS HASHEM

Contents

Preface

AUTHORS OF VOLUMES of collected papers often acknowledge serious doubts concerning the wisdom of having permitted their essays to be published in book form. And it must be admitted that the trepidation with which such volumes are sent to the publisher is often thoroughly justified. The present collection is offered not without uncomfortable awareness of these facts of life. Nonetheless, I yet dare to hope that the volume may be judged to have earned the right to appear, by virtue of the unity, the timeliness, and the importance of the theme shared by the papers it contains.

This theme—the role of entrepreneurship in market processes—might at first glance appear to concern merely one particular item in the theoretical apparatus of the economist. But the truth is that this theme points provocatively beyond itself toward nothing less than the need for a thorough revision of the very core of modern economic theory. That the time is ripe for such a revision appears clear from the unanticipated warmth of the reception the profession accorded my earlier book, *Competition and Entrepreneurship* (1973), to which the present volume is something of a sequel. That earlier book was written from a frankly "Austrian" perspective, one that had for thirty years been thoroughly out of fashion. Yet the argument of that work, appealing for a theory of price in which entrepreneurial market processes be accorded their rightful place, has found many unexpected sympathizers. During the past half-dozen years it has been enormously gratifying for me to witness, and a privilege for me to participate in, a remarkable resurgence of the Austrian tradition. The papers here presented have had their origin during these exciting years and represent an attempt to demonstrate further the profound significance of those entrepreneurial aspects of human action that are not captured in the standard models of economic decision making upon which so much of contemporary economics rests. One of the very real hazards of collected papers is repetition; the one discussion that indeed appears in many of these papers (and for which I beg the reader's indulgence) is precisely that emphasizing the difference between "Robbinsian" maximizing, economizing, decisions, and "Misesian" human action. While this discussion, being the heart of each of the papers in which it appears, has been unavoidably repeated throughout the book, the papers themselves apply it to an array of independent topics.

The opening chapter provides a review of certain leading ideas in the entrepreneurial approach and serves as a general introduction to the volume. Chapter 2 explores the source of our insights into the pattern of the entrepreneurial process. Chapter 3 and chapter 4 examine aspects of the history of economic thought for possible earlier recognition of the role of entrepreneurship. Chapter 5 relates the entrepreneurial idea, about which we have learned so much from Mises, to his views on capital and interest. Chapter 6 pursues further the implications of capital requirements for the scope for entrepreneurial activity. Chapter 7 relates the entrepreneurial role to the requirements of theories of economic development. Chapters 8, 9, and 10 contain perhaps the most important of the ideas on entrepreneurship the book contains. These chapters explore, more fully than I have done until now, the nature of economic error, entrepreneurial alertness, and their relation to pure entrepreneurial profit. The final section of the book (chaps. 11, 12, and 13) applies entrepreneurial insights to issues peripheral to economic theory itself: the ethics of private property, the meaning of economic justice, and the nature and consequences of economic freedom. In all these areas, it is shown, our insights into the entrepreneurial aspects of human action illuminate matters not fully understood by writers held captive by conventional economic paradigms.

The ideas presented in these papers have crystallized out of much thought and discussion carried on within the modern Austrian tradition—that line of economic reasoning going back to Böhm-Bawerk and, especially, to Menger and represented in our time by the lonely, courageous voices of Mises and Hayek. It will be a task for future historians and philosophers to explain why so sensitive and insightful a tradition came to be almost entirely submerged in the post–World War II decades and yet to enjoy its current remarkable, if modest, revival. If these papers can contribute to the furtherance of this revival, and thus to the much-needed revision of the core of contemporary economic theory to which this revival points, then the task of its preparation will have been well worthwhile.

It remains for me to express my warm thanks to many friends, both colleagues and students, whose advice and help have contributed to the publication of this book. It is not possible for me to list all those to whom I am indebted; while I apologize to those not mentioned here by name, I do assure them of my grateful appreciation. Among those whose help has been particularly valuable I recall my dear friend and colleague who has contributed so much to the resurgence of Austrian economics, Ludwig M. Lachmann; Gerald P. O'Driscoll, Jr., Mario J. Rizzo, Steven C. Littlechild, Louis M. Spadaro, Edwin G. Dolan, Laurence S. Moss, T. W. Schultz, J. Huston McCulloch, Karen Vaughn, Roger Garrison, Walter Block, and Walter E. Grinder, and all members of the Austrian Economic Seminar. To George H. Pearson I owe a great debt for his help and wise advice on so many matters. Leonard E. Read provided warm and deeply valued encouragement at a crucial stage in the work that led up to this volume. For generous financial assistance throughout the period of research for these papers, I am deeply grateful to Scaife Family Charitable Trusts. Additional assistance at an early stage was provided by the Earhart Foundation and by the Committee on Grants of the Glenmede Trust Company; the Institute for Humane Studies and the Liberty Fund generously helped underwrite and organize a number of "Austrian" conferences at which earlier versions of several of these papers were presented. Charles G.

Koch has for years been a staunch and stalwart source of support to the intellectual movement within which these papers have emerged. To all these I am thoroughly indebted and deeply appreciative for their encouragement and support. In respect to this book, even more than for my earlier works, I must record my singular debt to my wife for her patience, forbearance and encouragement, contributed during a particularly difficult time for our family.

Acknowledgments

NINE OF THE PAPERS in this volume have already appeared in earlier publications. Permission to republish these papers here is most gratefully acknowledged by the author and the publisher. Thanks are due, specifically, to the following:

1. The Institute for Humane Studies for permission to publish (a) "Equilibrium versus Market" (chapter 1 in this volume), which appeared in E. G. Dolan, ed., *The Foundations of Modern Austrian Economics*, 1976; (b) "Ludwig von Mises and the Theory of Capital and Interest" (chapter 5 in this volume), which appeared in L. S. Moss, ed., *The Economics of Ludwig von Mises*, 1976; (c) "Entrepreneurship and the Market Approach to Development" (chapter 7 in this volume), which appeared in *Toward Liberty: Essays in Honor of Mises*, 1971; (d) "Economics and Error" (chapter 8 in this volume), which appeared in L. Spadaro, ed., *New Directions in Austrian Economics*, 1978; (e) "Producer, Entrepreneur, and the Right to Property" (chapter 11 in this volume), which appeared in S. Blumenfeld, ed., *Property in a Humane Economy*, 1974.

2. *Atlantic Economic Journal* for permission to publish "The Entrepreneurial Role in Menger's System" (chapter 4 in this volume), which appeared in the September 1978 number of the journal.

3. Hillsdale College Press for permission to publish "Capital, Competition and Capitalism" (chapter 6 in this volume), which appeared in *Champions of Freedom: The Ludwig von Mises Lecture Series*, 1974.

4. *Eastern Economic Journal* for permission to publish "Entrepreneurship, Entitlement, and Economic Justice" (chapter

12 in this volume), which appeared in volume 4, number 1 (1978) of the journal.

5. *ORDO (Jahrbuch für die Ordnung von Wirtschaft und Gesellschaft)* and its publishers, Gustav Fischer Verlag, for permission to publish "Entrepreneurship, Choice, and Freedom" (chapter 13 in this volume), which appeared in volume 30, (1979) of the yearbook.

Part One

ENTREPRENEURSHIP AND DISEQUILIBRIUM

1

Equilibrium versus Market Process

A CHARACTERISTIC FEATURE of the Austrian approach to economic theory is its emphasis on the market as a *process*, rather than as a configuration of prices, qualities, and quantities that are consistent with each other in that they produce a market equilibrium situation.[1] This feature of Austrian economics is closely bound up with dissatisfaction with the general use made of the concept of perfect competition. It is interesting that economists of sharply differing persuasions within the Austrian tradition all display a characteristic disenchantment with the orthodox emphasis on both equilibrium and perfect competition. Thus Joseph A. Schumpeter's well-known position on these matters is remarkably close to that of Ludwig von Mises.[2] Oskar Morgenstern, in a notable paper on contemporary economic theory, expressed these same Austrian criticisms of modern economic theory.[3]

EQUILIBRIUM AND PROCESS

Ludwig M. Lachmann has indicated that his own unhappiness with the notion of equilibrium primarily concerns the usefulness of the Walrasian general-equilibrium construction rather than that of the simple Marshallian partial-equilibrium construction.[4] But it is precisely in the context of the simple short-run one-good market that I shall point out some of the shortcomings of the equilibrium approach.

In our classrooms we draw the Marshallian cross to depict

Presented at the Austrian Economic Conference held at South Royalton, Vermont, June 1974.

competitive supply and demand, then go on to explain how the market is cleared only at the price corresponding to the intersection of the curves. Often the explanation of market price determination proceeds no further—almost implying that the only possible price is the market-clearing price. Sometimes we address the question of how we can be confident that there is any tendency at all for the intersection price to be attained. The discussion is then usually carried on in terms of the Walrasian version of the equilibration process. Suppose, we say, the price happens to be above the intersection level. If so, the amount of the good people are prepared to supply is in the aggregate larger than the total amount people are prepared to buy. There will be unsold inventories, thereby depressing price. On the other hand, if price is below the intersection level, there will be excess demand, "forcing" price up. Thus, we explain, there will be a tendency for price to gravitate toward the equilibrium level at which quantity demanded equals quantity supplied.

Now this explanation has a certain rough-and-ready appeal. However, when price is described as being above or below equilibrium, it is understood that a single price prevails in the market. One uncomfortable question, then, is whether we may assume that a single price emerges before equilibrium is attained. Surely a single price can be postulated only as the result of the process of equilibration itself. At least to this extent, the Walrasian explanation of equilibrium price determination appears to beg the question.

Again, the Walrasian explanation usually assumes perfect competition, where all market participants are price takers. But with only price takers participating, it is not clear how unsold inventories or unmet demand effect price changes. If no one raises or lowers price bids, *how* do prices rise or fall?

The Marshallian explanation of the equilibrating process—not usually introduced into classroom discussion—is similar to the Walrasian but uses quantity rather than price as the principal decision variable.[5] Instead of drawing horizontal price lines on the demand-supply diagram to show excess supply or unmet demand, the Marshallian procedure uses vertical lines to mark off the demand prices and the supply prices for given quantities. With this procedure, the ordinate of a point on the demand curve indicates the maximum price at which a quantity (represented by the abscissa of the point) will be sold. If this price is greater than the corresponding supply price (the minimum price at which the same quantity will be offered for sale), larger quantities will be offered for sale. The reverse takes place when supply price exceeds demand price. In this way a tendency toward equilibrium is allegedly demonstrated to exist.

This procedure also assumes too much. It takes for granted that the market already knows when the demand price of the quantity now available exceeds the supply price. But disequilibrium occurs precisely because market participants do not know what the market-clearing price is. In disequilibrium "the" quantity is not generally known nor is the highest (lowest) price at which this quantity can be sold (coaxed from suppliers). Thus it is not clear how the fact that the quantity on the market is less than the equilibrium quantity assures the decisions of market participants to be so modified as to increase it.

Clearly, neither of these explanations for the attainment of equilibrium is satisfactory. From the Austrian perspective, which emphasizes the role of knowledge and expectations, these explanations take too much for granted. What is needed is a theory of the market process that takes explicit notice of the way systematic changes in the information and expectations upon which market participants act lead them in the direction of the postulated equilibrium solution. The Austrian point of view does, in fact, help us arrive at such a theory.

Robbinsian Allocation and Misesian Action

In developing a viable theory of market process it is helpful to call attention to the much-neglected role of *entrepreneurship*. The neglect of entrepreneurship in modern analysis is a direct consequence of the general preoccupation with final equilibrium positions. In order to understand the distinction between a process-conscious market theory, which makes reference to entrepreneurship, and an equilibrium market theory, which ignores entrepreneurship, it will help to compare the Misesian concept of human action with the Robbinsian concept of economizing, that is, allocative decision making.

It may be recalled that Lord Robbins defined economics as dealing with the allocative aspect of human affairs, that is, with the consequences of the circumstance that men economize by engaging in the allocation of limited resources among multiple competing ends.[6] Mises, on the other hand, emphasized the much broader notion of purposeful human action, embracing the deliberate efforts of men to improve their positions.[7] Both concepts, it should be noticed, are consistent with methodological individualism and embody the insight that market phenomena are generated by the interaction of individual decision makers.[8] But the two constructions do differ significantly.

Robbinsian economizing consists in using *known* available resources in the most efficient manner to achieve given purposes. It entails the implementation of the equimarginal principle, that is, the setting up of an allocative arrangement in which it is impossible to transfer a unit of resource from one use to another and receive a net benefit. For Robbins, economizing simply means shuffling around available resources in order to secure the most efficient utilization of known inputs in terms of a *given* hierarchy of ends. It is the interaction in the market of the allocative efforts of numerous economizing individuals that generates all the phenomena that modern economics seeks to explain.

The difficulty with a theory of the market couched in exclusively Robbinsian terms is that in disequilibrium many of the plans of Robbinsian economizers are bound to be unrealized. Disequilibrium is a situation in which not all plans can be carried out together; it reflects mistakes in the price information on which individual plans were made. Market experience by way of shortages and surplus reveals the incorrectness of the original price expectations. Now the Robbinsian framework suggests that the unsuccessful plans will be discarded or revised, but we are unable to say much more than this. The notion of a Robbinsian plan assumes that information is both given and known to the acting individuals. Lacking this information, market participants are blocked from Robbinsian activity altogether. Without some clue as to what *new* expectations will follow disappointments in the market, we are unable to postulate any sequence of decisions. All we can say is: if all the Robbinsian decisions dovetail, we have equilibrium; if they do not dovetail, we have disequilibrium. We lack justification within this framework for stating, for example, that unsold inventories will depress price; we may only say that with excessive price expectations Robbinsian decision makers will generate unsold inventories. As decision makers they do not raise or lower price; they are strictly price takers, allocating against a background of given prices. If all participants are price takers, how then can the market price rise or fall? By what process does this happen, if it happens at all?

In order for unsold inventories to depress price, market participants with unsold goods need to realize that the previously prevailing price was too high. Participants must modify their expectations concerning the eagerness of other participants to buy. But in order to make these assertions we must transcend the narrow confines of the Robbinsian framework. We need a concept of decision making wide enough to encompass the element of *entrepreneurship* to account for the way in which market participants *change* their plans. It is here that the Misesian notion of human action comes to our assistance.

Mises's concept of human action embodies an insight about man that is entirely lacking in a world of Robbinsian economizers. This insight recognizes that men are not only calculating agents but are also *alert to opportunities*. Robbinsian theory only applies after a person is confronted with opportunities; for it does not explain how that person learns about opportunities in the first place. Misesian theory of human action conceives of the individual as having his eyes and ears open to opportunities that are "just around the corner." He is alert, waiting, continually receptive to something that may turn up. And when the prevailing price does not clear the market, market participants realize they should revise their estimates of prices bid or asked in order to avoid repeated disappointment. This alertness is the entrepreneurial element in human action, a concept lacking in analysis carried out in exclusively Robbinsian terms. At the same time that it transforms allocative decision making into a realistic view of human action, entrepreneurship converts the theory of market equilibrium into a theory of market process.

THE ROLE OF ENTREPRENEURSHIP

There have, it is true, been other definitions of the entrepreneurial role. The principal views of the question have been those of Schumpeter, Frank H. Knight, and Mises. I have argued, however, that these alternative definitions upon analysis all have in common the element of alertness to opportunities.[9] Alertness should be carefully distinguished from the mere possession of knowledge. And it is the distinction between being alert and possessing knowledge that helps us understand how the entrepreneurial market process systematically detects and helps eliminate error.

A person who possesses knowledge is not by that criterion alone an entrepreneur. Even though an employer hires an expert for his knowledge, it is the employer rather than the employee who is the entrepreneur. The employer may not have all the information the hired expert possesses, yet the employer is better informed than anyone else—he knows where knowledge is to be obtained and how it can be usefully employed. The hired expert does not, apparently, see how his knowledge can be usefully employed, since he is not prepared to act as his own employer. The hired expert does not perceive the opportunity presented by the possession of his information. The employer does perceive it. Entrepreneurial knowledge is a rarefied, abstract type of knowledge—the knowledge of where to obtain information (or other resources) and how to deploy it.

This entrepreneurial alertness is crucial to the market process. Disequilibrium represents a situation of widespread market ignorance. This ignorance is responsible for the emergence of profitable opportunities. Entrepreneurial alertness exploits these opportunities when others pass them by. G. L. S. Shackle and Lachmann emphasized the unpredictability of human knowledge, and, indeed, we do not clearly understand how entrepreneurs get their flashes of superior foresight. We cannot explain how some men discover what is around the corner before others do. We may certainly explain—on entirely Robbinsian lines—how men explore for oil by carefully weighing alternative ways of spending a limited amount of search resources, but we cannot explain how a prescient entrepreneur realizes before others do that a search for oil may be rewarding. As an empirical matter, however, opportunities do tend to be perceived and exploited. And it is on this observed tendency that our belief in a determinate market process is founded.

ADVERTISING AS AN ASPECT
OF THE COMPETITIVE PROCESS

Characterization of the market process as one involving entrepreneurial discovery clarifies a number of ambiguities about the market and dispels several misunderstandings about how it functions. Advertising provides an excellent example on which to base our discussion.

Advertising, a pervasive feature of the market economy, is widely misunderstood and often condemned as wasteful, inefficient, inimical to competition, and generally destructive of consumer sovereignty. In recent years there has been somewhat of a rehabilitation of advertising in economic literature, along the lines of the economics of information. According to this view, advertising messages beamed at prospective consumers are quantities of needed knowledge, for which they are prepared to pay a price. The right quantity of information is produced and delivered by the advertising industry in response to consumer desires. For reasons having to do with cost economy, it is most efficient for this information to be produced by those for whom such production is easiest, namely, by the producers of the products about which information is needed. There is much of value in this approach to an understanding of the economics of advertising, but it does not explain everything. The economics of information approach tries to account for the phenomena of advertising entirely in terms of the demand for and supply of nonentrepreneurial knowledge, information that can be bought and sold and even packaged. But such an approach does not go beyond a world of Robbinsian maximizers and fails to comprehend the true role of advertising in the market process.

Let us consider the producer of the advertised product. In his entrepreneurial role, the producer anticipates the wishes of consumers and notes the availability of the resources needed for a product to satisfy consumer desires. This function might appear to be fulfilled when the producer produces the product and makes it available for purchase. In other words, it might seem that the entrepreneur's function is fulfilled when he transforms an opportunity to produce a potential product into an opportunity for the consumer to buy the finished product. Consumers themselves were not aware of the opportunities this production process represents; it is the superior alertness of the entrepreneur that has enabled him to fulfill his task. It is not sufficient, however, to make the product available; consumers must be aware of its availability. If the opportunity to buy is not perceived by the consumer, it is as if the opportunity to produce has not been perceived by the entrepreneur. It is not enough to grow food consumers do not know how to obtain; consumers must know that the food has in fact been grown! Providing consumers with information is not enough. It is essential that the opportunities available to the consumer attract his attention, whatever the degree of his alertness may be. Not only must the entrepreneur-producer marshal resources to cater to consumer desires, but also he must insure that the consumer does not miss what has been wrought. For this purpose advertising is clearly an indispensable instrument.

By viewing advertising as an entrepreneurial device, we are able to understand why Chamberlin's distinction between fabrication costs and selling costs is invalid.[10] Fabrication (or production) costs are supposedly incurred for producing a product, as distinguished from selling costs incurred to get buyers to buy the product. Selling costs allegedly shift the demand curve for the product, while the costs of fabrication (production) affect the supply curve only. The distinction has been criticized on the grounds that most selling costs turn out to be disguised fabrication costs of one type or another.[11] Our perspective permits us to view the issue from a more general framework, which embodies the insight that all fabrication costs are at once selling costs as well. If the producer had a guaranteed market in which he could sell all he wanted of his product at a certain price, then his fabrication costs might be only fabrication costs and include no sum for coaxing consumers to buy it. But there never is a guaranteed market. The producer's decisions about what product to produce and of what quality are invariably a reflection of what he believes he will be able to sell at a worthwhile price. It is invariably an entrepreneurial choice. The costs he incurs are those that, in his estimation, he must incur to sell what he produces at the anticipated price. Every improvement in the product is introduced to make it more attractive to consumers, and certainly the product itself is produced for precisely the same reasons. All costs are, in the last analysis, selling costs.

PROFITS AND THE COMPETITIVE PROCESS

The Austrian concept of the entrepreneurial role emphasizes profit as being the prime objective of the market process. As such, it has important implications for the analysis of entrepreneurship in nonmarket contexts (such as within firms or under socialism or in bureaucracies in general). I have already remarked that we do not know precisely how entrepreneurs experience superior foresight, but we do know, at least in a general way, that entrepreneurial alertness is stimulated by the lure of profits. Alertness to an opportunity rests on the attractiveness of that opportunity and on its ability to be grasped once it has been perceived. This incentive is different from the incentives present in a Robbinsian world. In the nonentrepreneurial context, the incentive is constituted by the satisfactions obtainable at the expense of the relevant sacrifices. Robbinsian incentives are communicated to others by simply arranging that the satisfactions offered to them are more significant (from their point of view) than the sacrifices demanded from them. Incentive is thereby provided by the comparison of known alternatives. In the entrepreneurial context, however, the incentive to be alert to a future opportunity is quite different from the incentive to trade off already known opportunities; in fact it has nothing to do with the comparison of alternatives. No prior choice is involved in perceiving an opportunity waiting to be noticed. The incentive is to try to get something for nothing, if only one can see what it is that can be done.

Robbinsian incentives can be offered in nonmarket contexts. The bureaucrat, employer, or official offers a bonus for greater effort. For entrepreneurial incentives to operate, on the other hand, it is necessary for those who perceive opportunities to gain from noticing them. An outstanding feature of the market system is that it provides these kinds of incentives. Only by analysis of the market process does this very important entrepreneurial aspect of the market economy come into view. The real economic problems in any society arise from the phenomenon of unperceived opportunities. The manner in which a market society grapples with this phenomenon cannot be understood within an exclusively equilibrium theory of the market. The Austrian approach to the theory of the market therefore holds considerable promise. Much work still needs to be done. It would be good to know more about the institutional settings that are most conducive to opportunity discovery. It would be good to apply basic Austrian theory to the theory of speculation and of the formation of expectations with regard to future prices. All this would enrich our understanding of the economics of bureaucracy and of socialism. It can be convincingly argued that Mises's famous proposition concerning economic calculation under socialism flows naturally from his "Austrianism." Here, too, there is room for further elucidation. In all this agenda, the Austrian emphasis on process analysis should stand up very well.

2
Hayek, Knowledge,
and Market Processes

THE RECENT WORK of a number of outstanding economic theorists reveals a most welcome, if muted, rediscovery of an aspect of Hayek's work that has for some time been thoroughly—and most unfortunately—neglected.[1] Economists have, it seems, found their way back to that series of remarkable papers written in the thirties and forties in which Hayek addressed himself decisively to the role of *knowledge* in economic theory. In these papers, the analysis of this role was developed with a clarity and power that ought well to have guided the development of subsequent economic thought along lines both fruitful and exciting. The failure of the profession, during the fifties and sixties, to follow Hayek's profoundly insightful guideposts must be counted one of the most disappointing features of postwar economic thought. The rediscovery, in the seventies, of these guideposts raises one's hopes that the lost momentum can perhaps at last be resumed.

For Hayek's own work, both in economics and in the broader range of social thought, his explorations into the role of knowledge have of course been both central and seminal. No examination, such as this paper seeks to offer, of any one aspect of Hayek's ideas on knowledge, dare lose sight of the overarching unity these ideas, in their entirety, confer on virtually all of his far-flung and many-faceted contributions. For this and for other reasons, therefore, it seems convenient and useful to present, at the very outset of our discussion, a brief catalog of the more fundamental Hayekian ideas concerning knowledge.

Presented at a session of the meetings of the Allied Social Science Associations, held at Dallas, Texas, December 1975.

Thereafter we will be able to identify more usefully the particular strand of thought, running through Hayek's views on the economic role of knowledge, to which we wish to direct critical attention.

THE ROLE OF KNOWLEDGE: SOME HAYEKIAN INSIGHTS

1. The notion of the market equilibrium, Hayek explained, depends crucially on the correctness of the expectations members of society hold concerning each other's actions. For equilibrium, the different plans the members of society have made for action must be mutually compatible. For this to occur, every person's plan must be "based on the expectation of just those actions of other people which those other people intend to perform," and "all these plans are based on the expectation of the same set of external facts, so that under certain conditions nobody will have any reason to change his plans. Correct foresight is then not, as it has sometimes been understood, a precondition which must exist in order that equilibrium may be arrived at. It is rather the defining characteristic of a state of equilibrium."[2] "The statement that, if people know everything, they are in equilibrium, is true simply because that is how we define equilibrium."[3]

2. The process whereby the market is understood to move from disequilibrium toward equilibrium is, it follows, to be similarly perceived in terms of knowledge. The assertion that a tendency toward equilibrium exists "can hardly mean anything but that, under certain conditions, the knowledge and intentions of the different members of society are supposed to come more and more into agreement or . . . that the expectations of the people and particularly of the entrepreneurs will become more and more correct."[4]

3. The economic problem facing society is one that rests on the fragmentation of knowledge. Thus this problem is *not* how to allocate given resources "if 'given' is taken to mean given to a single mind."[5] The economic problem rests on the fact "that the knowledge of the circumstances of which we must make use never exists in concentrated or integrated form but solely as the dispersed bits of incomplete and frequently contradictory knowledge which all the separate individuals possess."[6]

The problem is "how to secure the best use of resources known to any of the members of society, for ends whose relative importance only these individuals know." It is a problem of "the utilization of knowledge which is not given to anyone in its totality."[7]

4. The great debate surrounding the relative merits for the economic organization of society, of the market system, and of the centrally planned system, it follows, must perforce come to grips with the problems created by this social fragmentation of knowledge. "Which of these systems is likely to be more efficient depends mainly on the question under which of them we can expect that fuller use will be made of the existing knowledge. This, in turn, depends on whether we are more likely to succeed in putting at the disposal of a single central authority all the knowledge which ought to be used but which is initially dispersed among many different individuals, or in conveying to the individuals such additional knowledge as they need in order to enable them to dovetail their plans with those of others."[8] And it is therefore Hayek's perception of the market equilibrating process as effectively marshaling relevant information which led him to perceive the market price system as something of a "marvel"[9]—whose counterpart he was unable to discover in the socialized economy.

5. Hayek's insights as an economist into "the fact that no human mind can comprehend all the knowledge which guides the actions of society" led him more generally to an appreciation of "the impersonal processes of society in which more knowledge is utilized than any one individual or organized group of human beings can possess" and in particular toward his own "comprehensive restatement of the basic principles of a philosophy of freedom."[10] It is the essence of civilization that it "enables us constantly to profit from knowledge which we individually do not possess and . . . each individual's use of his particular knowledge may serve to assist others unknown to him in achieving their ends."[11] And indeed the "case for individual freedom rests chiefly on the recognition of the inevitable ignorance of all of us concerning a great many of the factors on which the achievement of our ends and welfare depends. . . . Liberty is essential in order to leave room for the unforeseeable and unpre-

dictable; we want it because we have learned to expect from it the opportunity of realizing many of our aims. It is because every individual knows so little and, in particular, because we rarely know which of us knows best that we trust the independent and competitive efforts of many to induce the emergence of what we shall want when we see it."[12]

Listing Hayekian ideas concerning the role of knowledge and of its fragmentation hardly does justice to the degree to which they support his entire system of thought; nonetheless this listing may serve to suggest the broader context within which Hayek's views on the market process are to be understood. It is with the role played in this process by the process of learning—as noted in the second of the listed propositions—that this chapter is specifically concerned. Some general remarks on the nature and significance of market process analysis may help us appreciate Hayek's contribution in this regard.

THE SIGNIFICANCE OF THE ANALYSIS
OF MARKET PROCESSES

It must remain something of a riddle for historians of modern economic thought that the mainstream of theoretical literature has, until perhaps the past half dozen years, virtually ignored the need to explain and to understand the *processes* occurring in the market. For decades theorists were, with extremely few exceptions, content to preoccupy themselves with the conditions for market equilibrium, without giving serious thought to what is to be understood as going on when these conditions do not prevail. For decades economists blithely assumed, in effect, that equilibrium situations are instantaneously attained.[13] As Patinkin has exhaustively documented, Walras's partial recognition of the problem of how the market might proceed toward equilibrium, and his imaginative, if unsatisfying, attempt to grapple with it through a theory of *tâtonnement*, were for three quarters of a century largely neglected by economic theorists.[14] As is well known, Hicks's *Value and Capital* treatment of the stability of equilibrium flatly assumed that adjustment processes are timeless.[15] And even the introduction into economic theory by Samuelson and others during the forties of a "truly dynamic" analysis of stability[16] left, as we shall see, the nature of the processes essentially unexplained and the full significance of their analysis only incompletely perceived.[17]

The truth is that the significance of the issue extends far beyond that usually associated with the question of the stability of general equilibrium—or for that matter partial equilibrium—states. Questions of stability turn on the possibility of demonstrating convergence toward the equilibrium state, whatever the context. But a theory of process must establish the determinateness of the course of market events, quite apart from the issue of whether this course of events does or does not tend toward an equilibrium state. Hahn has recently emphasized that the equilibrium concept by itself implies no tendency toward equilibrium. The equilibrium concept implies little more, Hahn writes, than the weak claim "that no plausible sequence of economic states will terminate, if it does so at all, in a state which is not in equilibrium."[18] The significant question, therefore, is whether we can conclude that the market achieves any *systematic* "sequence of economic states" at all.[19] It was this question that was ignored for so long.

The only voices raised in protest, during the decades of exclusive preoccupation with equilibrium, seem to have been those of the "Austrians," Mises and Hayek. Mises vigorously denounced the abuse of the (concededly highly useful) equilibrium concept by theorists who ignored the essentially process character of markets. Again and again he showed how the belief held by theorists that equilibrium states are actually attained led them to misunderstand grossly what markets in fact achieve.[20] For Mises, the essence of a theory of markets must be to explain the forces that generate *changes* in prices and quantities; the equilibrium concept is useful precisely in its offering, in its utterly hypothetical freedom from change, a contrast to the world of incessant change. Hayek's quite independent search for an understanding of market processes is the subject of this chapter. It was in 1936 that Hayek observed that while usual presentations of equilibrium analysis make it appear that the questions of how the equilibrium comes about have been solved, in fact these presentations do no more than assume what needs to be shown.[21] Again, in the course of his pioneering critique of the way theorists had come to use the notion of competition,

Hayek unerringly identified the difficulty as arising from the assumption that equilibrium already exists, that "the data for the different individuals are fully adjusted to each other, while the problem which requires explanation is the nature of the process by which the data are thus adjusted."[22]

It is of course true that in discussing competitive markets economists have always implied *some* kind of process. For many decades, this implied process was uncritically expressed as the "law of supply and demand." This was generally understood in terms of the explanation for the course of market price for a given single good; this simple context will suffice for most of our purpose.

When theorists sought to isolate more specifically the dynamics of this competitive process of supply and demand for the single good, they did so generally in what has come to be called the "Walrasian" version of simple stability analysis.[23] Freshman undergraduates have, in this version, been taught for decades that the intersection of the market supply curve and market demand curve yields the price and output toward which the market tends. Should price be below this equilibrium level, students have been told, the excess demand of competing unsatisfied buyers will force price up; if price is above equilibrium excess supply will bring about falling prices. The early discussions of the stability of equilibrium formalized this mechanism as follows:[24]

$$\frac{dp}{dt} = H(q_D - q_S),$$

where

$$H(0) = 0, \quad \text{and} \quad H' > 0.$$

The time rate of price change is declared to be a function of the excess demand generated by the going price. Price moves up so long as there is excess demand; it moves down with excess supply (i.e., negative excess demand); at zero excess demand price does not change. The Walrasian stability conditions (which associate positive excess demand with below-equilibrium prices) are then sufficient to guarantee convergence to equilibrium, provided the demand and supply curves are not themselves shifted by trading at disequilibrium prices. It will be helpful, in pointing out the problems inherent in this kind of process analysis, to spell out some of the well-known elements of the view of the market process this approach implies.

(1) This approach rules out the possibility of more than one price, even in disequilibrium. Each date is associated with one and only one price. (2) At each price, each market participant believes it is possible for him to buy or sell any amount he chooses without the price being changed as a result of his actions. This implication of perfect competition the approach assumes means that each participant reacts passively to price: He is a "price taker." (3) Price changes come about not through the deliberate decisions of any market participants, since everyone is a price taker, but in some unexplained way, such as through the agency of an imagined Walrasian auctioneer. This enumeration points directly to the difficulties that render this approach so thoroughly unsatisfactory. It is a welcome feature of the recent literature on market process that it has clearly recognized these difficulties.

Most disturbing among these difficulties has been the complete absence of explanation of how, lacking the mysterious auctioneer, prices in fact change, in a world in which no participant changes prices.[25] The difficulty, or one very close to it, has also been articulated by noticing that the approach under discussion fails to deduce price changes "as the maximizing response of economic units to changing data."[26] In other words, the theory of market process the approach provides us is not a "choice-theoretic" one and is thus a major departure from the microeconomic method usually associated with price theory. Another widely noted difficulty concerns the logical contradiction entailed in the assumption of perfect competition under disequilibrium conditions. In order to analyze the dynamics of price adjustment, it is "necessary to discard the perfectly competitive paradigm of the producer as price-taker."[27] One cannot, without logical strain, postulate market participants who at all times see themselves as price takers, able to buy and sell all they choose at going prices, while simultaneously discussing the excess demand or supply being continually generated by these prices until equilibrium has been reached. A further difficulty infrequently noticed in the recent literature is that the stability-theoretic approach we have been examining leaves room for only one price at each point in time, even during disequilibrium.[28] Since the disequilibrium markets we know in the real world are not quite as obligingly simple as this,[29] the approach fails to provide an explanation for an important aspect of the market process, namely, how during the course of the process, many prices converge, as entailed by Jevons's Law of Indifference, toward a single price. Moreover, the equilibrating process of price change that the approach postulates, being based on the single-price assumption, begs the question of how this process is to be understood in the context of that *other* converging process we must assume to be simultaneously at work, during which many prices are only gradually being shaken down toward uniformity.

It is against this background of long-time unconcern by economic theorists with the need for an adequate theory of market process that we turn now to consider Hayek's attempt, forty years ago, to throw light on the character of this process.

HAYEK, KNOWLEDGE, AND MARKET PROCESSES

The kernel of Hayek's contribution to an understanding of market processes consisted in his interpreting the assertion that a tendency exists toward equilibrium as meaning "that, under certain conditions, the knowledge and intentions of the different members of society are supposed to come more and more into agreement or . . . that the expectations of the people and particularly of the entrepreneurs will become more and more correct."[30] Equilibrium was defined, for Hayek, as the state of affairs characterized by universally correct anticipation of the actions of other people. A tendency toward equilibrium must therefore mean more than a particular converging pattern of price and quantity adjustments over time; it must mean a systematic process through which market participants replace sets of plans based on incorrect awareness of each other's plans by plans in which everyone more accurately anticipates what everyone else intends to do. The market process must, if it is to be in the direction toward equilibrium, be a process of mutual discovery.

Hayek pursued this theme further in a well-known paper on the role of competition in the market process. In that paper, Hayek sharply criticized dominant notions of competition. The truth is, Hayek argued, that "competition is by its nature a dynamic process whose essential characteristics are assumed away by the assumptions underlying static analysis."[31] The modern theory of competitive equilibrium "deals almost exclusively with a state . . . in which it is assumed that the data for the different individuals are fully adjusted to each other, while the problem which requires explanation is the nature of the process by which the data are thus adjusted."[32] And Hayek is emphatic in understanding this process as consisting in the discovery and dissemination of relevant information, that information which the theory of competitive equilibrium unhelpfully assumes to be already known. Knowledge of the lowest costs of production can be discovered only through the process of competition. The wishes and desires of consumers cannot properly be regarded as given facts to producers, "but ought rather to be regarded as problems to be solved by the process of competition." The knowledge consumers are supposed to possess cannot be assumed before the process of competition starts; "the whole organization of the market serves mainly the need of spreading the information on which buyers act."[33]

What happens in disequilibrium is, of course, different from what happens in equilibrium. During equilibrium, prices and quantities do not change; in disequilibrium they do. For Hayek the difference is far deeper. During equilibrium men act on the basis of correct knowledge; in disequilibrium they are, on the one hand, acting on the basis of partial ignorance and, on the other hand, engaged in a process of learning.

Hayek's insight into the nature of the market process enables us to avoid the difficulties that inhere in the simple Walrasian version of stability analysis. There need be no mystery about how prices change during equilibrium. Prices change because individual market participants have discovered they can do better for themselves by offering or asking prices dif-

ferent from those hitherto prevailing. A buyer who failed to find a
seller willing to sell to him at yesterday's prices has learned the
need to offer a higher price. A buyer who found that at yesterday's prices he was inundated with the offers of would-be sellers scrambling for his patronage realizes that he can obtain
what he seeks at a lower price. A buyer who purchased yesterday at a given price discovers that others were able to buy for
lower prices; he has learned that more than one price has been
prevailing, and he will adjust his bids accordingly. And so on.[34]
Similarly, once the analysis of the competitive process is
couched in terms of information discovery, the other difficulties cited in the preceding section can immediately be seen as
no longer relevant. All this attests to the power and fertility of
Hayek's insight. It was from this powerful insight that Hayek
proceeded to make a series of observations concerning
economic theory, which it is my purpose to examine critically.

PROCESS ANALYSIS, PURE LOGIC, AND EMPIRICAL SCIENCE

From the distinction that he drew between what is happening
during equilibrium and what is happening during the course of
the market process, Hayek proceeded to assert the existence
of a sharp difference between the epistemological character of
equilibrium analysis and that of process analysis. The analysis
of equilibrium is identical with the Pure Logic of Choice; it
consists essentially of tautologies that are necessarily true because they are merely transformations of the assumptions from
which we start. These tautologies by themselves tell us nothing
about the real world; they merely elaborate the conditions logically required for the equilibrium state to exist. What enables
us to pass from these exercises in pure logic to statements
about causation in the real world is only our analysis of the
tendency of market processes to lead toward equilibrium. In
fact, the only justification for our concern with the fictitious
state of equilibrium "is the supposed existence of a tendency
toward equilibrium. *It is only by this assertion that such a
tendency exists that economics ceases to be an exercise in pure
logic and becomes an empirical science.*"[35] And it is Hayek's
understanding of the market process as one of learning infor-

mation that enables him to argue that the assertion of a tendency toward equilibrium "is clearly an empirical proposition, that is, an assertion about what happens in the real world which ought, at least in principle, to be capable of verification."[36] The tautologies of equilibrium analysis "can be turned into propositions which tell us anything about causation in the real world only in so far as we are able to fill those formal propositions with definite statements about how knowledge is acquired and communicated."[37] For Hayek, the asserted tendency toward equilibrium depends upon assumptions "about the actual acquisition of knowledge" in the course of the market process. "The significant point . . . is that it is these apparently subsidiary hypotheses or assumptions that people do learn from experience, and about how they acquire knowledge, which constitute the empirical content of our propositions about what happens in the real world."[38] The assumptions necessary for these empirical propositions differ sharply in generality, Hayek argues, from those upon which rests the Pure Logic of Choice. The latter assumptions are "axioms which define . . . the field within which we are able to understand . . . the processes of thought of other people. . . . They refer to a type of human action (what we commonly call 'rational,' or even merely 'conscious,' as distinguished from 'instinctive' action) rather than to the particular conditions under which this action is taken. But the assumptions . . . which we have to introduce when we want to explain the social processes, concern the relation of the thought of an individual to the outside world, the question to what extent and how his knowledge corresponds to external facts."[39]

We may summarize Hayek's position as consisting in the following propositions: (1) Understanding of the separate plans individuals make, each on the basis of his own knowledge and anticipations, may be sought at a level that involves nothing more than the pure logic of choice. (2) In disequilibrium many individuals will not be able to carry out, or will come to regret their execution of, their plans, because the realized plans of others differ from those which had been anticipated. (3) Our understanding of the configuration of plans that is consistent with equilibrium (i.e., the global set of compatible plans, each of which reflects correct anticipation of the plans of others), is again an exercise in the pure logic of choice. (4) An assertion that the attempted execution of a set of incompatible plans will set in motion a systematic series of plan changes tending toward equilibrium *cannot* be made on purely logical grounds. Such an assertion must depend on a postulated propensity on the part of market participants to learn the correct lessons from their experiences. Such a propensity can be claimed to exist only as a matter of fact; it cannot be derived simply from the logic of conscious human action. (5) The epistemological character of economic theory is thus not uniform. That portion of economic theory that concerns itself with the conditions required for equilibrium is known a priori; it is an extension of the pure logic of choice, possessing no empirical content whatever. That portion of economic theory that attempts to explain the nature of equilibrating market forces possesses the character of an empirical science, since its propositions depend crucially on postulated factual relationships held to govern the way men learn relevant information. Several interrelated observations may be immediately made concerning Hayek's view of the epistemological character of economic theory.

First of all, we note what at least superficially appears to be an important disagreement between Hayek and Mises concerning the character of economics. Hayek is often coupled with Mises as espousing the view of economics as a completely a prioristic body of thought.[40] We have seen, on the contrary, that Hayek took great pains to emphasize his perception of economic science as being, with the exception of equilibrium analysis, empirical science.

We note further, perhaps with an implication casting doubt on the conclusiveness of our preceding observation, that the manner in which Hayek's empirical economic science links the purely logical propositions of economics with the phenomena of the real world is rather different from other perspectives on the same task. Ordinarily, attempts to use pure economic logic in the formulation of empirical statements seeking to describe the real world involve the translation of the formal categories of economic theory into applied form expressing the facts of particular situations. Empirical assertions are derived from statements concerning preferences and choices that are no longer pure, but which rather reflect observed (or postulated) specific patterns of tastes, or technological possibilities.[41] Despite Hayek's remarks about filling formal propositions with definite content concerning how knowledge is acquired, the truth is that propositions about individual plans that continue to presume no specific preference structures and no specific production possibilities must continue to be empty propositions, despite any postulated pattern of learning information. Indeed the empirical element introduced by Hayek not only fails to fill with factual content the empty formal propositions that make up the logic of choice, it leaves these propositions themselves exactly as empty as it finds them. The pure logic of choice explains the decisions a man makes in terms of his preferences and the price and technological constraints he perceives to be relevant to him. These explanations, being purely logical in character, are entirely general. They refer with equal validity to any specific set of preferences and to any sets of perceived prices and technologies. Hayek's empirical element does not, even in principle, provide concrete content to the empty set of perceived prices. It merely assures us that, *were* we to know specifically the various sets of prices individual agents perceived at any one date, we could, on the basis of our factual knowledge of learning processes, know what prices they would expect on future dates. Hayek's empirical element does not, therefore, introduce any specificity into our logical propositions concerning the choices at any given date. It merely provides an abstract pattern within which to *link* the purely formal propositions relevant to choices at one date to the equally purely formal propositions relevant to choices at later dates.

This observation may be presented somewhat differently. Suppose we knew the concrete structure of an individual's preferences at a given date, and we also knew with completeness the precise way that individual's perception of his constraints can be modified by experience. We would not yet, nonetheless, be able to predict his specific decisions at that date until we have, in addition, been provided with factual information concerning his perception of his constraints at that date or at least concerning the perception he had of his con-

straints at an earlier date, together with a history of his subsequent relevant experience. Hayek's empirical element does
not refer to this required additional information. Without it,
Hayek's empirical hypotheses concerning the way people learn
from experience leave the set of constraints perceived by an
individual decision maker as empty as before. What Hayek's
empirical element has introduced, therefore, is not a device for
translating, even in principle, any of the propositions of the
logic of choice into empirical statements; rather, it is a device
to explain, on empirical grounds, the way the set of choices
made at one date can be seen, ceteris paribus, to follow from
the set made at earlier dates.

I do not underestimate the significance of this accomplish-
ment; on the contrary, my principal purpose is to draw attention to the profound importance of these neglected Hayekian
insights into the learning process through which the market
achieves its tendency toward equilibrium. My observations
concerning the special and highly limited sense in which
Hayek's empirical element affects the purely logical character
of propositions in economic theory, were made to provide a
background for a critical examination of Hayek's own understanding of the epistemological implications of his contribution. To this examination we now turn.

ALLOCATIVE DECISION MAKING, HUMAN ACTION, AND MARKET PROCESS

Hayek has offered us a view of the market process that sees it
as made up of a succession of two diverse elements, logical
inevitability and empirical accident. At any given date, market
participants make their buying, production, and selling decisions as determined by their preferences and perceived
constraints, with these constraints reflecting the anticipated
decisions of others. We understand these allocative decisions in
terms of our immediate a priori access to the logic of choice.
Owing to the ignorance of market participants, these decisions
of a given date will not mesh. As a result, participants will
experience market phenomena such as surpluses or shortages
that will teach them more accurate information concerning the
preferences and decisions of others. The specific lessons market experience will impart are *not* understandable through the

logic of choice; they are to be understood by the economist only as empirical regularities—if regularities indeed prevail at all—that happen to be the way they are. Apart from the accident of such empirical regularities, there is nothing in the logic governing the set of choices made by market participants at one date to account for the set of choices they make at future dates. From a strictly logical perspective, the sets of allocative decisions made at different dates are unrelated. They are linked only by the accidents of the learning process. The Hayekian perception of the dynamics of the market process is like a somewhat peculiar motion film made up of a succession of static pictures. Each separate picture itself is entirely understandable in terms of the logic of choice; the changes between each picture and its successor can be explained only in terms of facts ungoverned by a priori considerations of any kind. It is with this dichotomous view of the market process that I will take issue. My position will rely a good deal on the distinction, drawn elsewhere at greater length,[42] between Robbinsian economizing and Misesian human action.

Economizing man engages in allocative decision making within a strictly given framework of ends and means. He "is endowed with the propensity to mold given means to suit given ends. The very concept presupposes some given image of ends and means. . . . Economizing behavior—or, more accurately, its analysis—necessarily skips the task of identifying ends and means. The economizing notion by definition presupposes that this task (and its analysis) has been completed elsewhere."[43] It follows that an analysis confined to allocative, economizing explanations must indeed fail to account for any continuity in a sequence of decisions, since each decision is comprehended purely in terms of its own relevant end-means framework. "With purely allocative explanations, no earlier decision can be used to explain later decisions on the basis of learning; if the pattern of ends-means held relevant by the individual at the later decision differs from that held relevant earlier, then there is, within the 'economizing framework,' nothing but a discontinuity. Such exogenous change has simply wiped out one decision-making situation and replaced it with a different one."[44]

What Hayek contributed was an insight into how continuity

can be accounted for in such a sequence of decisions. But, apparently working implicitly within an economizing framework, Hayek was able to introduce such continuity only from outside that allocative framework, from the empirical accidents of the learning process. The pure logic of economic analysis, seen as extending no further than the limits of the economizing framework, could, Hayek argued, be of no assistance in providing an understanding of continuity; the market process must call, for its analysis, on additional, empirical regularities. I will argue that insight into the nature of Misesian human action enables us to see matters somewhat differently.

> Human action, in the sense developed by Mises, involves courses of action taken by the human being "to remove uneasiness" and to make himself "better off." Being broader than the notion of economizing, the concept of human action does not restrict analysis of the decision to the allocation problem posed by the juxtaposition of scarce means and multiple ends. The decision, in the framework of the human action approach, is not arrived at merely by mechanical computation of the solution to the maximization problem implicit in the configuration of the given ends and means. It reflects not merely the manipulation of given means to correspond faithfully with the hierarchy of given ends, but also *the very perception of the ends-means framework* within which allocation and economizing is to take place...Mises' *homo agens*...is endowed not only with the propensity to pursue goals efficiently, once ends and means are clearly identified, but also with the drive and alertness needed to identify which ends to strive for and which means are available.[45]

This drive and alertness can be identified as the entrepreneurial element in human decision making. "In any real and living economy every actor is always an entrepreneur."[46]

For a world of Robbinsian economizers, the market process must indeed seem a discrete sequence of separate states linked, at best, accidentally by the extraeconomic facts of the learning process. But as soon as "we broaden our theoretical vision of the individual decision-maker from a 'mechanical'

Robbinsian economizer to Mises' *homo agens*, with the universally human entrepreneurial elements of alertness in his makeup, we can cope with the task of explaining the changes which market forces systematically generate"[47] without necessarily transcending the scope of the analysis of decision making. It will be helpful, in perceiving this, to emphasize the difference between learning facts, and discovering opportunities.

It is, of course, perfectly true that insight into the entrepreneurial element in human action does not by itself assure us that people necessarily learn the correct facts of their situations from their market experiences. While the recognition of universal human alertness provides grounds for presuming learning, it does not, it may seem, guarantee discovery of the truth. Can we be sure that, confronted with a surplus, would-be sellers will realize that they must accept lower prices in the future? Can we be sure that, when more than one price prevails for the same item, entrepreneurs will indeed learn of this and move toward the elimination of the price differential? The very existence of error suggests that men have not learned the correct lessons from experience or, at any rate, have not learned them sufficiently well.

But, having recognized that, despite their alertness to new information, people err, we must nonetheless point out that the alertness we have discovered in human action does carry us further than we may have realized. The entrepreneurial alertness with which the individual is endowed does not refer to a passive vulnerability to the impressions impinging on his consciousness during experience in the manner of a piece of film exposed to the light; it refers to the human propensity to sniff out opportunities lurking around the corner. What the notion of human action gives us is the recognition that people possess a propensity to discover what is useful to them. We have no assurance that a man walking down the street will, after his walk, have absorbed knowledge of all the facts to which he has been exposed; we do, in talking of human action, assume at least a tendency for man to notice those that constitute possible opportunities for gainful action on his part.

It has been the contribution of economic theory to show how

markets in disequilibrium offer market participants *opportunities for gain*. The absence of uniform price offers the possibility of pure arbitrage profit; shortages offer alert sellers the opportunity to obtain higher prices than hitherto prevailed, and so on. Our insight that opportunities do tend to be discovered assures us that a process is set in motion by disequilibrium conditions as these opportunities are gradually noticed and exploited. The process by which facts are hammered into human consciousness is not wholly ungoverned by the logic of human action; it fits naturally into the tendency for alert acting human beings to notice what is likely to be of service to them.

This perspective on the learning process that, as Hayek has taught us, constitutes the inner core of the market tendency toward equilibrium provides us, then, with a somewhat different view of its character from that which Hayek himself emphasized so strongly. Our identification of decision making with alert, entrepreneurial human action has provided us with *an explanation for the market process that does not, in principle, depend for its general pattern, upon any extraeconomic factual considerations whatsoever*. The market process emerges as the necessary implication of the circumstances that people act, and that in their actions they err, discover their errors, and tend to revise their actions in a direction likely to be less erroneous than before.

Note that we have not claimed a priori validity for our insight concerning man's propensity to discover opportunities. It is enough, for our purpose, to recognize this propensity as inseparable from our insight that human beings act purposefully. Recognizing that whatever learning occurs during the market process is likely to be a manifestation of man's propensity to discover opportunities, enables us, in fact, to use Hayek's own criteria to question the validity of his dichotomy. For Hayek the regularities governing the way people learn from experience are of a nature "in many respects rather different from the more general assumptions from which the Pure Logic of Choice starts."[48] The first way the latter, more general assumptions are not similar to those relevant to the learning process is that these "more general assumptions" are "common to all human thought. They may be regarded as axioms which define or delimit the field within which we are able to understand or mentally to reconstruct the processes of thought of other people."[49] Our insight concerning the alertness of human beings to information about opportunities renders this alertness fully as integral an aspect of human thought and action as are the purportedly more general assumptions to which Hayek refers.

All this, inconsistent though it may be with Hayek's sharply dichotomous view concerning the epistemological character of the market process, does not, one should observe, deny the relevance of such empirical regularities as may be discovered in the learning process. It is one thing to postulate an equilibrating tendency on the basis of the general character of human action; it is quite another to account for the concrete pattern of events in which this tendency happens to manifest itself. "Economists," Mises remarked, "must never disregard in their reasoning the fact that the innate and acquired inequality of men differentiates their adjustment to the conditions of their environment."[50] It is indeed empirical accidents, such as the differences in the entrepreneurial alertness of different men, that will govern the specific course of market events. But this circumstance does not remove the entrepreneurial, profit-seeking, driving force of the market, which propels this course of events, from the realm of those general assumptions whose relevance Hayek himself was prepared to recognize only in equilibrium analysis. The general logic employed in equilibrium analysis cannot, of course, by itself account for *specific* equilibrium values of prices and outputs; for this, we need additional empirical information. But it is nonetheless the general logic of choice that governs these specific equilibrium values. Similarly, without knowledge of the empirical patterns that characterize the learning processes of specific men, we cannot know the specific course of market events. But our insight into the general propensity of people to be alert to opportunities nonetheless provides us with an understanding of the overall tendencies governing these sequences of market events.

Our recognition of human purposefulness permits us to see the actions of people, the phenomena of social interaction, in terms of a calculus of choice. We explain bald facts in terms of such purposefulness. In the same way, surely, our recognition

that human purposefulness embraces alertness to hitherto unnoticed opportunities permits us to see the sequence of market
phenomena in terms of the universal propensity to notice what
may be useful.

To arrive at empirical propositions concerning the course of
market events, it is necessary to fill our general insights into
man's propensity to notice opportunities in precisely the same
way as the theorems of the logic of choice come to be translated into propositions of empirical science.

PERFECT KNOWLEDGE, ALERTNESS, AND THE EQUILIBRATING PROCESS

Largely as a result of Hayek's work, it is now well understood
that neoclassical price theory suffered seriously from its care-
free use of the assumption of perfect knowledge. The task of
economic theory, we now know, is precisely that of accounting
for the way information is brought to bear on the decisions of
market participants and on the extent to which the market
directs relevant information to those who can make the (socially) best use of it. The assumption of perfect knowledge
assumes away the central task of economic theory. In emphatically rejecting the perfect knowledge assumptions we
should not, however, lose sight of those considerations that
endow such an assumption with its superficial plausibility.

If an activity promises to yield a revenue more than
sufficient to cover all necessary costs, *including the costs of
buying relevant needed information,* our instinctive reaction as
economists is to feel sure that the activity will be carried on.
Upon reflection, we are likely to concede that, even if the
revenue is sufficient to cover the information costs as well,
ignorance may nonetheless block immediate exploitation of
this opportunity: no one may yet be aware of the existence of
the opportunity at all.[51] Despite this realization, our instinct
still assures us that the opportunity will sooner or later be
discovered and exploited. The perfect knowledge assumption
of neoclassical economics carried this instinctive assurance to
altogether unjustified lengths.[52] In rejecting this dangerous
assumption, we must take care not to expunge the entirely
healthy instinct on which it rested.

The truth is that at any given time people will, on the one hand, be blissfully ignorant of opportunities staring them in the face; on the other hand, they will be delightedly proceeding to exploit newly noticed opportunities of which they had been unaware yesterday. Our instinctive feeling of assurance that profitable opportunities will be noticed should not lead us to treat this tendency as being so powerful as to be instantaneously realized, as is implied in the perfect knowledge assumption. This would cause us to overlook, as neoclassical theory has indeed overlooked, the role of the market process in reinforcing this tendency. We must indeed not take for granted something it is our responsibility to explain. On the other hand, however, we must not consider the possibility of ignorance giving way to awareness as being entirely arbitrary, as a matter on which we can only patiently wait for empirical evidence. We must not fail to exploit to the fullest our assurance that there is indeed a tendency for opportunities to be noticed.

What is significant in all this is that our insight into the existence of such a tendency provides us with an approach to the analysis of equilibrating processes. We need not wait for evidence on the way information comes to spread through a society. We can, instead, employ our logic of choice to identify, within disequilibrium markets, the opportunities for gain that disequilibrium conditions themselves create. Postulating a tendency for such opportunities to be discovered and exploited, we can then explain the way such gradual discovery and exploitation of opportunities in turn gradually alters the pattern of opportunities presented in the market as the process unfolds.[53]

This approach leaves ample room for applied empirical work directed at the specifics of the tendency for opportunity discovery, at the possibility of the tendency's being slowed down by incompetent entrepreneurial activity, and so on. It has been my purpose to argue that such empirical work not be viewed as embracing all or even the principal share of the economics of market processes, that Hayek's pioneering view of market process as being one of information dissemination and discovery be exploited for what it has given us: the guidepost to an entrepreneurial perspective on market processes.

Part Two

ENTREPRENEURSHIP
AND CAPITAL
IN THE HISTORY OF
ECONOMIC THOUGHT

3

Classical Economics and the Entrepreneurial Role

ONE OF THE BETTER-KNOWN aspects of the theoretical system known as classical economics is that it suffered from a failure to identify the entrepreneurial role separately from the role of the capitalist. In the classical system the capitalist received profits, and there was little understanding that the latter "confused and garbled concept"[1] is in fact to be seen as a complex of analytically separate items. One writer has sweepingly, but not inaccurately, observed that "until the last quarter of the nineteenth century economists in Britain had only the vaguest conceptions of the undertaker's function."[2]

This failure to recognize the entrepreneurial role does call for explanation. As we shall see, the figure of the entrepreneur was fairly well recognized in the eighteenth century world of commerce. Moreover, in other earlier and contemporary systems of economic thought the function of the entrepreneur was identified and, indeed, even emphasized. Why then, one must ask, did the English classical economists construct their system in a fashion that so completely submerged the entrepreneurial function, jumbling it so unhelpfully with that of the capitalist? The purpose of this chapter is not so much to offer a new answer to this question as to report on a search of the literature for recognition of the difficulty and for the alternative explanations that have been offered.

Presented at a session of the meetings of the History of Economics Society, held at Cambridge, Massachusetts, May 1975.

THE ENTREPRENEUR IN EIGHTEENTH-CENTURY ENGLISH COMMERCE

Scholars researching the history of entrepreneurship have traced early references to the entrepreneurial role in eighteenth-century commercial literature. As we shall notice, French writings show perhaps more widespread awareness of the entrepreneur than do eighteenth-century English authors. But the research has nonetheless turned up enough references to convince us that the entrepreneurial figure was by no means unnoticed in England. As early as 1697, we find the term "projector" used by Daniel Defoe in the sense of someone rather similar to Schumpeter's "creative" entrepreneur.[3] Postlethwayt's *Universal Dictionary of Trade and Commerce* (London, 1751–55) uses the term "honest projector" to include both the inventor and the creative entrepreneur as contrasted with "idle, roguish and enthusiastical projectors" whose activities reflect "whim and knavery."[4] Hoselitz, noting a 1705 usage of the term "projector" to refer to Sir Walter Raleigh in his capacity of discoverer and colonizer, remarks that the term had an "invidious flavor and was applied to either fraudulent or highly speculative enterprisers."[5] The term "undertaker" had its origins in sixteenth-century usage to refer to contractors, and in particular to government contractors. Gradually, it came to be used synonymously with projector, serving as the English counterpart of the French entrepreneur. By the middle of the eighteenth century, an undertaker was simply a big businessman or an ordinary businessman. However, Hoselitz discovered, "by the time of Postlethwayt and Smith the more general meaning to the word tended to become obsolete and only the special meaning of an arranger of funerals survived. The undertaker in English economics was replaced by the capitalist who only toward the end of the nineteenth century again gave way to the entrepreneur."[6] Smith himself did use both projector and undertaker. By undertaker he apparently meant primarily capitalist. The price of output, Smith argued, must cover not only the cost of labor and materials, but also something "for the profits of the undertaker of the work who hazards his stock in this adventure."[7] At one place Smith discusses the higher wages that must be offered to attract workers when "a projector attempts to establish a new manufacture."[8] And he remarks, in this regard, that the "establishment of any new manufacture, of any new branch of commerce, or of any new practice in agriculture, is always a speculation, from which the projector promises himself extraordinary profits."[9]

THE ENTREPRENEUR IN EIGHTEENTH-CENTURY FRANCE

Recognition of the entrepreneurial role was even clearer in eighteenth-century France. Although it was once thought that J. B. Say in 1803 was the first to use the term entrepreneur, it is now well known that the term was familiar to French economists from Cantillon to Turgot to Quesnay. Hoselitz has discovered a whole series of French writings indicating that the term was used in France as early as the Middle Ages in the sense of *actor* (with apparant special reference to warlike action). In particular, the entrepreneur was in charge of large-scale construction projects such as cathedrals, bearing no risks but simply carrying the task forward until resources were exhausted. By the seventeenth century the term was used to designate the risk bearer, typically "a person who entered into a contractual relationship with the government for the perfor-mance of a service or the supply of goods. The price at which the contract was valued was fixed and the entrepreneur bore the risks of profit and loss from the bargain."[10] During the eighteenth century, the French writers on economic matters used the term in a variety of senses. In 1729 Belidor, like Cantillon in 1725,[11] used entrepreneur to mean risk bearer. For Quesnay, an entrepreneur is, less colorfully, "simply a tenant farmer who rents property at a fixed rent and produces a given output with given factors at given prices." On the other hand, for Beaudeau (1767) and Turgot, the risk-bearing aspect of the entrepreneur is again emphasized with attention also to his ownership, planning, organizing, and supervising.[12] In addi-tion, the entrepreneur appears to have typically been wealthy. One turn-of-the-century American profit theorist has inter-preted the physiocratic surplus theory as reflecting recognition of enterprise as the dominant productive factor.[13]

ADAM SMITH AND THE ENTREPRENEUR

There is a certain ambiguity in the literature concerning
whether Smith failed completely to identify the entrepreneurial
role separately from the role of the capitalist. We have already
seen, of course, that on occasion Smith made passing reference to the undertaker[14] and the projector. And one writer has
claimed that Smith took the next step (beyond the position of
the physiocrats) in differentiating the function of the entrepreneur.[15] Knight has pointed out that Smith and his followers
"recognized that profits even normally contain an element
which is not interest on capital. Remuneration for the work and
care of supervising the business was always distinguished.
Reference was also made to risk, but in the sense of risk of loss
of capital, which does not clearly distinguish profit from interest."[16] Despite Smith's indirect references to the entrepreneurial role, therefore, his discussion of profits on stock tended to
confuse any possible distinction between the pure interest of
the capitalist and the pure profit of the entrepreneur.[17] Although Smith explicitly recognizes that gross profit on stock
leaves the producer with a net profit after he pays interest to
the lenders of the capital,[18] it is made quite clear that profits on
stock are "regulated altogether by the value of the stock
employed, and are greater or smaller in proportion to the extent of this stock."[19] Whatever the "labour of inspection and
direction" the producer may himself furnish, profits "bear no
proportion to the quantity, the hardship, or the ingenuity of this
supposed labor."[20] Thus, Smith led the way for the general
classical approach to the distribution question, in which no
separate share of output is recognized as accruing to a separate
function of entrepreneurship. In fact, one modern writer has
considered Smith's treatment of profit as "the income of the
capitalist entrepreneur" to be worthy of applause. He criticizes
those writers from Say on who have "with all the resources of
excessively atomistic analysis, dismembered Smith's basic
idea."[21]

On the other hand, this "basic idea" of Smith was criticized
in the years following publication of the *The Wealth of Nations*.
Redlich[22] has drawn attention to an open polemic letter written
to Smith by Jeremy Bentham, in which Smith is accused of not

seeing the importance of the projector (used in the sense of creative entrepreneur). J. B. Say was explicit in criticizing Smith for having involved himself in great difficulty by not separating the profits of the entrepreneur from the profits of his capital.[23] And Blaug has drawn attention to several British economists of the early nineteenth century who did more or less accurately distinguish entrepreneurial profit.[24]

Our problem therefore emerges fairly clearly. Eighteenth-century writers on commercial affairs, including Smith himself, both in England and France, recognized the entrepreneurial figure. At least in France, the economists had already emphasized a distinct entrepreneurial role in production. And yet Smith and his followers failed to make the necessary analytic distinction between the profits captured by the pure entrepreneur and the profits on capital itself. Instead, the classical economists were led to search for a theory of distribution in which a single entity, profit, was perceived as accruing to a single factor class, capital. Some explanation is surely called for to account for what, from a present perspective, appears as an analytic blunder. The need for explanation is greater by virtue of the circumstance that the concepts needed for a more careful treatment were, as we have noticed, so obviously at hand. Before canvassing the literature for attempts to provide this explanation, I shall digress briefly to notice the way Smith treated one particular type of entrepreneur.

THE INDEPENDENT WORKER

We have seen how the entrepreneurial role came, in Smith's system, to be seen as inseparable from the role of the capitalist. It is worth noting that Smith was in fact not prepared to recognize a separate entrepreneurial role even where it manifested itself quite apart from any capitalist function. "In some parts of Scotland," Smith reported, [25] "a few poor people make a trade of gathering, along the seashore, those little variegated stones commonly known by the name of Scotch Pebbles. The price which is paid to them by the stone-cutter is altogether the wages of their labor; neither rent nor profit make any part of it."

Since these gatherers of pebbles require no capital for their operations, since their pebbles come from ownerless land and are free goods, Smith can discover no elements of profit or rent in the market value of the pebbles when delivered to the stonecutter. It did not occur to Smith that the pebble gatherers may be exercising entrepreneurship. And this despite Smith's belief, noticed by Cannan,[26] that no worker would accept a master unless he were unable to set himself up as an "independent workman."

Half a century before Smith, Cantillon had explicitly drawn attention to the role of "Undertakers of their own Labour who need no Capital to establish themselves, like Journeyman artisans, Copper-smiths, Needlewomen, Chimney Sweeps, Water Carriers" and to "Undertakers of their own labour in Art and Science, like Painters, Physicians, Lawyers, etc."[27] It makes no difference to the entrepreneurial role, Cantillon points out, "whether (Undertakers) set up with a capital to conduct their enterprise, or are Undertakers of their own labour without capital."[28] When Smith considers the high profits made by apothecaries on the drugs they sell, higher than the prevailing rate of profit on capital, he is quick to point out the special skills of the apothecaries which may account for a high implicit wage, but fails to consider the possibility that an apothecary may be treated in Cantillon's terminology as an undertaker of his own labor.[29]

Smith's treatment of the independent worker confirms that, in spite of his insight into the entrepreneurial role, he was unable to perceive it in isolation from the role of capitalist or laborer with which the entrepreneurial role comes packaged in the real world. It is for an explanation of this failure that we turn to the literature.

SOME REMARKS ON THE LITERATURE

It would not be correct to say that the literature of the history of thought has ignored this problem. In fact, as we shall see, the literature yields a surprising number of explanations for the failure of classical economics to accord the entrepreneurial element its due. But, it must be observed, the literature has hardly treated the problem as a serious one calling for careful research. Many of the explanations seem to have been suggested quite casually, as if they were almost self-evident. And the surprising number of explanations to be found appear, in part, to arise precisely out of this casualness with which they were offered. The possibility of alternative explanations was apparently not seriously entertained, nor was any search made in the literature for such alternatives. The result has been that the different explanations to be found in the various writings on classical economics are neither carefully developed nor offered with awareness of competing interpretations.

In what follows, the different attempts at explanation and interpretation are grouped around several leading themes that seem to repeat themselves again and again.

Explanations in Terms of Current Business Practice

Probably the most popular explanation for the classical neglect of the role of the entrepreneur is one that depends on the pattern of business organization characteristic of the classical period. As long ago as 1855, Mangoldt sought the explanation for the insistence of the French economists following Say on separating profit from interest in the "different character of typical French industry, and the greater relative importance of the manager's personality in it relatively to the capital sector."[30] Both Schumpeter[31] and Hoselitz[32] have suggested that Say's own insistence on separating the entrepreneurial function from that of the capitalist was related to his personal experience in and knowledge of the entrepreneurial role, which the other classical economists lacked.

There exist two somewhat different emphases in the explanation in terms of contemporary business practice. It is pointed out that in Smith's time the entrepreneurial role was, in practice, generally merged with that of the capitalist. Some writers, like Blaug, emphasize that entrepreneurship typically involved the entrepreneur's own capital.[33] "Until the 'railway mania' of the 1840's, trading on the stock exchange was largely confined to government bonds and public utility stocks. The domestic capital market was poorly organized and virtually all new industrial investment was financed out of undistributed profits. There was, consequently, little basis in practice for considering the investment function independently of the level of saving. Without distorting reality, it was possible to think of the active entrepreneur as identical with the inactive investor of capital."[34] Schumpeter similarly saw the distinction between the entrepreneur and the capitalist facilitated during the second half of the nineteenth century "by the fact that changing methods of business finance produced a rapidly increasing number of instances in which capitalists were no entrepreneurs and entrepreneurs were no capitalists."[35]

Other writers emphasize the related circumstance that, during the classical period, the corporate form of business organization, in which the capitalist role of stockholders is sharply distinguished from the decision-making role of managers, was not yet widely prevalent.[36]

In this regard, it is of interest to notice that one historian of thought has emphasized an almost precisely opposite chain of causation. The failure of the British classical economists to identify a separate entrepreneurial profit has been related by Haney not to the relative absence of the joint-stock company, but to its relative frequency. Contrasting Hermann's treatment of undertaker's gains with that of the British economists, Haney writes of this being "an interesting illustration of the close relation between the industrial environment and economic thought."[37] In England the growing importance of joint-stock companies controlling large commercial and industrial concerns meant that a considerable class was receiving an income other than rent or wages, which suggested the idea of profits as a return on business capital. On the other hand, in Germany, industry was carried on in smaller units with the handicraftsman using his own relatively small capital, being his own manager and businessman. "Thus the function of the business undertaker—as the Germans called the entrepreneur or enterpriser—was relatively more dominant than in England."[38]

Explanation in Terms of the Wage-Fund Theory

An interesting explanation of the classical schema was advanced by Edwin Cannan, reflecting his own view of entrepreneurship as a particular kind of labor and of entrepreneurial profit as a kind of wage. The classical economists, Cannan argued, were unable to realize this because they were trapped by the wage-fund theory. This theory, Cannan explains, denied that wages are derived from output, maintaining instead that they are advanced from the capital of employers. The classical economists, therefore, could not possibly make wages "include income received by undertakers not by way of advance but as a consequence of the success of their undertakings." It was only when "at last the wage-fund theory of wages expired" that "the way was open for the classification of the earnings of undertakers' labour along with that of other kinds of labour."[39]

In Cannan's opinion, Marshall's view of entrepreneurial profit as "earnings of management" was the natural consequence of this liberation from the wage-fund theory.[40] According to this view, the classical economists had every reason to distinguish the entrepreneurial role from the role of the capitalist. What prevented them from properly treating this role as a special category of labor was that they could not see wages as income derived from labor. They "denied that the produce had anything to do with the level of earnings except in so far as, conjoined with saving or accumulations, it affected the magnitude of the capital devoted to the payment of wages."[41] Although, therefore, entrepreneurial labor may indeed be reflected in the size of the volume of output, entrepreneurial profit could not be explained by the classical economists as wages reflecting that entrepreneurial productivity. On the other hand, entrepreneurial profit could not, clearly, be seen, as other wages were held to be, as advanced out of capital, since the entrepreneurs were themselves the capitalists. The consequence was that while the "English economists of the first three-quarters of the nineteenth century" were prepared "to throw out of 'profits of capital' all that the undertaker gets in consequence of his personal activity rather than his possession of capital," they "threw it into the air instead of finding a place for it in their treatment of income derived from labour."[42]

Explanation as a Deliberate Theoretical Effort

Several writers seem to have viewed the suppression of the entrepreneurial role in classical economics not as an analytical lapse calling for excuse, but as arising from a deliberate, and at least partly meritorious, theoretical advance. In this view, Adam Smith was consciously reacting against the earlier ways of seeing the productive process. "Before Smith...," Meek has observed, "'profit' had usually been regarded either as a mere synonym for 'gain,' or as a sort of superior wage or as a surplus over cost whose level varied (as Stewart put it) 'according to circumstances.' With one bold stroke Smith cut through the difficulties involved in these earlier approaches to the problem. He postulated profit as the income of the class of employers of labor... he argued that competition would tend to reduce this profit to 'an ordinary or average rate' on the capital employed."[43] Many years ago, Hawley saw Smith as reacting against physiocratic errors. The physiocrats, Hawley explained, are entitled to the credit of recognizing enterprise as the dominant productive factor. But they erred in thinking that "because enterprise was dominant the other productive factors existed only for its benefit, and that the community was prosperous in the proportion in which the 'surplus' was enhanced at the expense of wages and interest."[44] Hawley sees Smith and his followers as properly revolting against this but as falling, consequently, into the opposite error of "practically ignoring enterprise."

Explanation in Terms of Emphasis on Labor

Some writers have attributed the classical neglect of entrepreneurship to the dominance, in the classical paradigm, of labor. Schumpeter wrote that natural-law preconceptions were to blame for Smith's emphasizing the role of labor "to the exclusion of the productive function of designing the plan according to which this labor is being applied."[45] As a result, the role of the businessman came to be reduced to that of advancing capital.

This interpretation of Schumpeter is to be contrasted with that of Cannan, cited earlier. For Cannan, the contribution of the entrepreneur is seen as a special kind of labor. Smith, according to Cannan, saw this too but was prevented by the wage-fund theory from pursuing the necessary implications. For Schumpeter, on the other hand, the entrepreneurial contribution is to be sharply distinguished from that of labor, and it was the classical preoccupation with labor, therefore, that prevented perception of the entrepreneurial function.

Kuenne, in a few short sentences, has adumbrated an explanation for the classical submersion of the entrepreneur that, while pointing to the dominance of the labor and, generally, cost of production theory of value, is somewhat different from the explanations both of Cannan and of Schumpeter. The classical theories of value, Kuenne asserts, "tempted theorists to resolve capital goods into their labor or primary factor content"[46] and thus to merge the capitalist with an entrepreneur whose contribution could be explained as labor of superintendence.

Explanation in Terms of Emphasis on Capital

In sharp contrast to explanations that stress the classical emphasis on labor must be classed a recent explanation that depends on a postulated central role in classical thought for capital. Eagly has recently sought to present the classical economists as, like the physiocrats, placing capital at the center of the stage. As a result of this pivotal role, the capitalist came to be seen as the dominant decision maker in the system. He is seen as setting labor into motion. Laborers and landlords are assigned negligible roles as decision makers compared with the capitalists, who control, allocate, and accumulate capital. As a consequence, what we now identify as the purely entrepreneurial function was perceived as inseparably bound up in the capitalist function. It was not until the classical paradigm was replaced by the Walrasian and other neoclassical ways of looking at the economic system that entrepreneurs could emerge as analytical figures in their own right. Their emergence was possible only because the new paradigm reduced the capitalist to one who merely owns stock, on an equal footing with laborers and landowners.[47]

Did the Classics View Production as Automatic?

Eagly's interpretation of the classical economists as treating the capitalist as the *dominant decision maker* in the system contrasts with alternative views of the classical system in yet another respect. A number of writers have treated the classical neglect of entrepreneurship as reflecting an approach that sees production as being *an automatic process not calling for active decision making at all*. If one accepts this interpretation of classical thinking, then one has, it can be argued, in effect a new explanation of the absence of the entrepreneur from the classical system. In this explanation, the entrepreneurial role is missing from the classical system because the classical economists did not assign any central importance to the decision-making element in the production process. The economic regularities they believed they saw did not depend on any such decision-making element. Therefore, their analysis did not have to encompass the entrepreneur.

Most emphatic in regard to the automaticity of the classical production process was Schumpeter. Schumpeter, writing of the Ricardians and of Senior, remarks that they "almost accomplished what I have described as an impossible feat, namely, the exclusion of the figure of the entrepreneur completely. For them—as well as for Marx—the business process runs substantially by itself, the one thing needful to make it run being an adequate supply of capital."[48] Of Smith's view of the economic process, Schumpeter has remarked that a reader of Smith is "bound to get an impression to the effect that this process runs on by itself."[49]

We have seen that, for Eagly, the dominance of the capitalist in the classical schema does *not* mean that active decision making is absent from the system, merely that such decision making is located within the capitalist function. Blaug appears to be thinking similarly when he writes of the classical perspective as making it "possible to think of the active entrepreneur as identical with the inactive investor of capital."[50] Cannan's view seems to be slightly more complicated.

In some passages Cannan might, on a superficial reading, appear to attribute to the classical economists, as do Eagly and Blaug, a view of the capitalist role that includes active decision making. Thus Cannan writes of the displacement, in late nineteenth-century economics, of capital from the "triad of productive requisites." This would not, he comments, have been of much importance if capital had not, in the classical system, been "represented as the most active element in the triad. As it is, the change is immense. No longer is capital supposed to decide whether industry shall be set in motion or not, and whether it shall flow into this or that channel when it is set in motion. Capital takes its proper place as an inanimate stock of goods and machinery.... The power of 'managing' industry is attributed not to the mute and inanimate capital, nor even to the owners of the capital, but to the 'entrepreneurs.' "[51]

Here Cannan might be understood as seeing the classical production process not as automatic but as one in which the decision initiatives derive from capital and its owners.[52] On the other hand, Cannan's references to a classical view of decision making as contrasted with mute, inanimate capital may be significant. It may be said with truth, Cannan argued at one point, "that it is the capitalists or owners of the capital who for the most part take the 'initiative' in industrial enterprise, and so in a way 'put labor into motion.' But it certainly is not the capital itself, a mere mute mass of objects, which puts industry into motion."[53] Here Cannan appears to be implying that the classical economists had a view of production in which it is indeed automatic in the sense that all direction flows from the "mere mute mass" of capital itself. Again, in the passage cited above, (in which Cannan remarks on the displacement of capital from the classical triad) Cannan goes on to remark that even the entrepreneurs who, now that the dominance of capital has been broken, are seen as managing industry, "can only direct industry into particular channels by virtue of their intelligent anticipation of the orders of the consumers, whose demands they have to satisfy on pain of bankruptcy."[54]

It thus seems more accurate to read Cannan as charging the classical economists, as we have seen Schumpeter do, with an automatic view of the process of production. This automaticity is to be understood, however, as being closely related to the classical neglect of demand as an active force directing production. Whereas modern economics, in Cannan's view, sees the pattern of the allocation of resources directed by entrepreneurs responding to dictates of consumer demand, the classical vision saw production as somehow automatically determined by the availability of stock, of labor, and of land. According to this interpretation of Cannan, his references to capital as, in the classical system, deciding whether and how to set industry into motion, should not be understood as emphasizing the capitalist as being, for the classical economists, the active decision maker. Rather Cannan, in these passages, is underlining the awkwardness of a view that sees production, which Cannan himself sees to be obviously the result of active entrepreneurial decision, as flowing *without* anyone being assigned the specific role of decision making, just as if the decisions were made by themselves.

What emerges from this reading of Cannan, then, is a possible explanation for the classical neglect of the entrepreneur. This interpretation ascribes to the classical economists a view of production that, because it had little recognition of the sovereign role of demand, saw it as automatic and therefore in no need of the entrepreneurial role that anticipates consumer wishes. Cannan himself seems not to have considered this interpretation. Nonetheless, such an interpretation may have some merit.

Explanation in Terms of Long-run and Equilibrium Emphasis

Running through several discussions of the weakness of classical economics on profit theory and on the entrepreneurial role is at least a hint of yet another explanation. This one accounts for the classical failure to emphasize the entrepreneur by referring to the classical failure to distinguish carefully between long-run, normal equilibrium states of affairs and real world market conditions. Knight was the most explicit of these writers. In seeking to explain the earlier weaknesses in profit theory, Knight wrote: "A further source of confusion was the indefiniteness of the conception and use of the ideas of natural and market prices in the minds of the early writers. Only recently...has the analysis of long-time normal prices by Marshall and of the 'static state' by Clark and Schumpeter begun to give to economists a clearer notion of what is really involved in 'natural' or normal conditions. To the earlier classical writers this obscurity hid the fundamental difference between the total income of the capitalist manager and contract interest."[55]

Cole appears to have had a similar explanation in mind when, in discussing Ricardo's failure to follow Cantillon and Say in distinguishing the entrepreneur, he blames Ricardo's emphasis on long-run conditions and on static analysis as distracting attention from short-run forces that produce change. Such an explanation may perhaps be supported from Adam Smith's discussion of speculators' profits. "The speculative merchant," Smith observes, "exercises no one regular, established, or well-known branch of business. He is a corn merchant this year, and a wine merchant the next, and a sugar, tobacco, or tea merchant the year after. He enters into every trade when he foresees that it is likely to be more than commonly profitable.... His profits and losses...bear no regular proportion to those of any one established and well-known branch of business. A bold adventurer may sometimes acquire a considerable fortune by two or three speculations."[56] Smith explains very carefully that the general tendency for wage and profit rates to be equal throughout the market may be thwarted by unusual events such as wartime conscription of sailors that forces up wages of merchant sailors, or a public mourning that raises the price of black cloth, and that in new industries wages and profits may be above normal. It is not difficult, then, to perceive that Smith's view of the normal long-run tendencies in production can afford to ignore the bold new adventurous speculator-projector. The circumstance that post-Walrasian emphasis on equilibrium has, in our times, led to the role of the entrepreneur being virtually expunged from economics, lends further plausibility to this explanation.

Earlier in this chapter, we noticed that eighteenth-century English usage distinguished between the "honest projector" and the "idle, roguish, and enthusiastical projectors" whose activities reflect "whim and knavery." Without knavery, the ordinary course of commerce tends to preclude above-normal profit. The more permanent forces of the market tend to eliminate temporary sources of entrepreneurial gain. Permanent gains flow from the ownership of capital; temporary gains unrelated to the size of capital stock can be ignored as either temporary or the fruit of knavery. The classical unconcern with the entrepreneur therefore need not be criticized at all; it can be perceived as the altogether consistent implication of classical attention to the more powerful, permanent, and enduring forces in the economic system.

4

The Entrepreneurial Role in Menger's System

IT IS BY NOW fairly well recognized that the mainstream of modern equilibrium microeconomics has, particularly since its decisive absorption of Walrasian influence, assumed a form in which scope for the entrepreneurial role is conspicuous by its absence.[1] One broad modern tradition in which the entrepreneur was never squeezed out drew its source from Carl Menger and his followers. Writers with such sharply varied approaches to economics as Schumpeter and Mises shared, at least, a high disdain for the dominant perfectly-competitive-equilibrium view of price theory, and a lively sense of the crucial significance of entrepreneurship for an understanding of the capitalist-market process. Yet the history of economic thought does not, in its treatment of the place of entrepreneurship in economic theory, assign much importance to the founders of the Austrian school. In the considerable economic literature, from the 1880s on, in which entrepreneurship and entrepreneurial profit were discussed, there were few contributions from the founding Austrians.[2] It is of some interest, therefore, to examine the writings of Carl Menger to determine rather carefully the extent to which his system, explicitly or implicitly, found room for the entrepreneurial role or to which his system might, at the hands of his followers, be expected to lead to the clear identification and explication of this role.

This interest is perhaps heightened by the existence of some intriguing discussions concerning the extent to which Menger's work influenced later writers on the problems of entrepreneur-

Presented at a session of the meetings of the Atlantic Economic Society, held at Washington, D.C., October 1977.

ship. Knight, in his highly unsympathetic introduction to the first English translation of Menger's *Grundsätze,* remarked that, on the questions of entrepreneurship and profit, "Later economists got little help from Menger or his contemporaries, or even his successors in the Austrian School."[3] On the other hand, Streissler recently expressed the view that, though Menger's immediate followers ignored his emphasis on problems of information, Schumpeter built his own theory of entrepreneurial innovation largely on Menger's foundations.[4]

Now Streissler's view that Schumpeter built on Mengerian foundations is difficult to document. In his 1911 book, where his distinctive ideas on entrepreneurship were most definitively stated early in his career, Schumpeter hardly referred to any Austrian literature. Beyond a disparaging reference to Mataja,[5] Schumpeter cited only Böhm-Bawerk's "friction" theory of entrepreneurial profit;[6] Menger's writings are not mentioned at all in regard to the entrepreneurial function. Even more revealing is Schumpeter's indirect, but very clear, dismissal—in his *History of Economic Analysis,* written so many years later—of Menger's work on entrepreneurship. Again, referring to Böhm-Bawerk's theory of entrepreneurial profit, Schumpeter remarked that "excepting Böhm-Bawerk, the Austrians had very little to say about the matter."[7] Nonetheless, Streissler's conjecture that Menger's ideas on information *may have* provided a broad source for Schumpeter's later ideas—even if it were to prove that they did not so serve—remains a fascinating possibility.

We turn, then, to Menger's view of the market process in order to explore Streissler's conjecture and also to confront this paradox: on the one hand, we have a flourishing modern Austrian tradition claiming its paternity from Menger even more emphatically than from Böhm-Bawerk,[8] emphasizing entrepreneurial processes, while, on the other hand, we have in Menger's own work what appears at first glance to be a decided lack of attention to the nature of the entrepreneur, of his role, and of entrepreneurial profit.

In what follows, we shall successively discuss (1) Menger's treatment of the entrepreneurial role; (2) Menger's recognition of the importance of knowledge, of error, and of uncertainty in economic process; (3) Menger's position with respect to the role of equilibrium analysis of economic phenomena, and (4) Menger's understanding of the nature of competition and of product quality variation in market processes. We will then, in the light of these discussions, return to appraise Menger's system from the perspective of the purposes of this chapter. It should be mentioned at the outset that this chapter owes a great deal to several important papers by Streissler.[9] Although I shall have occasion to take serious issue with several of his conclusions, it is to Streissler, rather than to the earlier and better-known surveys of Menger's contributions,[10] that we owe an awareness of Menger's unique understanding of the crucial importance of knowledge, error, and uncertainty. Ultimately, any examination of the place of entrepreneurship in Menger's system must, as mine will, take this awareness as its point of departure.

MENGER ON ENTREPRENEURSHIP

Menger's explicit treatment of entrepreneurship is brief, consisting of two or three passages in his *Principles of Economics*, the longest of which is a footnote.[11] For Menger, entrepreneurial activity is a special kind of labor service. Such activity is, as a rule, valuable to economizing men. However, since these kinds of services cannot be bought and sold,[12] they do not have a market price.[13] A necessary prerequisite for the provision of such services, moreover, is possession of the appropriate amounts of capital. Menger listed the specific functions constituting entrepreneurial activity as involving "(a) *information* about the economic situation; (b) economic *calculation*—all the various computations that must be made if a production process is to be efficient...; (c) the *act of will* by which goods of higher order... are assigned to a particular production process; and finally (d) *supervision* of the execution of the production plan so that it may be carried through as economically as possible."[14] Menger is explicit in rejecting Mangoldt's view that risk bearing is the essential function of entrepreneurship.[15]

Entrepreneurship is a good of higher order, that is, one of the complementary higher-order goods needed for production. The "prospective value of the product determines the total [of the complementary goods of higher order] only if the value of entrepreneurial activity is included in the total."[16]

It seems fair to understand Menger's entrepreneurial activities as being quite similar, say, to those of Marshall's entrepreneur-manager.[17] Despite the special, and quite unusual, attention paid by Menger to the information, and to the act of will involved in the entrepreneurial function, we find no attempt (such as we find later in Schumpeter or in Knight) to distinguish the entrepreneurial role from that of the hired manager. And Menger had no qualms about treating entrepreneurial profit as a species of factor return, as the value of a useful service. In a long footnote discoursing on the morality of property incomes, in which Menger simply pointed out that given the social conditions of the moment, the efficient market simply assigns each factor its true economic value, whether or not we approve of it aesthetically, Menger finds no need to give pure entrepreneurial profit any separate treatment. Nor is there any hint of a relentless competitive market process continually and repeatedly operating to grind down entrepreneurial profit to zero, or of the associated possibility that in equilibrium there might be a situation in which no scope at all would exist for the entrepreneur. Certainly, insofar as any *deliberate* discussion of entrepreneurship finds a place in Menger, it is understandable that Schumpeter and Knight saw little from which either could draw inspiration.

MENGER ON KNOWLEDGE, ERROR, AND UNCERTAINTY

Despite the limited explicit attention Menger paid to the entrepreneurial function, it is nonetheless possible that Menger's exposition of the operation of the market system may embody implicit understanding of the pivotal role the pure entrepreneur plays in the capitalist process. Such implicit understanding must, if it is indeed found to exist, relate especially to the importance of changing *knowledge* as the propelling force behind the process; to the concomitant continual discovery in the market of earlier *errors* by decision makers; and to perception of the closely related phenomenon of *uncertainty* that necessarily conditions and suffuses all market decisions. We shall, that is, be searching for possible signs that Menger recognized the systematic tendencies generated in the market by the dynamics of interacting decisions that are made under a wide range of degrees of mutual ignorance.

Menger's system provides, indeed, a fascinating opportunity for such a search. As Streissler emphasized, Menger's *Grundsätze* provides numerous instances of his "constant stress on problems of information" with its variability "over time and, at any given moment, over individuals."[18] Moreover, Menger's emphasis on the time dimension led him to pay a good deal of attention to the *uncertainty* this dimension entails.[19] This Mengerian emphasis on the role of knowledge is a remarkable feature of his work, one to which commentators before Streissler unaccountably failed to draw attention. And even Streissler, one may argue, does not quite do complete justice to the extent to which Menger's whole system revolves around questions of knowledge.

MENGER ON KNOWLEDGE

Menger's *Grundsätze* is not merely a treatise containing scores of references to knowledge. Nor is the crucial role of knowledge in Menger's system quite captured, one may argue, even in his "remarkable sentence, 'the quantities of consumption goods at human disposal are limited only by the extent of human knowledge.'"[20] Menger's awareness of the importance of knowledge is central to an impressive variety of different aspects of his theory, including—perhaps, for our purposes, most significantly—the very foundation of his system, that of economizing activity.

Menger stated, of course, that it is the *perceived* usefulness of goods that makes them goods in the first place, and that it is upon this that the notion of economic value depends.[21] Changes in perception, correct or otherwise, change value.[22] To the extent to which planful provision for the future occurs, it must depend on foresight and expectations.[23] As mentioned, economic progress depends for Menger, in the last analysis, on the progress of human technical understanding.[24] The very first component of entrepreneurial activity, we have seen in a previous section, involves "information about the economic situation."[25] Opportunities for mutually beneficial exchange, Menger made very clear, can be expected to be acted upon only if both parties are able to *perceive* the existence and worthwhileness of these opportunities.[26] Of particular interest, in this last respect, is Menger's footnote reference to advertising as a means whereby producers can make their products known to potential customers.[27] Menger has a highly impressive analysis of the spontaneous market process by means of which a money can emerge. This process is one of spontaneous discovery, and is worth quoting at some length:

> The exchange of less easily saleable commodities for commodities of greater marketability is in the economic interest of *every* economizing individual. But the actual performance of exchange operations of this kind presupposes a knowledge of their interest on the part of economizing individuals.... This knowledge will never be attained by all members of a people at the same time. On the contrary, only a small number of economizing individuals will at first recognize the advantage accruing to them from the acceptance of other, more saleable, commodities in exchange for their own whenever a direct exchange of their commodities for the goods they wish to consume is impossible or highly uncertain.... Since there is no better way in which men can be enlightened about their economic interests than by observation of the economic success of those who employ the correct means of achieving their ends, it is evident that nothing favored the rise of money so much as the long-practiced, and economically profitable, acceptance of eminently saleable commodities in exchange for all others by the most discerning and most capable economizing individuals.[28]

Of special interest for our purpose is the place knowledge occupies in relation to the activity of *economizing*. This is the basic activity upon which Menger's elaborate microeconomic theoretical structure is built. (I shall later have further occasion to comment on the character of the Mengerian "economizing individual.") Knowledge appears to enter Menger's elaboration of the requirements and characteristics of economizing activity in at least two ways, although Menger does not himself articulate these differences.

First, for economizing activity to take place, it is necessary that the individual *perceive* that his needs exceed his means.

> Wherever . . . men recognize that the requirements for a good are greater than its available quantity they achieve the further insight that no part of the available quantity, . . . may lose its useful properties or be removed from human control without causing some concrete human needs, previously provided for, to remain unsatisfied. . . . A further effect . . . is that men become aware . . . that any inappropriate employment of particular quantities of this good must necessarily result in part of the needs that would be provided for by appropriate employment of the available quantity remaining unsatisfied.[29]

At this level, *knowledge* of scarcity is called upon to impress upon the individual the very need to economize, to *realize* that he lives not in a land of Cockaigne, but under conditions in which avoiding waste is of some importance.

Second, to effectively engage in provident economizing activity, the individual must know not merely that he lives in a world of scarcity, but also the specifics of his anticipated requirements and of the expected quantities of goods that will be at his disposal. It is at this level of discussion that we encounter some of Menger's remarks on uncertain expectations. It is in relation to this kind of specific knowledge that Menger discussed the deliberate efforts of men *to obtain knowledge*. "To the degree to which men engage in planning activity directed to the satisfaction of their needs, they endeavor to attain clarity as to the quantities of goods available to them at any time."[30] And it is here that Menger, no doubt drawing on his own earlier experience as an economic journalist surveying the state of the markets for the *Wiener Zeitung*, discussed the various concrete methods by which reports on commodity stocks in grain, sugar, and cotton markets are assembled and used by traders.[31] And, in perhaps his closest linking of knowledge to entrepreneurship, Menger explains how a widening

market permits "the development of a special professional
class ... [that has an interest] in compiling data about the quantities of goods, currently at the disposal of the various people
and nations whose trade they mediate .... They have, moreover, an interest in many other general kinds of information."[32]

Menger's emphasis on knowledge is certainly significant,
and it acquires even greater significance in the context of his
parallel emphasis upon *ignorance* and *error*. Nonetheless, it is
not enough, in order to declare Menger a pioneer in entrepreneurial theory, to cite his ubiquitous references to knowledge.
It seems more likely that this aspect of Menger's system stems
from his central concern to establish the *subjectivist* perspective on economic phenomena as the starting point in economic
theory. According to the subjectivist point of view, economic
changes arise not so much from the *circumstances* relevant at
the moment of decision as from man's *awareness* of these circumstances. So that Menger's carefully constructed
methodological individualism required him at each turn to emphasize the decision maker's knowledge and awareness of
economic constraints, rather than the force exercised by those
constraints in and of themselves. This does not, at least without further extension, imply that a systematic process of adjustment exists in the market, set in motion and fueled by
continual entrepreneurial discovery. We shall find ourselves
compelled to recognize the validity of this restrained interpretation of Menger by a consideration of his treatment of ignorance and error, to which we now turn.

MENGER ON IGNORANCE AND ERROR
As almost a corollary of his emphasis on knowledge in
economizing activity, Menger called attention to error and uncertainty.[33] If man's valuation of goods depends on his knowledge of his need and of their availability, then it follows that
"men can be in error about the value of goods just as they can be
in error with respect to all other objects of human knowledge."[34]

Moreover, at one point Menger recognizes that the gains
from new trade, between individuals or between nations, are
clearly related to ignorance. If, Menger explains, "the full
gains from the new trade are sometimes not immediately forth-

coming, the reason is that...knowledge of the trading opportunities and power to carry through exchange operations recognized to be economic, are ordinarily acquired by the participants only after a certain period of time."[35] While the context of this sentence clearly shows that Menger did *not* see that the high initial gains from new trade are associated with the very imperfection of knowledge to which he refers, the passage does view the market process as one that gradually overcomes ignorance.

One recent writer has in fact treated Menger's recognition of the possibility of error as a major characteristic of his system, distinguishing him sharply from his fellow pioneers, Jevons and Walras, in the so-called marginal revolution. Thus, William Jaffé writes, "Veblen's strictures upon what he considered the Austrian preconception of human nature fit Jevons' or Walras' theory much better than they do Menger's. In Menger, man is not depicted as a hedonistic "lightning calculator of pleasures and pains." Man, as Menger saw him, far from being a "lightning calculator" is a "bumbling, erring, ill-informed creature, plagued with uncertainty, forever hovering between alluring hopes and haunting fears, and congenitally incapable of making finely calibrated decisions in pursuit of satisfactions."[36]

Jaffé's interpretation of Menger's economizing individual is suggestive. To the extent that we can agree with Jaffé's interpretation, we can attribute to Menger's economizing individual scope for precisely the same kind of "entrepreneurship" that, for Mises, is contained in the notion of individual human action.[37] This is not the place to embark on a full-scale analysis of the role of economizing man in Menger's writings. Nonetheless, we may remark that Jaffé's position seems to be closer to the truth than that apparently taken by Knight in his introduction to Menger's *Principles*. In that essay, Knight understands (or rather misunderstands) Menger's use of the notion of the economizing individual as "naive economism." Menger's "economizing man" is the "economic-man who has been the butt of so much sarcasm."[38] Moreover, Knight appears to argue that error plays no role in Menger's theory! "Menger notwithstanding," Knight writes quite astonishingly, "economic behavior is more than mechanical cause and effect. Its indubitable affection by error proves that."[39] Certainly Jaffé's quite different understanding of Menger is closer to the truth.[40]

It is tempting, then, to seize on Jaffé's interpretation of Menger as the basis for maintaining that Menger's perception of the market process was indeed an entrepreneurial one, one that understands the market process to be a systematic modification of error on the part of market participants and of steadily improving mutual knowledge. Unfortunately, it does not seem possible to sustain such a reading of Menger.

This becomes apparent in Menger's famous fifth chapter, "The Theory of Price," the chapter Hayek describes as the "crowning achievement" of the entire work and as revealing "the clear aim which directs [Menger's] exposition" from the very beginning.[41] In Menger's entire theory of price, error is carefully excluded, completely confirming Knight's reading of Menger! At all the stages of the argument, Menger abstracts from error—in the discussion of bilateral monopoly, of one-sided competition, and of bilateral competition. The possibility of error in the decisions that determine price, is not forgotten; it is deliberately brushed aside. Moreover, the possibility is not simply assumed away as a matter of analytical convenience, it is assumed away as being an abnormality! In concluding the theory of monopoly price policy, Menger declares that "of course, error and imperfect knowledge may give rise to aberrations, but these are the pathological phenomena of social economy and prove as little against the laws of economists as do the symptoms of a sick body against the laws of physiology."[42] Menger's discussion of competition, too, explicitly proceeds on an assumption "barring error and ignorance on the part of the economizing individuals involved."[43]

Clearly, Menger's willingness to incorporate error into his system was neither as totally absent as Knight believed nor as complete as claimed by Jaffé. Either we have here a curious inconsistency in Menger, or else there is some subtlety here that has yet to be plumbed. Certainly a theory of price in which error is assumed away as a pathological abnormality cannot qualify as a process theory of the modern Hayekian variety, involving *discovery* in some essential way. We turn our attention now to Menger's position on the role of equilibrium analysis of economic phenomena.

MENGER ON EQUILIBRIUM AND DISEQUILIBRIUM

The discussions in the preceding section (and in particular our remarks on the apparent inconsistency in Menger's treatment of error in his price theory as compared with his emphasis on error elsewhere) have considerable bearing on the question of the extent to which Menger's economics can be described as "disequilibrium economics." If it were indeed possible to show that Menger's theory was primarily "disequilibrium theory," then indeed Menger's credentials as a forerunner of the entrepreneurial theory of the market process would be strengthened considerably.

The view that Menger's economics is disequilibrium economics has been put forward recently by Streissler[44] and strongly endorsed by Jaffé.[45] An *apparently* contradictory statement by Schumpeter: "We must see in the Jevons-Menger utility theory an embryonic theory of general equilibrium"[46] is itself too terse and its context is not sufficiently clear to enable us to be sure that Schumpeter is disagreeing with Streissler. In any event, against Schumpeter's statement we may balance the recent statement by Hayek that there is in Menger's work an "absence...of the conception of a general equilibrium. If he had continued his work it would probably have become even more apparent...that what he was aiming at was rather to provide tools for what we now call process analysis than for a theory of static equilibrium."[47]

Neither Hayek, Streissler, nor Jaffé offers explicit citations from or references to Menger's work to support his view. Evidently they base their views on a general reading of Menger in which they found him, in Streissler's phrase, both "shirk[ing] away from too precise a statement of equilibrium theorems,"[48] and denying in certain passages "that one and the same good had at a given moment of time *everywhere the same price*."[49] Streissler and Jaffé both understand the disequilibrium economics they attribute to Menger not primarily as offering scope for an entrepreneurial process, or as evidence that

Menger saw the market process as an entrepreneurial one, but simply as a refusal "to glorify entrepreneurial ability into a high speed adjustment mechanism."[50] As Jaffé puts it, "With his attention unswervingly fixed on reality, Menger could not, and did not, abstract from the difficulties traders face in any attempt to obtain all the information required for anything like a pinpoint equilibrium determination of market prices to emerge."[51]

Nonetheless, even if the emphasis is more on the *delay* in the communication of information reflected in disequilibrium than on the process of learning that equilibrium might represent, the Mengerian refusal to be trapped in the equilibrium mold could at least open the way to a theory of the market process based on learning. Streissler does in fact refer to a *tâtonnement* process in Menger, one that takes a century, in contrast to Walrasian *tâtonnement* that takes a minute.[52] And this Mengerian *tâtonnement* is, as Streissler explains, a kind of social learning process involving the standardization of goods, the creation of institutions for gathering information, and the emergence of a class of middlemen.

But here again we encounter the very same puzzle in Menger that we found earlier. Surely Menger's theory of prices, monopolistic or competitive, is emphatically *not* a disequilibrium theory! An examination of Menger's fifth chapter on the theory of price provides no hint of any time-consuming market process (entrepreneurial or otherwise) through which prices are systematically formed. On the contrary, Menger explicitly assumed the absence of all error, an assumption guaranteeing instantaneous equilibrium and one that starts out by giving entrepreneurs little to do.

Now Streissler does seem to have been aware, at least to some extent, of this difficulty. "If Menger did not believe in equilibrium," Streissler asks, "how is it possible that we find in his founding treatise all the laws of the determination of the prices of productive inputs?"[53] This is not, however, a clear statement of the difficulty we have encountered. Our difficulty is not so much that Menger offered a theory of price determination; our problem is that, in Menger's theory, prices are shown to be determined instantaneously and inexorably by the

ruling economic circumstances. It follows that our puzzlement
is not immediately lessened by Streissler's attempted answer
to his question: "Menger would have replied that he had to
show the fundamental causes that determined economic processes," to which Streissler adds the even more puzzling remark that "Menger did not try to outline the equilibrium
points, the solutions of a set of differential equations." *Our*
difficulty is that Menger's price theory surely *is* an outline of
the equilibrium situation!

THE ROLE OF ERROR AND DISEQUILIBRIUM IN MENGER: A SUGGESTION

We have encountered what appears to be a fundamental inconsistency between Menger's price theory and the rest of his
Grundsätze. Except for his chapter on price, Menger's book
displays a sensitive awareness of the inescapable influence of
error and ignorance, and of the resulting continuous state of
flux in which the economic system must always find itself. Yet
in his chapter on price Menger seems unaccountably to lapse
into a world in which equilibrium prices are instantaneously
determined, under conditions for which any suspicion of less
than perfect omniscience is dismissed as pathological. A possible solution to this difficulty may be suggested. The solution
depends on the distinction which Menger implies at several
points between "economic prices" and "uneconomic prices."

Menger's chapter on the theory of price does indeed assume
the absence of error, and is therefore *not* a disequilibrium
theory. But Menger does not claim that market prices will at
any time correspond to the prices whose determination this
chapter explains. This chapter deals only with *economic*
prices, *the price that would emerge if economizing individuals
acted in their own best mutual interests without the hindrance
of incomplete information*. Menger is fully aware that the world
will, at any given moment, display prices that are, to greater or
lesser degree, *uneconomic*. And Menger's later chapter 7,
dealing with the "marketability" of commodities, is the locus for
his insights concerning the imperfectly economic character of
market prices in the real world.

So that the prices discussed in Menger's chapter 5 are not

primarily *equilibrium* prices in the sense that at any given moment Menger is especially concerned to postulate a powerful tendency for actual market prices to converge toward them. Rather, they are "correct" prices in a normative sense—that is, the prices sensible market participants would (each in his own interest) immediately agree to were they aware of all the relevant circumstances. "Uneconomic prices" are, in this sense, "wrong" prices.

The century-long *tâtonnement* to which Streissler has referred should be understood as a social process in which people devise institutions, and in the course of which specialists emerge that help uneconomic prices to be avoided. Owing to the complicated character of trading relationships, Menger explains in a footnote to his chapter on prices, "the formation of economic prices becomes virtually impossible" without the institutions of markets, fairs, and exchanges.[54] "The speculation that develops on these markets has the effect of impeding uneconomic price formation."[55] This idea is expanded upon in his chapter 7 in the course of the discussion on marketability. "The institution of an organized market for an article makes it possible for the producers . . . to sell . . . at any time at economic prices."[56] In the successful achievement of economic prices *knowledge* is explicitly accorded an important role. "If every consumer knows where to find the owners of a commodity, this fact alone increases to a high degree the probability that the commodity will, at any time, be sold at an economic price." The absence in retailing of local concentrations of sellers "constitutes the major cause of less economic prices being established in this branch of commerce."[57]

Most fundamentally, "economic prices" are those that faithfully reflect the underlying valuations, by market participants, of the relevant goods or resources. Uneconomic prices incorrectly, or in a distorted fashion, reflect these valuations. In a remarkable footnote to his chapter on the theory of value, in the course of which Menger declares the moral character of rent and interest to be beyond the scope of economics, he explains that wherever "the services of land and of capital bear a price, it is always as a consequence of their value, and their value to men is . . . a necessary consequence of their economic character. The prices . . . are therefore the necessary products of the economic situation under which they arise, and will be more certainly obtained the more developed the legal system of a people and the more upright its public morals."[58]

It follows from all this that Menger had *every reason not* to introduce error into his chapter on the theory of price. For the determination of economic price, error is indeed to be viewed as a pathological aberration. The absence, therefore, of any hint in that chapter of the need and scope for an equilibrating process should not be a source of bewilderment.

It should not be thought, despite our attempt to solve the apparent contradiction in Menger, that Menger's theory of *market* price determination is fully absolved from difficulties. Although Menger's theory has, as we have seen, been described as disequilibrium theory by several writers, it cannot be said that he gave us an adequate theory of price equilibration. The century-long *tâtonnement* that Streissler identified certainly does not give us such a theory. Rather, that glacial *tâtonnement* consists of slow but ultimately dominant forces that for Menger generate a climate in which the costs of avoiding error are reduced toward zero. This process is not therefore a learning process in the course of which prices are, through entrepreneurial grasping of arbitrage opportunities, gradually shaken down toward equilibrium. It is instead a process that brings change to the environment within which prices are on each day, instantaneously, determined.

In this view of the market there appears no systematic process linking today's prices directly to those that prevailed yesterday. Yesterday's prices were struck in reflection of yesterday's valuations, possibly as distorted by yesterday's ignorance or lack of "upright public morals." Today's prices are struck in reflection of today's valuations possibly as distorted by today's ignorance. There is no hint that today's prices might reflect any process of learning about other people's valuations that might have been set off by the experience of yesterday's prices. If any link at all is to be seen in Menger's system between present prices and those of the past, this must be merely in that the superior present institutions aiding the communication of information (for example, organized markets) evolved out of the inadequate results experienced in earlier environments.

Our conclusion, then, is that, at least as far as concerns the role of entrepreneurial alertness to existing error in bringing about adjustments in prices not yet in equilibrium, Menger's theory was *not* a disequilibrium theory at all. It did *not* make use of the phenomena of ignorance and error. This conclusion, it will be observed, does not necessarily deny the validity of what might seem the contrary view of Streissler and of Jaffé, that Menger's theory was distinguished precisely by its recognition of scope for the entrepreneur, of error, and of disequilibrium. That no such denial is necessarily involved can be shown most effectively by recalling Hayek's sharp criticism of Schumpeter on a matter closely resembling those features of Menger's theory to which I have been drawing critical attention.

In one of the papers in which Hayek developed his ideas of the role of knowledge in market processes, he pointed to Schumpeter's view "that the possibility of a rational calculation in the absence of markets for the factors of production follows for the theorist 'from the elementary proposition that consumers in evaluating ("demanding") consumers' goods *ipso facto* also evaluate the means of production which enter the production of these goods.'"[59] Hayek reacts sharply:

> What Professor Schumpeter's *"ipso facto"* presumably means is that the valuation of the factors of production is implied in, or follows necessarily from, the valuation of consumers' goods. But this...is not correct. Implication is a logical relationship which can be meaningfully asserted only of propositions simultaneously present to one and the same mind.... To assume all the knowledge to be given to a single mind in the same manner in which we assume it to be given to us as the explaining economists is to assume the problem away.[60]

Most significantly, Hayek can find an explanation for the circumstance that "an economist of Professor Schumpeter's standing should thus have fallen into a trap" only in that "there is something fundamentally wrong with an approach which habitually disregards an essential part of the phenomena with which we have to deal: The unavoidable imperfection of man's knowledge and the consequent need for a process by which knowledge is constantly communicated and acquired."[61] That such a criticism can be leveled against Schumpeter in no way destroys our view of him as a pioneer in the explication of the entrepreneurial role. Quite similarly, our criticism of Menger's theory of market price determination—that it reveals no insight into Hayek's "process by which knowledge is constantly communicated and acquired"—does not rule out a possibly pioneering role for Menger in the economics of entrepreneurship, or of imperfect knowledge, or of disequilibrium.

MENGER ON COMPETITION AND PRODUCT VARIATION

Another aspect of economic analysis in which we may detect adumbrations of entrepreneurial processes in Menger's system concerns the nature of competition and product variation. Both competitive activity, in general, and product variation as a form of competitive activity, in particular, can be understood as manifestations of entrepreneurial search and experiment.[62] In fact, perhaps the most powerful force that pushed entrepreneurship out of post-Marshallian price theory was the attempt to confine that theory within the perfectly competitive mold, within which product variation was excluded by definition, and in which competition became a state of affairs, not an activity at all.

Here, too, Streissler and Jaffé have emphasized the difference between Menger and his non-Austrian contemporaries. "The important point to be remembered about Menger's vision of the market structure of an economy is that in contrast to most economists he did not consider monopoly as an odd exception to a world of competition. He much rather thought of *monopoly as the general state of the market and competition as a limiting* case to 'monopolies.' . . . [M]ore precisely, Menger considers *isolated exchange* as the basic type of economic intercourse, . . . a particular case of *bilateral monopoly*."[63] Moreover, "Menger, as far as he thought of competition generally thought of it as *imperfect* competition in the modern sense: Again and again he stresses *product differentiation* and *qualitative* dimensions in competition."[64]

For Streissler, in fact, product variation emerges as the *very central theme* of Menger's entire system. "Much more than a dissertation on utility," Menger's *Grundsätze* "is an *enquiry into the diversity of goods*. Its central thesis is the following: *The increase in the variety of goods* . . . enhances the wealth of nations just as much as the division of labor."[65]

Now it must be observed that this latter view of Streissler's not only is bizarre but appears to be wholly unfounded. A passage in Menger's opening chapter[66] vigorously disputes Adam Smith's thesis that the economic progress of mankind is primarily the result of the increasing division of labor. Menger argues that, historically, progress has resulted from the willingness of people to extend their attention to providing goods of progressively higher order instead of confining their activity to acquiring naturally available goods of lowest order. If "men abandon this most primitive form of economy, investigate the ways in which things may be combined in a causal process for the production of consumption goods, take possession of things capable of being so combined, and treat them as goods of higher order . . . the available quantities of [consumption] goods will no longer be independent of the wishes and needs of men."[67] In this process, Menger points out, not only will the volume of consumption goods expand, but the more *varied* will also become the kinds of goods produced. Menger appears to be moved to make this observation in order to explain the increasing importance of Smith's division of labor *as a result* of economic progress. There is *no* suggestion here, as Streissler repeatedly asserts, that it is product variation that *is responsible for* economic progress. Moreover, this entire passage, in which Menger takes issue with Smith, was in the second edition of the *Grundsätze* (1923) removed from the opening chapter and inserted toward the end of the fourth chapter, where it appears on pages 94–96, which hardly supports the view that this passage is of central importance to Menger's system as a whole.

But Streissler's emphasis on product variation as a recognizable feature of Menger's economics is, of course, untouched by our criticism of Streissler's own excessive emphasis on this feature. And since entrepreneurial innovation is surely responsible for experimentation with new products, new qualities, and varieties of products, this feature of Menger's analysis certainly invites our examination.

Unfortunately, Menger's perspective on the market—while it unquestionably transcends the perfectly competitive model with respect to numbers of market participants and to product homogeneity—offers little direct support for any discovery that Menger recognized the entrepreneurial role. While the perfectly competitive model later came to be viewed as the very core of neoclassical price theory, the truth is that the early post-1870 theorists worked with more realistic perceptions of the market.[68] Menger certainly had his feet planted firmly in a world of heterogeneous products and of exchanges taking place between finite numbers of market participants and, as Streissler points out, often between isolated buyers and sellers. But all this is, after all, entirely consistent with a perfect knowledge view of the universe in which no scope is permitted to exist for entrepreneurial alertness.

THE ENTREPRENEURIAL ROLE IN MENGER'S SYSTEM

Our survey of the various aspects of Menger's economic system that relate to the entrepreneurial role has yielded somewhat paradoxical conclusions. There can be no doubt that Menger, as shown and emphasized by Streissler, displayed remarkable insights about the role of *knowledge*, the phenomenon of *error* in economic activity, and the resulting shadow of *uncertainty* in which economizing activity is carried on. Nor, again, can we doubt that Menger perceived the economic world as an arena of dynamic, rivalrous competition, a world totally unlike the equilibrium world of the perfectly competitive model. Certainly Menger's world was one in which we would have expected the entrepreneurial role to have been not only clearly perceived but boldly underlined. That we have found this *not* to be the case is paradoxical enough.

This paradox becomes all the more puzzling when Menger's theory of price is examined. This theory, we see, appears to be constructed only through the careful *exclusion* of all error and ignorance. The prices explained by Menger's theory become, therefore, prices fully consistent with equilibrium and totally

inconsistent with competition understood as an entrepreneurial process generated by error and its spontaneous discovery.
How are we to account for this surprising gap in Menger? How
could a writer so steeped in nonequilibrium perspectives on the
economic process fail to recognize the pivotal character of the
entrepreneurial role in this process?

Streissler, though he does not directly confront this question, has already provided, it might be maintained, an answer.
In a discussion of the sociological milieu from which the early
Austrian economists sprang, Streissler attributes to them a
political bias that must have operated against any thorough
recognition of the role of the entrepreneur. The early Austrians
faced the problem of explaining the great Austrian economic
revival in the third quarter of the last century, especially after
the military defeat of 1866. The question was: "To which social
group does Austria owe its prosperity? In similar contexts the
English classicists would have replied without hesitation: To
the businessmen, the entrepreneurs. But this kind of answer
could not be given by the three founders of the Austrian
School, all of them sons of noble civil servants. This answer
could only be given by Schumpeter, the son of a wealthy
businessman. The answer would furthermore have enclosed
political dynamite of the highest explosiveness. For who would
have been responsible for the sole successes? An entrepreneurial class which in Austria was particularly strongly socially disparaged and which was, to boot, nearly exclusively of
alien extraction: Germans, Protestants, Jews! Who would, on
the other hand, have failed in their specific, the political, task?
Their own class, the bureaucracy and the crown, the 'House of
Austria.'"[69] In this vein, Streissler explains the emphasis of
the Austrians, particularly of Wieser, upon marginal utility as
ideologically inspired. "In the shift of responsibility for
economic prosperity from the embarrassing businessmen to
the innocuous consumers, to everybody, the ideological charge
of the idea of marginal utility can be found."[70] But this approach can hardly be deployed to answer our question.

Not only is Streissler's suggestion little more than pure
conjecture—and a conjecture not only bizarre but also highly
uncomplimentary to the intellectual integrity of the early

Austrians—it would not even be fully consistent with his own
view of Menger's system. For Streissler, marginal utility was
not at all the central theme of *Menger's* economics; it was only
the later followers, particularly Wieser, who chose to emphasize this aspect of their system.[71] In Menger himself,
Streissler maintains, the "idea of marginal utility is only of
more or less secondary importance."[72] In this regard, it is
therefore not quite clear why Streissler finds it important or
even relevant to document that Menger, like Wieser and
Böhm-Bawerk, belonged to the class of noble civil servants.

A more intriguing explanation for the "entrepreneurial gap"
in Menger has been suggested (in personal conversation with
me) by Professor Lachmann. Schumpeter's recognition of the
role of the entrepreneur, Lachmann argues, arose out of his
profound preoccupation with the Walrasian general equilibrium model. Precisely because of the more than obvious discrepancies between this model and the real world, Schumpeter
discovered the source of these discrepancies in the dynamic
role of the entrepreneur. Menger, on the other hand, not being
encumbered by excessive attention to general equilibrium
conditions, was not led to emphasize the specifically dynamic
role of the entrepreneur; he had no need to do so. Lachmann's
suggestion is highly attractive, but it does not appear to take
into account the extent to which Menger's theory of price *is* an
equilibrium theory and the extent to which he does find it
necessary to account for a process of *institutional* change that
bears on the degree to which the real world has not yet attained
the full equilibrium of Menger's "economic prices."

Perhaps a more simple but plausible understanding of the
unevenly profound recognition of scope for entrepreneurship in
Menger may be gained from the traditional view of Menger's
system that Streissler finds so unacceptable. Surely the traditional view of Menger is wholly correct, if not in its emphasis
on "marginal utility" as being the central theme of Menger's
system, then at least in its emphasis upon subjective value. It
is almost impossible to see how any reader of the *Grundsätze*
can fail to agree that its single theme is the way all valuation in
an economic system takes its source from the final valuations
of those to whose desires the system is to minister. This theme

was so profoundly important and exciting for Menger, and one
so revolutionary, he believed, that it consumed all his energy
and attention. Precisely because of this, Menger's view of
economizing man is so complete, so sensitive to notions of
knowledge, error, and alertness. Nonetheless, in pursuing this
theme with single-minded concentration, Menger was simply
not led to see the market *process* as an entrepreneurial one; he
was not led to see how his own profound insights into the scope
for error in economizing decisions provided the key to a view of
the market as a process of social discovery, the very process
through which the valuations of Menger's consumers come to
be translated into complex chains of production decisions
ministering to their desires. It remained for later followers of
the Mengerian tradition, in particular Mises and Hayek, to
perceive the exact character of this process. In this task, they
were unquestionably able to draw upon a tradition, Mengerian
in origin, in which error, uncertainty, diversity, and rivalrous
competition were always, to some degree, in sight. But the
process itself was not seen by Menger.

It should come as no surprise that Menger himself was unable to see how his own ideas pointed to these powerful insights into the entrepreneurial process. It is always so with
great pioneers. And with Menger we have direct evidence that
he himself saw how this was occurring! In his 1923 review
article of the second German edition of Menger's *Grundsätze*,
Franz X. Weiss recalled an illuminating and touching conversation with Menger in 1910, when the latter was not quite
seventy. When Weiss suggested certain ideas to Menger, built
on Menger's own foundations, for the advancement of the
theory of the value of money, Menger replied that he too saw
how those ideas are the implications of his own teachings, yet
he was unable to accept them![73] Weiss uses this remark to
throw light on Menger's general failure to cite or to use almost
any of the work of his followers. The intellectual effort required
to escape and to overthrow the deeply entrenched classical
view of the economic system, Weiss believes, may have hin-
dered Menger from being able to see and accept all the implications drawn from his work by his followers. This appears to

be the case, I would argue, in regard to entrepreneurship. As Weiss emphasizes,[74] one's realization of this circumstance in no way diminishes the greatness of Menger's own pioneering contribution to the history of economic thought and, for that matter, to the development of the theory of the entrepreneurial market process.

5

Ludwig von Mises and the Theory of Capital and Interest

STUDENTS OF MISESIAN ECONOMICS often agree that the theory of capital and interest occupies a central and characteristically Austrian position in the general Misesian system. That is the reason Frank H. Knight, in his lengthy and critical review article of the first complete exposition of that system,[1] chose to concentrate on "the theory of capital and interest" after deciding to confine his review to "some one main problem which at once is peculiarly central in the structure of theory, and on which [his] disagreement with the author reaches down to basic premises and methods."[2] In that article, Knight identified Mises as the foremost exponent of the Austrian position on capital and interest. In a 1945 article, Friedrich A. Hayek also alluded to Mises as the most thoroughgoing among the Austrians on these problems.[3]

And yet, in his published works, Mises appears to have devoted little attention to the theories of capital and interest until relatively late in his career. His influence on these matters was largely confined to his oral teaching and seminar discussions. As late as 1941, presumably without having seen Mises's *Nationalökonomie*, published in 1940, Hayek remarked in his *Pure Theory of Capital* that, while Mises's "published work deals mainly with the more complex problems that only arise beyond the point at which [this book] ends," Mises had nonetheless "suggested some of the angles from which the more abstract problem is approached [in this book]."[4]

Apart from a 1931 *Festschrift* paper on inconvertible capital,[5]

Presented at a session of the meetings of the Southern Economic Association, held at Atlanta, Georgia, November 1974.

Mises's published work on capital and interest prior to 1940 is confined (apart from casual obiter dicta) to a few brief pages in his *Socialism*.[6] On the other hand, there is an intriguing, somewhat cryptic footnote in the second (1924) edition of his *Theory of Money and Credit*.[7] It makes clear that, since 1912, Mises (1) had given much critical thought to the theory of interest, (2) now considered Eugen von Böhm-Bawerk, while "the first to clear the way that leads to understanding of the problem," nonetheless to have presented a theory that was *not* satisfactory, and (3) hoped to publish "in the not-too-distant future" his own special study of the problem. It is certainly unfortunate that Mises never published such a study and that we are forced to rely on a relatively meager collection of scattered remarks in his larger works in order to understand what he considered unsatisfactory about Böhm-Bawerk's position. Fortunately, while his later works do not include a detailed critical discussion of Böhm-Bawerk's writings, they do provide us with a complete theoretical treatment of the problems of capital and interest, thereby justifying Knight's claim that the theory of capital and interest occupies a central position in the Misesian system. In what follows I shall first summarize Mises's own views on the problems of capital and interest and then discuss the extent to which his views differed from those of Böhm-Bawerk and Knight. In so doing, we shall discover that Mises's later position is, as was noted by both Knight and Hayek, characteristically and consistently Austrian.

MISES ON CAPITAL AND ON INTEREST

Mises's views on capital and interest may be conveniently summarized as follows:

1. Interest in *not* the specific income derived from using capital goods,[8] nor is it "the price paid for the services of capital."[9] Instead, interest expresses the universal ("categorial") phenomenon of time preference and will therefore inevitably emerge also in a pure exchange economy without production.

2. Since production takes time, the market prices of factors of production (which tend to reflect the market prices of the consumer goods they produce) are themselves subject to

considerations of time preference. Thus the market in a production economy generates interest as the excess *value* of produced goods over the appropriately discounted values of the relevant factors of production.

3. The concept of *capital* (as well as of its correlative *income*) is strictly a tool for economic calculation and hence has meaning only in the context of a market in which monetary calculation is meaningful. Thus, capital is properly defined as the subjectively perceived monetary value of the owner's equity in the assets of a particular business unit. *Capital* is therefore to be sharply distinguished from *capital goods*.

4. Capital goods are produced factors of production; they are "intermediary stations on the way leading from the very beginning of production to its final goal, the turning out of consumers' goods."[10]

5. It is decidedly *not* useful to define capital as the totality of capital goods. Nor does the concept of a *totality* of capital goods provide any insight into the productive process.

6. Capital goods are the results of earlier (i.e., higher) stages of production and therefore are not factors of production in their own right apart from the factors employed in their production. Capital goods have no productive power of their own that cannot be attributed to these earlier productive factors.

In his discussion about capital and interest, Mises did not, to any extent, name the specific authors with whom he took issue. As Knight observed, with respect to the entire volume that he was reviewing, Mises's exposition of capital and interest "is highly controversial in substance, and in tone, though the argument is directed toward positions, with very little debate or *Auseinandersetzung* with named authors."[11]

The hints Mises himself gave, together with a careful comparison of his own stated views with those of other capital theorists, enable us to understand how his views relate to the more widely known theories of capital and interest against which he was rebelling. Such an understanding is of the utmost importance in order to fully appreciate Mises's contribution. In the following analysis I shall indicate the points of disagreement between Mises and the two major contesting approaches of his time on the issue of capital and interest. I shall consider the Böhm-Bawerkian tradition first and then move on to review the [John Bates] Clark-Knight point of view.

MISES AND THE BÖHM-BAWERKIAN THEORY

We have already seen that, as early as 1924, Mises had expressed dissatisfaction with Böhm-Bawerk's theory. This may come as a surprise to those who—quite mistakenly—believe the Austrian position on most questions of economic theory, and especially on the theory of capital and interest, is a monolithic one. The truth of the matter is that, while the suggestive brilliance of Böhm-Bawerk's contribution won international recognition as typifying the work of the Austrian School, it was by no means acceptable to other leading representatives of that school. It is by now well known, as reported by Joseph A. Schumpeter, that Carl Menger considered Böhm-Bawerk's theory of capital and interest to have been "one of the greatest errors ever committed."[12] Referring specifically not only to Menger but also to Friedrich von Wieser and to Schumpeter himself, Hayek remarked that those "commonly regarded as the leaders of the 'Austrian School' of economics" did not accept Böhm-Bawerk's views.[13] So we should not be overly surprised at Mises's disagreement with his own mentor's teachings.

Mises's disagreements with the Böhm-Bawerkian theory reflect a consistent theme. Mises was concerned with distilling Böhm-Bawerk's basic ideas from the nonsubjective, technical, and empirical garb in which they had been presented. Mises tried to show that Böhm-Bawerk's basic ideas flowed smoothly out of his own praxeological approach, or, in other words, that they could be cast in a strictly subjectivist mold. Knight correctly characterized Mises as taking an extreme Austrian position on interest by refusing to attribute any explanatory role to the objective, or physical, conditions governing production in a capital-using world. As the Austrian theory of value depends on utility considerations, with no recognition accorded objective costs, so too, Knight explained, the Misesian theory of interest depends entirely on subjective time preference, with no influence attributed to physical productivity.[14] One is reminded of Hayek's penetrating comment concerning the nature of Mises's contribution to economics. Remarking that "it is probably no exaggeration to say that every important advance in economic theory during the last hundred years was a further step in the consistent application of subjectivism,"[15] Hayek cited Mises as the economist who most consistently carried out this subjectivist development: "Probably all the characteristic features of his theories... follow directly... from this central position."[16] More specifically, Mises's theory of capital and interest is in disagreement with Böhm-Bawerk's on the following points:

1. *On the role of time.* Mises, while paying tribute to the "imperishable merits" of Böhm-Bawerk's seminal role in the development of the time-preference theory, sharply criticized the epistemological perspective from which Böhm-Bawerk viewed time as entering the analysis. For Böhm-Bawerk time preference is an empirical regularity observed through casual psychological observation. Instead, Mises saw time preference as a "definite categorial element... operative in every instance of action."[17] In Mises's view, Böhm-Bawerk's theory failed to do justice to the universality and inevitability of the phenomenon of time preference. In addition, Mises took Böhm-Bawerk to task for not recognizing that time should enter analysis only in the ex ante sense. The role time "plays in action consists entirely in the choices acting man makes between periods of production of different length. The length of time expended in the past for the production of capital goods available today does not count at all.... The 'average period of production' is an empty concept."[18] It may be remarked that here Mises identified a source of perennial confusion concerning the role of time in the Austrian theory. Many of the criticisms leveled by Knight and others against the Austrian theory are irrelevant when the theory is cast explicitly in terms of the time-conscious, *forward-looking decisions* made by producers and consumers.[19]

2. *On the role of productivity.* As already mentioned, Mises sharply deplored the concessions Böhm-Bawerk made to the productivity theorists. To Mises, it was both unfortunate and inexplicable that Böhm-Bawerk, who in his critical history of

interest doctrines had "so brilliantly refuted" the productivity approach, himself fell, to some extent, into the same kinds of error in his *Positive Theory*. There is some disagreement in the literature on the degree to which Böhm-Bawerk in fact allowed productivity considerations to enter his theory. The issue goes back at least to Frank A. Fetter's remark in 1902 that it "has been a surprise to many students of Böhm-Bawerk to find that he has presented a theory, the most prominent feature of which is the technical productiveness of roundabout processes. His criticism of the productivity theories of interest has been of such a nature as to lead to the belief that he utterly rejected them.... [But] it appears from Böhm-Bawerk's later statement that he does not object to the productivity theory as a partial, but as an exclusive, explanation of interest."[20] Much later Schumpeter insisted that productivity plays only a subsidiary role in what is in fact wholly a time-preference theory.[21] It is of some interest to note that when Böhm-Bawerk considered the alternative roles for productivity in a time-conscious theory, he came out squarely for an interpretation that placed productivity and "impatience" on the same level.[22] Böhm-Bawerk made it very clear that he was not willing to identify his position with that of Fetter, who espoused a time-preference theory of interest without any mention of productivity considerations. Böhm-Bawerk remarked that "Fetter himself espouses a [theory which] places him on the outermost wing of the purely 'psychological' interest theorists—'psychological' as opposed to 'technical.' He moves into a position far more extreme than the one I occupy."[23]

Certainly Mises offered a theory of interest fully as extreme as the one developed by Fetter. Later we shall consider Mises's denial that capital productivity has any role in interest theory.

3. *On the definition of capital.* Böhm-Bawerk defined capital as the aggregate of intermediate products (i.e., of produced means of production)[24] and in so doing was criticized by Menger.[25] Menger sought "to rehabilitate the abstract concept of capital as the money value of the property devoted to acquisitive purposes against the Smithian concept of the 'produced means of production.'"[26] As early as his work on *Socialism* (1923), Mises emphatically endorsed the Mengerian

definition.[27] In *Human Action* he pursued the question even more thoroughly, though without making it explicit that he was objecting to Böhm-Bawerk's definition. Economists, Mises maintained, fall into the error of defining capital as *real capital*, as an aggregate of physical things. This is not only an empty concept but one that has been responsible for serious errors in the various uses to which the concept of capital has been applied.

Mises's refusal to accept the notion of capital as an aggregate of produced means of production expressed his consistent Austrian emphasis on forward-looking decision making. Menger had already argued that "the historical origin of a commodity is irrelevant from an economic point of view."[28] Later Knight and Hayek were to claim that emphasis on the historical origins of produced means of production is a residual of the older cost-of-production perspectives and inconsistent with the valuable insight that bygones are bygones.[29] Thus, Mises's rejection of Böhm-Bawerk's definition reflects a thoroughgoing subjective point of view.

In addition, Mises's unhappiness with the Böhm-Bawerkian notion of capital is due to his characteristically Austrian skepticism toward economic aggregates. As Mises wrote, "[The] totality of the produced factors of production is merely an enumeration of physical quantities of thousands and thousands of various goods. Such an inventory is of no use to acting. It is a description of a part of the universe in terms of technology and topography and has no reference whatever to the problems raised by the endeavors to improve human well-being."[30] Lachmann suggested that a similar objection to the questionable practice of economic aggregation may have been the reason for Menger's own sharp disagreement with Böhm-Bawerk's theory.[31]

In place of the Böhm-Bawerkian notion of capital, Mises took over Menger's definition of the term. Thus, in *Human Action*, Mises emphasized at great length that the measurement of capital has significance only for the role it plays in economic calculation. The term denotes, therefore, an accounting concept and depends for its measurement upon a system of market prices. Mises explained that "the capital concept is operative as far as men in their actions let themselves be guided by capital accounting."[32] At another place, Mises wrote: "Capital is the sum of the money equivalent of all assets minus the sum of the money equivalent of all liabilities as dedicated at a definite date to the conduct of the operations of a definite business unit."[33] It follows, in Mises's words, that capital "is inescapably linked with capitalism, the market economy. It is a mere shadow in economic systems in which there is no market exchange and no money prices of goods of all orders."[34] We shall return to several implications of Mises's substitution of the Mengerian capital concept for Böhm-Bawerk's definition.

MISES AND THE CLARK-KNIGHT TRADITION

If Mises's writings on capital and interest diverge from Böhm-Bawerk's theory, they certainly imply a total rejection of the principal alternative to that tradition, the approach developed in the writings of both Clark and Knight. The Clark-Knight concept of capital and the productivity theory of interest came under sharp attack in Mises's major (later) works. As we have mentioned, Knight's review article of Mises's *Nationalökonomie* consisted almost entirely of an attack on Mises's theory of capital and interest, coupled with a restatement and clarification of Knight's own position. By enumerating Mises's various objections to the Clark-Knight view, we acquire, at the same time, a more complete understanding of Mises's disagreement with Böhm-Bawerk. The reason is that the Knightian theory of interest is, as Knight proclaimed, completely opposed to the "absolute Austrianism" of Mises's approach. And what Mises found objectionable in Böhm-Bawerk's theory were, again, just those points in it that he saw as incompatible with a consistently Austrian perspective. So it is entirely understandable why Mises's position with regard to Böhm-Bawerk's theory is clarified by his criticisms of Clark's and Knight's views. We may group Mises's objections to the Clark-Knight position as follows:

1. *The Clark-Knight concept of capital.* Mises had little patience with the notion of capital as a self-perpetuating fund, which he (and others) declared to be sheer mysticism.[35] "An

existence," Mises wrote, "has been attributed to 'capital,' independent of the capital goods in which it is embodied. Capital, it is said, reproduces itself and thus provides for its own maintenance.... All this is nonsense."[36]

It is easy to see how foreign the notion of the "automatic maintenance of capital" must have appeared to Mises. An approach that concentrates analytical attention—as Austrian economics does—on the purposive and deliberate decisions of individual human beings when accounting for all social economic phenomena must treat the notion of capital as a spontaneously growing plant as not merely factually incorrect but simply absurd.[37] Moreover, Mises sensed that such Knightian ideas can lead men to dangerous mistakes in public policy when they ignore the institutional framework and incentive system needed to encourage those deliberate decisions necessary for maintaining the capital stock and enhancing its continued growth.[38]

The Misesian critique of the Clark-Knight view and his endorsement of the Mengerian capital concept suggest what Mises might have said about Hicks's recent classification of the views of economists concerning the aggregate of productive assets as being either "fundist" or "materialist."[39] Mises would have rejected a fundism that, by submerging the separate physical capital goods, ends up concentrating on some supposed quality apart from the goods themselves. He would have argued that the recognition of the time-conscious plans of producers does not require that we submerge the individualities of these goods into, say, a notion such as the average period of production. And, as we have seen, he rejected out of hand the Clarkian view—in Hicks's opinion a "materialist" view—that, by abstracting from the multiperiod plans needed to generate output with capital goods, sees these goods spontaneously generating perpetual flows of net income. In fact, Mises would argue, the entire fundist-materialist debate is predicated on the quite unfortunate practice of directing attention to the aggregate of physical goods. The only useful purpose for a capital concept consists strictly in its accounting role as a tool for economic calculation, a role enormously important for the efficient operation of a productive economy. It was, Mises would insist, Böhm-Bawerk's failure to see all this, and his willingness to accept the basis for a fundist-materialist debate, that lent credence to a Clark-Knight view of the real-capital concept, which implied the mythology of a kind of fundism ("perpetual capital") that Böhm-Bawerk himself did *not* accept. In rejecting Böhm-Bawerk's definition of capital in favor of the Mengerian definition, Mises rendered the Hicksian classification inapplicable to his own work.

2. *Trees and fruit.* Mises's adoption of Menger's concept of capital made it possible for him to avoid the pitfalls in interest theory that stem from the *capital-income* dichotomy. In everyday lay experience the ownership of capital provides assurance of a steady income. As soon as capital is identified as some aggregate of factors of production, it becomes tempting to ascribe the steady income that capital ownership makes possible as somehow expressing the *productivity* of these factors. This has always been the starting point for productivity theories of interest. Knight's permanent-fund-of-capital view of physical capital is simply a variant of those theories that view interest as net income generated perpetually by the productivity of the abstract capital temporarily embodied in particular lumps of physical capital. The capital stock, in this view, is a permanent tree that spontaneously and continuously produces fruit (interest).[40] Mises was explicit in concluding that this erroneous view of interest results from defining capital as an aggregate of produced factors of production. "The worst outgrowth of the use of the mythical notion of real capital was that economists began to speculate about a spurious problem called the productivity of (real) capital." It was such speculation, Mises made clear, that is responsible for the "blunder" of explaining "interest as an income derived from the productivity of capital."[41]

The Mengerian concept of capital as an accounting tool enables us to steer clear of such blunders. The accounting concept comes into play only as reflecting a particular motive that calculating human beings display: "The calculating mind of the actor draws a boundary line between the consumer's goods which he plans to employ for the immediate satisfaction of his wants and the goods . . . which he plans to employ for providing by further acting, for the satisfaction of future wants."[42] There is no implication whatsoever that the flow of income thus achieved for consumption—through the careful deployment of capital—is the automatic fruit of the productivity of capital.

3. *The structure of the productive process.* Perhaps at the core of Mises's rejection of the Clark-Knight productivity theory of interest lies his wholehearted support of the Mengerian insight that the productive process consists of deploying goods of higher order toward the production of goods of lower order. "It is possible to think of the producers' goods as arranged in orders according to their proximity to the consumers' good for whose production they can be used. Those producers' goods which are the nearest to the production of a consumers' good are ranged in the second order, and accordingly those which are used for the production of goods of the second order, in the third order and so on."[43] The purpose of such a scheme of classification is to demonstrate "how the valuation and the prices of the goods of higher orders are dependent on the valuation and the prices of the goods of lower orders produced by their expenditure."[44] This fundamental approach to the pricing of productive factors is able, Mises explained, to lay aside the reasoning of the productivity theorists. *The prices of capital goods must reflect the services expected from their future employment.*[45] In the absence of time preference the price of a piece of land or of a capital good—that is, the price in terms of consumer goods—would equal the undiscounted sum of the marginal values of the future services attributed to it. The productive capacity of a factor cannot, without time preference, account for a flow of interest income on its market value. The phenomenon of interest arises because, as a result of time preference, factor prices reflect only the *discounted* values of their services. "As production goes on, the factors of production are transformed or ripen into present goods of a higher value."[46] For Mises, the important economic characteristic of capital goods is not merely that they can be employed in future production, but that the relationship they bear to their future products is one of higher-order goods to those of lower order. It is this factor that vitiates the productivity theory.

Knight's refusal to grant merit to this reasoning must be seen as a consequence of his rejecting Menger's position that factors of production are really *higher-order* goods. "Perhaps the most serious defect in Menger's economic system...is his view of production as a process of converting goods of higher order into goods of lower order."[47] Because the Knightian view of the productive process emphasizes the repetitive "circular flow" of economic activity while denying the paramount importance of a *structural order* linked to final consumer demand, it is possible to simply ignore the Austrian critique of the productivity theory of interest. In essence, this is what Knight did.

MISES, CAPITALISTS, AND ENTREPRENEURSHIP

One final observation concerning Mises's theory of capital and interest is in order. At all times Mises stressed what he termed the "integration of catallactic functions" that takes place in the real world. Real-world capitalists, Mises constantly reminds us, must of necessity—like landowners, laborers, and consumers—be also *entrepreneurs*. "A capitalist [besides investing funds] is always also virtually an entrepreneur and speculator. He always runs the chance of losing his funds."[48] It follows that "interest stipulated and paid in loans includes not only originary interest but also entrepreneurial profit."[49]

In other words, entrepreneurship exists in capital-using production processes, not only in the usual sense that an entrepreneur-producer borrows or otherwise assembles capital as part of his entrepreneurial function, but also in the more subtle sense that the capitalists themselves, in lending their capital to entrepreneur-producers, are necessarily acting entrepreneurially. While this does not prevent us from analytically isolating the pure capitalist and pure entrepreneurial functions, it does mean that in the real world originary interest and entrepreneurial profit are never found in isolation from one another.

Part Three

THE ENTREPRENEURIAL ROLE

6

Capital, Competition, and Capitalism

NOTHING IS MORE FUNDAMENTAL to capitalism than competition, its very lifeblood. It is the interaction of consumers, resource owners, and entrepreneur-producers in free competitive markets which achieves the allocative efficiency and the affluence we take for granted in capitalist societies. At the same time, nothing can be more integral to the definition of capitalism than private ownership of the tools of production. It is, therefore, with puzzled surprise that one finds that private ownership of capital resources has been judged either unnecessary to, or incompatible with, the competitive market's operation.

On one hand, Professor K. Lancaster has recently asserted that a competitive market system does not require private ownership of capital. All the virtues of the system, he claims, could be achieved equally well in a system in which the state was the sole source of capital, providing it at a market-clearing price to all comers.[1] On the other hand, it is more often asserted that private ownership of capital, especially capital necessary to modern industry, operates as a barrier against the entry of new competition. The result is incompatible with the allocative efficiency usually found in the competitive market economy. I shall critically examine the second assertion, but our discussion will reveal certain weaknesses in the first assertion as well. The analysis will reaffirm the vital role private ownership of capital plays in the competitive market pro-

Presented as a lecture at Hillsdale College, Hillsdale, Michigan, February 1974.

cess by elucidating the way it supports the efficiency, flexibility, and resourcefulness of the capitalist system.

COMPETITION AND EFFICIENCY

The theory of the competitive market process teaches that where resources within a society leave opportunities for improvement via exchange, production, or some combination of both, they will appear as opportunities for entrepreneurial profit. The lure of profit will lead entrepreneurs to discover these opportunities and pursue them until, through the competitive entrepreneurial process, resources have been reallocated in an equilibrium that eliminates both the profit opportunities and the misallocation. Freedom of entry is crucial to this process. The process depends heavily on the likelihood that, whenever anyone perceives an opportunity for improvement, he will be motivated by the lure of profit to exploit that opportunity. For this actually to occur it is necessary that no one who has perceived such an opportunity be barred from exploiting it. Efficiency in resource allocation might fail to be achieved if the resource is monopolized. Where access to a resource is blocked by its monopolized ownership, the monopolist-owner may find it to be in his own interest to limit production, even where the opportunities for utilization of the resource are fully perceived by other would-be producers. Critics claim that the institution of private ownership of capital serves as an obstacle to competitive market entry, arguing that capitalism is incompatible with competition. Let us state these criticisms more fully.

CAPITALISM AND COMPETITION: THE CRITICISMS

Critics argue that lack of capital may prevent the entrepreneur who has the better idea from following it through. Resources will continue to be used for producing less urgently needed products; resources will continue to be combined less efficiently in production, not because superior modes of utilization cannot be perceived (at least by some potential entrepreneurs), but because these visionary pioneers lack the capital resources needed to implement their projects.[2] As a special example, when a poor youth shows unmistakable signs of exceptional native ability, if he cannot afford an education, he may never take advantage of his talents, and thus society may never enjoy the fruits of his ability. Absence of access to capital has left a valuable resource unexploited.[3] If entrepreneurs who lack capital are unable to compete, then the ideas that do become implemented in production are not necessarily those whose superiority in serving consumers has been proved in the crucible of competition.

It is argued that incumbent firms, by virtue of their ownership of capital—a resource not accessible to many potential competitors—are able to enjoy a monopolistic or oligopolistic position. Capital requirements, serving as a barrier to entry, operate to confer imperfectly competitive market structures upon industries. Inefficiency in resource allocation is seen as inevitable because, given the imperfectly competitive structure of an industry, firms will find it in their self-interest to produce less than the competitive ideal. As E. S. Mason objects, "The capital resources necessary to establish a new firm in an effective competitive position may be so large as to eliminate potential competition as a practical consideration."[4]

This line of criticism, especially when advanced by laymen, is often unhelpfully jumbled with other arguments based on the size of incumbent firms. Many argue that monopoly power is granted by the necessity for a firm to be large in order to take advantage of the economies of scale. With a market limited in total size by demand conditions, economies of scale tend to keep down the number of firms in the market, a circumstance which, in the common view, defines the industry as imperfectly competitive. But this version of the criticism is based on confusion. While the argument that capital requirements constitute a barrier to entry is strengthened by the existence of scale economies,[5] since these will increase the amount of capital needed to compete effectively, the argument does not depend on the superficial identification of large size with monopoly power (an identification derived from considerations of limited size of markets). It depends, in its clearest form, strictly on the contention that capital requirements serve to bar entry into industries. We shall appraise capital requirements in this form.

OWNERSHIP, ENTREPRENEURSHIP, AND PROFITS

Critical discussion of the thesis of capital as barrier against entry requires that we first clarify several widely misunderstood aspects of entrepreneurial profits. The common view sees profits as ordinarily accruing to the owner of an enterprise.[6] The entrepreneur is seen as capturing profits through his successful deployment of the resources of his firm. This identification of the owner as the recipient of entrepreneurial profit has been responsible for difficulties economists purport to have discovered in the modern corporation. The modern large corporation is owned by stockholders who exercise virtually no day-to-day control over the use of the corporate resources. Ownership apparently has come to be divorced from control over firm assets. In the Berle-Galbraith view of things, this circumstance shatters the traditional view of profit's role in shaping the pattern of production. In the traditional view, the lure of profits spurs producers to serve consumers; in the corporation the production decisions are not made by owners, to whom profits accrue, but by a new class of corporate managers who find little personal incentive in providing corporate profits for stockholders. It is not our purpose to expose the fallacies in this Berle-Galbraith doctrine on the corporation at this point. We merely note that it rests on an uncritical acceptance of the view that entrepreneurial profits go to the owners of business firms. It is only because profits are believed to accrue only to owners that the stockholders' lack of power appears to contradict the assumption that corporate production decisions are actuated by the profit motive. Later on, we will revert critically to this aspect of the Berle-Galbraith view of the modern corporation.

In contrast to this widespread position linking profit with the ownership of assets, there flows from the Misesian analysis of the market process an entirely different view of entrepreneurial profits. Entrepreneurial profits, in this view, are not captured by owners, in their capacity of owners, at all. They are captured, instead, by men who exercise pure entrepreneurship, for which ownership is *never* a condition.

The Misesian theory of entrepreneurial profit can be described as an "arbitrage" theory of profit.[7] "What makes profit emerge is the fact that the entrepreneur who judges the future prices of the products more correctly than other people do buys some or all of the factors of production at prices which, seen from the point of view of the future state of the market, are too low."[8] Profits arise, then, from the absence of adjustment between the prices on different markets. Entrepreneurship does not consist in exchanging (or physically converting) owned assets of low value into assets of higher value. It consists in exploiting the difference between two sets of prices for the same goods. It consists in buying at the low price and selling at the higher price. Where the opportunities to buy and to sell are, as in pure arbitrage, truly simultaneous, in principle no initial resources are needed at all. The higher price obtained from the sale is more than sufficient to pay the low price that must be paid simultaneously for the purchase. In the more general case of entrepreneurship exercised across time, purchase must precede sale; the capture of profit requires the investment of capital.

> But it is still correct to insist that the entrepreneur qua entrepreneur requires no investment of any kind. If the surplus (representing the difference between selling price and buying price) is sufficient to enable the entrepreneur to offer an interest payment attractive enough to persuade someone to advance the necessary funds, it is still true that the entrepreneur has discovered a way of obtaining pure profit, without the need to invest anything at all.[9]

Recognition that entrepreneurship, in the pure sense, does not require any prior ownership should not prevent us from seeing how an entrepreneur *may*, at the same time, be an owner. Instead of employing resources in a standard, routine use for which its productivity at the margin is widely known and is already precisely reflected in its own market price, an owner of a resource may deploy it in a new, imaginative fashion yielding a sales revenue far in excess of its own current market price. But clearly the same entrepreneurial success might have been obtained by a nonowner purchasing the same resource in the market at its low price and deploying it in the novel way.

Where the resource owner himself acted entrepreneurially in production, we should see him as having "purchased" the resource from himself at the current market price. When an entrepreneur has purchased a good for subsequent resale, he has become the owner of the good. When he does subsequently sell the good at a profit-yielding price, it might appear that it is as an owner that he has captured that profit. But reflection will confirm that the successful decision to which the entrepreneur must attribute his profit was made at a time when he was not yet the owner of the good he has now sold. The entrepreneurial decision is that which inspired him to buy the good in the first place for the sake of its expected sale at a later date. Clearly, then, while we see profits captured by owners, we must perceive that ownership has nothing to do with these profits, and by the same token, essentially nothing to do with the exercise of entrepreneurship.

CAPITALISTS AND ENTREPRENEURS

From the foregoing discussion there emerges with clarity the very important distinction that separates the role of the entrepreneur from that of the capitalist. The capitalist's role in the production process derives wholly from his ownership of resources. The capitalist is the resource owner who, in return for the promise of interest payments, is willing to permit his resources to be used in economic processes extending over time. The entrepreneur is one who perceives in a way the capitalist himself does not how these resources can be deployed in a way that can justify contractual interest payments to prospective investors. It is the entrepreneur who acquires these resources from the capitalist at the "low" price including interest in order to yield an even higher sales revenue at a later date.

To fulfill the capitalist role in production, it is necessary to own resources that can be offered in the market to producers, and to be prepared to wait for payment until these resources generate revenue in relatively time-consuming processes of production. Without prior ownership of productive resources, or funds able to command resources, it is as impossible to be a capitalist as to be a laborer without possessing the capacity to work. But to fulfill the entrepreneurial role, as we have seen, no prior ownership of any resources is needed. It is necessary for the prospective entrepreneur merely to be alert to the possibility of securing the means of production from capitalists and other resource owners to produce a final sales revenue greater than the sum of the amounts he must offer them in return.

It is true that, in the complexity of the real world, we must not expect to discover pure analytical categories. Those exercising entrepreneurship in the real world are likely to be resource owners at the same time. A laborer may borrow capital and produce a product which, after full payment of the costs of capital, leaves a surplus higher than the market value of his labor. And we have already noticed that the exercise of entrepreneurship will render the entrepreneur an owner of that which he has purchased, for the period between its purchase and its later sale. So those who have exercised entrepreneurship appear as current owners of assets. But this does not in any way diminish the power of our conclusion that entrepreneurship as an analytical category does *not* call for the prior ownership of anything as a prerequisite.

Acceptance of this important conclusion may be hampered by the circumstance that we may be unlikely to discover a pure entrepreneur or a pure capitalist. As Mises has pointed out, "every action is embedded in the flux of time and therefore involves a speculation";[10] the decision to lend capital is itself partly an entrepreneurial one, because it involves the possibility that the borrower may be unable to carry out his side of the contract. "A capitalist is always also virtually an entrepreneur and speculator."[11]

But the fact that every capitalist must be an entrepreneur does not in any way logically entail that to become an entrepreneur one must be a capitalist. Even where an entrepreneur happens to be a resource owner, we have seen that the entrepreneurship he has exercised has not depended in any essential way upon the accident of his being an owner of resources.

I emphasize here the sharpness of the distinction between the capitalist and the entrepreneurial roles not only for the sake of the economic insight the distinction confers. (A fascinating chapter in the history of economic thought concerns

the gradual emergence of this insight.) My emphasis also il-
luminates the question with which this chapter is directly concerned, namely, the possibility that the capital requirements of
modern industry operate as a barrier to competition. Let us see
how this is the case.

BARRIERS TO ENTRY

For competition to be eliminated from any branch of production, prospective competitors must somehow be prevented
from entering that branch of production. In the absence of
institutional barriers erected by governmental authority, one
can imagine prospective competitors being unable to enter an
otherwise profitable line of activity *only as a result of barred
access to needed resources*. Only if the needed resources for a
particular line of production are monopolistically owned and
barred to newcomers can producers feel secure from new
competition. Obstacles to competition in production must have
their source in monopolized resource ownership. It is important to perceive the implications of this way of looking at
things.

If the resources needed for production are not monopolized,
no one can be said to be barred from competing by his lack of
resources. If oranges are widely available for purchase, no
prospective producer of orange juice is barred from entering
the industry if it promises profits merely because he lacks
oranges. Nor does any one owner of oranges, in such circumstances, possess any kind of entrepreneurial advantage
over nonowners: "If the supply of an important factor is not
controlled monopolistically, ownership conveys no economic
power."[12] No prior ownership of oranges is needed in order to
capture, by the exercise of entrepreneurial imagination, the
profits waiting to be won through the production of orange
juice. Entrepreneurial entry into the orange juice industry can
be barred only through monopolistically barred access to
oranges.

The case is not one whit different for one said to be barred
from competing by his lack of capital. Unless access to capital
is monopolistically restricted, lack of capital can in no way be
seen as barring competition; nor can ownership of non-

monopolized capital resources be seen as conferring any special economic power. Capital resources, where they are not monopolized, are available to entrepreneurs who perceive how they can be turned to a profit. It is because the entrepreneurial role requires no prior ownership, being sharply distinguished from that of the capitalist, that entrepreneurial competition can never be said to be barred by lack of capital. However, further qualifying observations are in order.

Capital and Entry

Despite our theoretical conclusion that the lack of capital resources cannot, unless they are monopolized, form a barrier to entrepreneurial competition, it will be objected that casual business experience supports the contrary position. In everyday business experience, it will be argued, it is commonplace to find potential entrepreneurs unable to assemble the capital needed to finance promising projects. Apparently capital requirements do hamper competition.

We shall see, however, that the facts presented by casual empiricism can be reconciled with our theoretical conclusion in a number of ways. In fact, such reconciliation will be useful in further clarifying the insights embodied in that conclusion, as well as in guarding us against applying it in inappropriate contexts.

1. What may deter a would-be entrepreneur from implementing what he believes to be a good idea may not be the inaccessibility of capital, but merely its high cost. Clearly, where an idea that seems profitable with capital available at zero cost turns out to be unprofitable under actual capital market conditions, the idea is not in fact a very competitive idea. "The necessity of having to raise large amounts of capital,...cannot be said to prevent entry, since if sufficient profits were anticipated the capital would be forthcoming."[13]

2. Of greater relevance are those circumstances in which an entrepreneur is fully prepared to offer market rates of interest for capital and yet finds it impossible to finance his project. The late F. H. Knight observed years ago that "demonstrated ability can always get funds for business operations."[14] But what if funds are available only at above market rates of inter-

est that render proposed operations no longer profitable? And what if the prospective competitor is an entrepreneur who happens not to have had the opportunity to demonstrate his ability?

Economists have fallen into the habit of recognizing these kinds of possibilities as "capital market imperfections." Put in this way, these possibilities seem to support the charge which we are here rebutting. Even without monopoly in the ownership of capital, it is implied, distortions in resource allocation may be generated by the absence of perfect markets in capital. Moreover, in specific cases imperfection in the capital market may be ascribed to monopoly. In a valuable but neglected paper, G. J. Stigler has carefully collected examples of statements by economists alleging imperfections in the capital market and has demonstrated that all too frequently such allegations reflect nothing but careless thinking.[15] I will briefly report Stigler's criticism and will subsequently point out an aspect of capital markets to which Stigler has not drawn attention.

Stigler explains that market perfection—permitting "all exchange which the traders prefer to non-exchange"—requires a single price throughout the market for a given good. The existence of more than one price implies that "one seller is receiving less than some other buyer is paying, and both would prefer to trade with one another than with whomever they are trading." Thus economists who discover cases where capital can be obtained only at rates higher than those obtainable elsewhere, describe these as cases of market imperfection. But, Stigler points out, "this is surely not sufficient evidence to allow us to conclude that capital is being allocated inefficiently—any more than the fact that some people walk is proof of an imperfection in the automobile market."[16] The existence of trading costs such as costs of transportation, of acquiring information on products and other traders, inspecting quality, collecting funds, may make the absence of a single price fully consistent with market perfection. "There is no 'imperfection' in a market possessing incomplete knowledge if it would not be remunerative to acquire (produce) complete knowledge."[17]

In other words, if capital can be obtained for a project only at rates higher than those available elsewhere, this is not necessarily evidence of market imperfection, nor does it follow that capital requirements somehow operate to hamper competition. Thus, to use one of Stigler's examples, if an investment in college education is likely to yield a 12 percent return, no necessary "imperfection" in the capital market is demonstrated by the fact that a would-be student cannot borrow funds at "the" interest rate of 6 percent. After all, it is possible that the likely default rate—clearly a very significant transaction cost—on student loans may make even a 12 percent interest rate unprofitable to lenders. So the difficulty would-be students find in competing in the market for those with college degrees, under such conditions, could not be attributed to lack of access to capital. Instead, it should be clear, capital fails to flow into investment in education simply because when costs of transactions are appropriately taken into account, such investment turns out not to be the most profitable use of funds.

To pursue the point a little further, suppose an unknown, penniless would-be entrepreneur has a genuinely good idea but cannot put it into operation because capitalists do not wish to risk their capital on a venture in which they must rely on both his unproved judgment and his undemonstrated integrity. We have here a good idea which, if the entrepreneur had been independently wealthy, he would have plunged into with enthusiasm; it will now fail to be implemented solely because he is penniless. We have seen that it would be wrong to describe this as the result of an obstacle in the competitive process. What we may be seeing in such a situation may merely be the efficient translation of very real transactions costs (namely, the cost of securing recognition for one's entrepreneurial judgment and personal integrity) into the appropriate allocation of resources.[18] These costs of securing recognition of one's competence and trustworthiness are truly social costs. They would exist under any system of economic organization; thus under socialism, too, planners would face the problem of determining the competence and integrity of those to whom to entrust social capital. It is true, of course, that were the penniless entrepreneur a wealthy man, these costs would be absent. So it may be argued that, given the existing pattern of resource ownership, capital requirements operate to restrict entrepreneurial entry. But such an objection would be quite without force. It would be similar to an objection charging inefficiency on the grounds that, on the West Coast, there are unexploited opportunities for the utilization of skilled laborers who reside on the East Coast, whose transportation costs are not justified by the opportunities. Were the initial pattern of the geographical distribution of labor supply different, these transportation costs would indeed not have been needed. Given the existing state of the world, they *are* needed; to ignore them is to fall into miscalculation. Quite similarly, given the asset ownership pattern at any date, a true social cost must be incurred in order to entrust scarce valuable capital to penniless, unknown entrepreneurs. This hardly qualifies as an obstacle to entrepreneurial entry.

3. The preceding paragraphs, based substantially on the work of Stigler, go far to demonstrate why it is wrong to negate our theoretical conclusion because of the difficulties found in practice in assembling capital for a given project. But still further considerations must be adduced, not mentioned in Stigler's treatment, which lend additional support to my position.

Let us suppose, again, that a bright, unknown, penniless entrepreneur finds it difficult to finance his good idea. Let us suppose that his idea is so good that it justifies incurring all the transaction costs previously mentioned, and that it is profitable even after making ample allowance for the costs of proving the entrepreneur's competence and integrity to potential investors. But, despite all this, he still finds it impossible to raise the necessary capital. Our treatment so far merely suggests, with Stigler, that such cases have yet to be proved to exist. But, as we shall see, we need not be satisfied with this stance. What can be shown is that, even if such cases do exist, the case arguing the existence of a barrier to competition is not one whit the stronger. The clue to the matter lies in the circumstance that, as cited earlier from Mises, a "capitalist is always also virtually an entrepreneur and speculator."

If a new idea holds forth promise, even after all trading costs have been taken into account, of a yield to capitalists higher than they can obtain elsewhere, their failure to exploit it constitutes an entrepreneurial error on their part. To describe such a situation, as Stigler, by implication, seems forced to do, as the manifestation of imperfection in the capital market is to assume, quite erroneously, that absence of entry barriers assures instantaneous attainment of equilibrium; or at any rate, the term "imperfection" is used in a way misleading to laymen. In fact, whenever there exist—without entry barriers—two prices for the same good, this represents, rather than some sinister market "imperfection," nothing but a disequilibrium situation created by entrepreneurial errors, which the competitive entrepreneurial process tends to correct. Two prices for the same good, for which transaction costs are unable to account, are the result of imperfect information on the part of market participants. It is the essence of the entrepreneurial process that a two-price situation provides the incentives for entrepreneurial arbitrage, tending to eliminate the discrepancy. Such processes are the essence of markets, and they can be relied upon wherever entrepreneurial entry is not blocked. Errors by capitalists constitute no exception to these general market laws.

If capitalists have, every one of them, failed to assess correctly the profitability of an idea advanced by a penniless entrepreneur, because they have underestimated the competence or the integrity of its promoter, this creates, for capitalist-entrepreneurs, an opportunity for profit. Unless capital is monopolistically owned, capitalists will tend to compete among themselves with respect to the true measure of the competence and integrity of penniless, unknown would-be entrepreneurs. We have no reason to doubt that capitalists do frequently misjudge the ability of entrepreneurs vying for their capital. We have no reason to doubt, either, that entrepreneurial competition among capitalists always operates to generate a tendency toward equilibrium—that is, for present purposes, toward a state of affairs where the competence and integrity of prospective men of ideas are correctly assessed.

CORPORATIONS, ENTREPRENEURS, AND THE BERLE-GALBRAITH THESIS

Our discussion permits us to return to the problem of fitting the modern corporation into our theoretical framework. We have seen that the Berle-Galbraith thesis perceives the modern corporation as destroying the traditional paramountcy of the profit motive in allocating resources. With the ownership of the corporate capital separated from its control, the argument runs, the profit motives of the owners can hardly control the way corporate resources are allocated. In fact, in Galbraith's view, the modern corporation marks a highly significant shift of economic power away from the owners of capital, who dominated in earlier periods, to the "organized intelligence" that constitutes Galbraith's "technostructure" in the economy of today.[19]

The perspective developed here enables us to see things with greater clarity. For our present purposes, we do not need to engage the Berle-Galbraith thesis on its principal premise, namely, the validity of a separation between corporate ownership and control. Shorey Peterson and others[20] have shown how fuzzy such an alleged separation must be. For present purposes, it is sufficient to differ drastically with Galbraith on what the significance of any such separation must be.

My position is, briefly, that where the corporate form of business organization permits a measure of independence and discretion to corporate managers, this is an ingenious, unplanned device that eases the access of entrepreneurial talent to sources of large-scale financing. Instead of the entrepreneur having to borrow capital—with all the transactions costs we have seen this to involve—the corporate form of organization permits would-be entrepreneurs to hire themselves out to owners of capital as corporate executives. The capitalists retain formal ownership, permitting them, if they choose, to divest themselves easily of their shares in badly managed firms or, in the last resort, to oust incompetent management. Yet the executives, to the limited extent that they do possess discretionary freedom of action, are able to act as entrepreneurs and implement their ideas without themselves becoming owners at all.

Space does not permit an elaboration of this way of seeing the modern corporation. But this brief glimpse of it should reveal the remarkable institutional flexibility of capitalism. With no entry into markets blocked by institutional intervention, the market is incredibly ingenious in successfully encouraging new forms of entrepreneurial competition in the deployment of social capital resources to their most valuable uses. So, far from the modern corporation reflecting any weakening of entrepreneurial profit's role, it exemplifies the subtle ways the lure of profits permeates markets in the highly capitalized industrial forms of our time.[21]

CAPITALISTS AND COMPETITION

My main purpose has been achieved. We have seen how the capitalist role in modern market economies cannot in any way be described as incompatible with the competitive process. But our discussion also permits us to dissent vigorously from a related critical assertion. At the outset I cited the argument that, to enjoy the well-recognized advantages of a competitive market economy, private ownership of capital is not at all necessary. This view argues that all the virtues of a competitive market can be achieved equally well in a system in which the state is the sole source of capital, providing it at a market clearing price to all comers. There are a number of difficulties with this line of argument, as there are with all similar proposals for "market" systems under socialism; we will deal here only with one of them.

We have seen how important a role, in the market for capital, is played by the special trading costs associated with the entrusting of capital into entrepreneurial hands. In the assessment of these costs, we saw a new scope for the exercise of entrepreneurship. The Misesian insight that every capitalist must at the same time be an entrepreneur permitted us to see how entrepreneurial competition among capitalists plays a vital role in the selection of which would-be entrepreneurs shall be entrusted with society's scarce and valuable capital resources. Were the state to be the sole source of capital, this level of entrepreneurial competition would be eliminated. We need not stress the potential abuses lurking in such a state monopoly of capital ownership. We may assume for the sake of argument that such a monopoly would not create those very barriers to entrepreneurial entry that critics of capitalism erroneously claim are erected by capital needs of modern industry. But certainly state control of capital resources would mean that private capitalists would no longer compete with one another in entrepreneurship to identify would-be entrepreneurs of the competence and integrity needed to put massive quantities of capital to work implementing their ideas. Without the profit motive to guide those who select the men of action, initiative, and leadership—even if the profit motive is retained for the level at which men of action, initiative, and leadership themselves operate—we will have abandoned one crucial segment of the market process that tends to allocate capital to the entrepreneurs most likely to succeed.[22]

We conclude, then, not only that private ownership of capital is not inconsistent with the competitive market process, but that it is in fact essential to the efficiency of the competitive market process.

7

Entrepreneurship and the Market Approach to Development

IT IS BEGINNING to be evident that the vast literature on growth and development conceals a yawning gap. This void refers to an understanding of the role of the entrepreneur in economic development, both at the theoretical level and at the level of past and prospective economic history. The entrepreneur, Baumol remarks,[1] has "virtually disappeared from the theoretical literature." In a penetrating essay on the entrepreneur's role in economic development, Leibenstein discovers that the "received theory of competition gives the impression that there is no need for entrepreneurship."[2]

In the literature dealing more narrowly with growth models,[3] this hiatus is almost complete and is hardly surprising in view of its predominant concern with macroeconomic relationships.[4] In contrast, the literature dealing with development proper gives some attention to entrepreneurship, although little effort has been devoted to formulating a clear theoretical understanding of the entrepreneurial role. Discussion has revolved primarily around the possibilities of an "entrepreneurial climate" emerging in hitherto primitive economies, around whether the motivation to seek profits is as weak in underdeveloped countries as frequently assumed, around the feasibility of relying upon foreign entrepreneurs, and around similar issues.[5] However valuable, these discussions appear either to lack an explicit theoretical framework within which to examine the relevant issues or, at best, to be founded rather shakily on the theory of entrepreneurship in development as expounded

Presented at a meeting of the Mont Pelerin Society, held at Caracas, Venezuela, September 1969.

by Schumpeter in his justly famous work.[6] Frequent, somewhat vague references to Schumpeterian innovators and entrepreneurs are apparently considered sufficient to indicate the
theoretical background that is being assumed. Consequently,
the real function of the entrepreneur in a developing market
economy seems often to have been poorly understood, and the
plausibility of rapid development under alternative economic
systems seems to have been uncritically accepted.

I will attempt here to reconsider the role of the entrepreneur
in the theory of the developing market economy. Schumpeter's
approach, for all its brilliant and valuable insights, will be
criticized at a fundamental theoretical level—both his approach to the notion of entrepreneurship itself and his approach to capital-using production. Finally, I will attempt to
outline the far-reaching implications of these criticisms for the
economic policy of developing nations.

DECISIONS AND DECISIONS

At the heart of microeconomics lies the individual decision.
This decision is usually conceived of as an "economizing" one,
that is, one in which the individual—whether consumer, producer, or resource owner—seeks to achieve his ends to the
fullest extent possible within the constraints imposed by the
available means. It involves buying where price is lowest, selling where price is highest, balancing the marginal gain from
each proposed step against the associated marginal sacrifice,
and so on. This essentially allocative, efficiency-oriented,
economizing type of decision is the subject of exhaustive
analysis in the theory of price. The theory of the market
explores the extent to which economizing decisions of many
independent market participants can be carried out simultaneously. The conditions necessary for all such decisions to
dovetail, so that none need be disappointed, constitute the
conditions for market equilibrium. The market process enables
a state of affairs in which the conditions for equilibrium are
absent to lead toward the state of equilibrium.

The essential feature of the economizing decision, and the
feature that renders it amenable to analysis, is its "rationality"
or, more helpfully, its purposefulness. But this purposefulness

is viewed exclusively as imposing upon the utilization of means the importance assigned to the various relevant ends. In particular, these ends and means are viewed as given and known, the act of decision making being seen as essentially *calculative*, as though the resulting action were *already implicit* in the relationship between given ends and means.

But economists cannot confine their attention to this narrow notion of the decision. Attention must also be paid to an element in decision making that cannot be formalized in allocative, calculative terms. Purposefulness in human decision making manifests itself along a dimension that is ignored in the analysis of economizing decision making. In addition to the exploitation of perceived opportunities, purposive human action involves a posture of alertness toward the discovery of as yet *unperceived* opportunities and their exploitation. This element in human action—the alertness toward new valuations with respect to ends, new availability of means—may be termed the *entrepreneurial* element in the individual decision.[7] Awareness of this element in human action leads to the recognition that knowledge by the outside observer of the data surrounding a decision-making situation is not sufficient to yield a prediction of the decision that will be made. The observer's calculation of the optimum choice relevant to the data may be profoundly irrelevant. The crucial question concerns what knowledge of the data is possessed—effectively possessed—by the decision maker. In fact, the essence of the entrepreneurial decision consists in *grasping* the knowledge that might otherwise remain unexploited.

Equilibrium, Disequilibrium, and Entrepreneurship

It is not difficult to understand the traditional neglect by economists of this entrepreneurial element. Much economic analysis was developed against the background of an assumed world of perfect knowledge. The theory of perfect competition and, more generally, the theory of market equilibrium were developed in terms of perfect knowledge. Decisions were seen as strictly economizing decisions. Indeed, the world of perfect knowledge precludes the entrepreneurial element in decision making.

Most important, for a market to be in equilibrium, perfection of knowledge emerges as the essential condition. Equilibrium simply means a state in which each decision correctly anticipates all other decisions. In such a situation, decision making involves nothing more than the calculation of the optimum course available to the chooser, within the constraints imposed by the correctly anticipated decisions of others. No room exists for the entrepreneurial element.

In contrast, a disequilibrium market means a state of affairs in which decisions do not correctly anticipate all the other decisions being made. Clearly, scope exists here for exercise of the entrepreneurial alertness to opportunities for more advantageous decisions than those currently embraced.

It is here that the appropriateness of this concept of an entrepreneurial element in the individual decision becomes apparent. It is well known that in price theory the entrepreneur has no place in the state of equilibrium. Only in disequilibrium are there opportunities for entrepreneurial profit, for the purchase of inputs at a cost lower than the revenue obtainable from the sale of their potential output. In equilibrium all profits have been squeezed out, costs and prices have become fully adjusted. To imagine that all decisions correctly anticipate all others is to assume away all opportunities for capturing a margin between resource costs and product revenues. For the existence of such a margin is inconsistent with the knowledge assumed of resource sellers concerning the higher product revenues, and of the knowledge assumed of product purchasers concerning the lower resource costs. The perfection of knowledge, which rules out the entrepreneurial element in the individual decision, also rules out all entrepreneurial profit opportunities. The imperfection of knowledge that obtains in the disequilibrium market creates the price divergences between resource costs and product revenues that constitute the opportunities for profitable entrepreneurship in the more usual sense. And the exploitation of entrepreneurial opportunities for profit involves precisely that element in decision making that we have termed the entrepreneurial element. To win pure entrepreneurial profits, it is necessary to perceive price divergences that have gone unnoticed. What is required is an alertness to the existence of opportunities that have been overlooked—because their continued existence must mean they have been overlooked.

Entrepreneurship—Equilibrating or Disequilibrating?

All this is elementary enough, although not always clearly perceived, and is not inconsistent with the framework within which Schumpeter develops his entrepreneur-innovator. While, unlike Schumpeter, I have couched my discussion primarily in terms of decisions (and the knowledge possessed by decision makers of others' decisions), my analysis can easily be seen to correspond to Schumpeter's discussion of the entrepreneurless circular flow and of the way the entrepreneur injects change into the system.

But the emphasis in Schumpeter's presentation, quite apart from its failure to stress the importance to decision makers of knowledge of the decisions of others, slurs over an important aspect of entrepreneurial activity. In Schumpeter it appears that the entrepreneur acts to *disturb* an existing equilibrium situation. Entrepreneurial activity *disrupts* the continuing circular flow. While each burst of entrepreneurial innovation leads eventually to a new equilibrium, the entrepreneur is presented as a disequilibrating force. "Development...is... entirely foreign to what may be observed in...the tendency towards equilibrium."[8]

In contrast, our discussion here indicates that the existence of an as yet unexploited opportunity for entrepreneurial profit means that the existing state of affairs, no matter how evenly it seems to flow, is a disequilibrium situation. It is a situation in which some decision makers are at least partly ignorant of the decisions being made by others. This situation is bound to change, and the existence of profit opportunities is the leaven that gives rise to the fermentation of change. Thus in our discussion the entrepreneur is seen as the equilibrating force. More precisely, we see the entrepreneur as bringing into mutual adjustment those discordant elements that constitute the state of disequilibrium. His role is created by the state of disequilibrium and his activities ensure a tendency toward equilibrium. While it is true that without him a disequilibrium state of affairs might continue indefinitely, so that one could hardly insist upon calling the situation one of disequilibrium, nonetheless it is important to recognize that the changes he initiates are *equilibrating* changes, that is, away from the maladjusted state of affairs that invites change and toward the state of affairs in which further change is unnecessary or even impossible.

This contrast, between Schumpeter's vision of the entrepreneur as a spontaneous force pushing the economy *away* from equilibrium and my view of the entrepreneur as the prime agent in the process from disequilibrium *to* equilibrium, is particularly important in the context of economic development. We must first, however, explicitly extend our discussion of entrepreneurship to the multiperiod level, in which Schumpeter's exposition suffers further.

Single-Period Equilibrium and Intertemporal Equilibrium

In an analysis confined to single-period decisions, equilibrium means the state of affairs in which all the single-period decisions made will correctly anticipate the other such decisions being made. Entrepreneurship, in single-period analysis, consists in grasping profit opportunities to buy and sell at different prices in a disequilibrium market within the same period.

In an analysis extending to multiperiod decisions, the notion of equilibrium is more complex. In such an analysis, decisions extend to plans to buy or sell in the future. A man invests now in his education, intending to sell in the future the skills he is learning. Another man erects a shoe factory now, intending to buy regular supplies of leather during the future periods of time. The equilibrium that would result from perfect dovetailing of these multiperiod plans must be an *intertemporal equilibrium*. Plans made today must fit not only with plans made by others today, but also with plans made in the past and other plans to be made in the future.[9] A state of disequilibrium will exist wherever any plan being made at any date fails to dovetail with other relevant plans of whatever date in the entire system being considered. A man who erects a shoe factory and who discovers in later periods that shoe leather is unobtainable, or that consumers no longer wish to buy shoes, made his decision in ignorance of the plans of others on which his own depended. A man who educates himself in a profession for which later demand is lacking has made a plan based upon incorrectly anticipated plans of others.

Clearly, entrepreneurship has its place in the intertemporal market in a way analogous to that occupied in the simpler single-period analysis. Where existing plans do not satisfy the conditions for intertemporal equilibrium, the relevant ignorance by the decision makers has created opportunities for entrepreneurial profit that can be grasped by those who are able to see what others fail to see. These opportunities, available to market participants with that alertness we have identified as the entrepreneurial element in individual decision making, consist in the availability of resources today at prices lower than the present value of the prices at which outputs can be sold in the future. This difference between buying prices and selling prices is similar to entrepreneurial profit in simpler contexts. This profit margin is the result of the failure by those selling the resources today at the lower prices to perceive the possibilities for selling at higher prices in the future. Entrepreneurial alertness to these opportunities will capture this difference as profit and thereby generate the universal tendency toward the elimination of profit. Their buying and selling activities in the intertemporal market will tend to bring resource prices of one date into line with output prices of later dates until only pure interest will be left separating them.

Thus, in the multiperiod context, as in the single-period analysis, the entrepreneur finds scope for his specific role in opportunities for the profitable use of resources that others have not perceived. We see him tending to bring about the exploitation of production possibilities no one has yet noticed. These insights may be extended very smoothly to encompass capital-using production plans.

Entrepreneurship and the Use of Capital

Everyone knows that economic growth and development requires capital. Our discussion of the entrepreneurial role in the context of the intertemporal market will help us to understand the relation between the entrepreneur and the capitalist.

We have seen that the intertemporal production opportunities involve the acquisition of inputs at one date and the subsequent sale of products at a later date. In the context of capital-using production we say that the producer "locks up" resources in the form of capital goods, or goods in process, until the completion of the period of production. For such time-consuming, capital-using productive processes it is necessary for someone to forgo the alternative outputs available by using the inputs in less time-consuming processes of production. That is, someone must perform the capitalist role. If the input sellers—laborers—are not willing to wait for payment (wages), someone else must advance the funds for the purchase of the inputs and wait until the end of the productive process for the return of his investment. The producer who borrows the funds to finance his capital-using process of production finds it worthwhile to undertake the commitment necessary to persuade the capitalist to invest. The more productive processes of production, insofar as these involve more investment of capital, will be undertaken only to the extent that the producer sees the profitability of these processes. All this is trivial enough. But it focuses attention on the role of the entrepreneur in a way that is important for our purposes.

The technical availability of profitable capital-using methods of production and of savings to provide the necessary capital is not sufficient to ensure that these methods will be undertaken. They constitute an opportunity for intertemporal exchanges *that may never be exploited if no one is aware of it*. If, at any time, such an opportunity remains as yet unexplained, it offers opportunity for entrepreneurial profit. An entrepreneur will be able to borrow capital, buy resources, and produce output at a market value that will more than repay the capitalist's investment together with the interest necessary to persuade him to advance the capital funds. Only in intertemporal equilibrium (which, in the context of capital accumulation, certainly does *not* mean a stationary state), will capital-using methods of production yield no surplus over the resource costs plus interest. In the world of imperfect knowledge—and in the multiperiod context lack of prescience is hardly a rarity—harnessing of capital to more productive processes of production must involve entrepreneurial recognition of an opportunity that has hitherto gone unperceived.

Entrepreneurship is necessary in economic development, therefore, for the quite pedestrian purpose of ensuring a tendency toward the adoption of the socially advantageous long-term capital-using opportunities available. So far from being a kind of exogenous push given to the economy, entrepreneurial innovation is the grasping of opportunities that have somehow escaped notice. So far from Schumpeter's "spontaneous and discontinuous change in the channels of the flow," disturbing and displacing "the equilibrium state previously existing,"[10] the development generated by entrepreneurial activity is to be seen as the *response* to tensions created by unfulfilled opportunities, by the unexploited information already at hand.

SCHUMPETERIAN DEVELOPMENT: A CRITICISM

We have brought the discussion to a point where our dissatisfaction with Schumpeter's view of the role of entrepreneurship in development emerges in clear focus. Samuelson has captured the spirit of the Schumpeterian vision with an admirably apt metaphor. "The violin string is plucked by innovation, without innovation it dies down to stationariness, but then along comes a new innovation to pluck it back into dynamic motion again. So it is with the profit rate in economic life."[11] Development is *initiated* by innovators who are *generating* new opportunities. The Schumpeterian innovators stir the economy from its sluggish stationariness. The imitators compete away the innovational profits, restoring the stationary lethargy of a new circular flow, until a new spurt of innovational activity emerges to spark development once again.

In spite of the brilliance and power of Schumpeter's analysis, my own view of entrepreneurial development is quite different. For me entrepreneurship is an *equilibrating* force in the economy, not the reverse. *My* entrepreneur, whether at the single-period level or at the multiperiod level, is seen as fulfilling existing opportunities, as the one who generates the tendency toward the satisfaction of the conditions for equilibrium consistent with available information. His role is to fulfill the potential for economic development that a society already possesses.

My dissatisfaction with the Schumpeterian scheme is as follows. At all levels of human action, whether in the market economy or the centrally planned economy, we must distinguish *two* separate problems associated with ensuring that the best possible course of action will be adopted. The first concerns planning the best available course of action and is essentially a matter of calculation from the relevant data. The second problem is how to ensure that this best course of action, which *can* be carried out, *will* be carried out. At the level of the individual decision, economic analysis has all too frequently assumed that the second problem will take care of itself. The decision maker is simply assumed to seek the optimum position. In other words, the analysis overlooks the need for the entrepreneurial element in the individual decision, assuming the relevant ends and means are known. But as soon as one recognizes the problem of ensuring that the individual sees the optimum course of action, the importance of this entrepreneurial element, of ensuring alertness to and awareness of the data, becomes apparent.

When we consider the economic prospects of developing societies, the same two problems present themselves, and again we find the second problem ignored. The first problem is the determination of the best course of economic development available to the society. In principle, it is a matter of calculating, of comparing alternative possibilities consistent with available resources and technology, in the light of relevant scales of value whether of individuals or of planners, and including the relevant time preferences. No matter how elaborately this kind of calculation is carried out, the solutions obtained relate only to the first problem of determining what is best in the light of what is possible. We are still left with the second problem of ensuring that the opportunities thus computed will be fulfilled. No matter what the form of economic organization, laissez-faire or central planning or some attempted mixture, the second problem must be faced: What can ensure that the opportunities that exist will be seen and embraced? It is here, in the market case, that the entrepreneurial element comes in.

In the market system the existence of opportunities is signaled by profit opportunities in the form of price differentials. Now signals may not always be seen but the kernel of market theory is that a *tendency* exists for them to be seen. The profit incentive is viewed as the attractive force. It is a force that not only provides the incentive to grasp the opportunities once perceived, but ensures a tendency for these opportunities *to be perceived*. Entrepreneurship is seen as the *responding* agency; the alertness of the entrepreneur to profit possibilities is seen as the social mechanism ensuring that society will capture the possibilities available to it. What the entrepreneurial element in individual decision making is to the individual, the entrepreneur is to the market economy. All this is missing in Schumpeter's scheme.

The literature on growth and development consists of careful, elaborate discussions of what possibilities exist for raising the productivity of labor, for increasing the volume of resources, for accumulating physical and human capital, for making gains through foreign trade, foreign capital, and so on. The problem of entrepreneurship in this literature seems to be treated in much the same way as are economic resources in general. Although a difference is recognized between the entrepreneur and the manager, the former still appears to be treated as an element that *extends the range of possible opportunities*, rather than the element needed to ensure a tendency toward the fulfillment of opportunities available in principle without him. Schumpeter's picture of the entrepreneur as the initiator and author of development seems to be at least partly responsible for this failure to grasp the real significance of entrepreneurship. (In this regard, Leibenstein makes a valuable distinction between allocative efficiency and "X-efficiency," and recognizes entrepreneurship as being concerned with the latter rather than with the former.[12])

My objections to Schumpeter may be summed up briefly. The Schumpeterian view of development is one of spontaneous, disjointed change. The circular flow from which such change occurs is one in which intertemporal plans seem to be somehow suppressed, so that changes, say, in the capital intensity of production are associated specifically with entrepreneurial activity. This view directs attention from the possibility of intertemporal equilibrium in the sense of an economy fully adjusted, with no scope for entrepreneurship, to a definite pattern of increasingly capital-intensive activity. The role of the entrepreneur *to ensure a tendency toward the fulfillment* of such a pattern is thus suppressed. Instead of entrepreneurs *responding* to intertemporal profit possibilities through alertness to possibilities of commanding additional capital resources, the entrepreneur is pictured as *creating* profits ("the child of development").[13] Instead of entrepreneurs grasping the opportunities available, responding to and healing maladjustments due to existing ignorance, the entrepreneur is pictured as generating disturbances in a fully adjusted circularly flowing world in which all opportunities were already fully and familiarly exploited.

THE IMPLICATIONS OF THE CRITICISM

Does this criticism of the Schumpeterian view make much difference, or is it another way of seeing the same thing? There are strong grounds for insisting that our criticism does indeed have important implications.

The great neglected question in development economics concerns the existence of a social apparatus for ensuring that available opportunities are exploited. Its solution requires a way to ensure that the decision makers become aware of the existence and attractiveness of these opportunities. We have noticed that the market possesses exactly such an apparatus in the freedom with which it permits entrepreneurs to exploit opportunities for profit of which they become aware. Profit, in the market system, is not merely the incentive to lure entrepreneurs into grasping the opportunities they see, it is the incentive upon which the market relies to ensure that these opportunities will be seen in the first place. *One of the major arguments in favor of a market approach to economic development consists precisely in this crucially important element of the system.* Whatever advantage the price system possesses as a computer, facilitating an optimum intertemporal allocation of resources, these advantages depend utterly on the entrepreneurial element we have identified. And it is precisely such an element that appears to be lacking in alternative systems of social economic organization.[14] It is here, I submit, that Schumpeter's scheme fails us.

For Schumpeter's picture of economic development depends, after all, upon entrepreneurship. Yet, though he has within his grasp this enormously important insight, Schumpeter lets it go. His picture fails to bring out the power of entrepreneurship to ensure a tendency toward the fulfillment of socially desirable opportunities. It fails to throw into relief how the tension generated by the existing maladjustments draws the corrective entrepreneurial activity. It fails to reveal how it is the *market* that permits all this to occur. On the contrary, the entrepreneurship around which Schumpeter builds his system is in principle equally applicable to the centrally planned economy.[15] The notion of circular flow and the possibility of its disturbance through creative spontaneous decisions are in principle entirely relevant to the nonmarket economy. What Schumpeter's picture of innovational development fails to explain is that the existence of a possibility is not enough, that a social mechanism is needed to ensure that possibilities are perceived and embraced. Schumpeter fails to show how the nonmarket economy can grapple with this central problem.

Schumpeter's brilliant insights into the nature of innovation and entrepreneurship thus need to be recast into an ex ante mold. Instead of seeing only changes the entrepreneur has wrought, we must focus on the opportunities that were *waiting* to be grasped by the entrepreneur. Instead of identifying the profits captured ex post by the entrepreneur, we must focus attention on the profit *possibilities* that serve to attract him. Instead of seeing how the entrepreneur has disturbed the placid status quo, we must see how the status quo is nothing but a seething mass of unexploited maladjustments crying out for correction. Instead of seeing entrepreneurship as jerking the system out of equilibrium, we must see it as fulfilling the tendencies within the system *toward* equilibrium. My belief is that only such a theoretical scheme can be helpful in the great policy questions that face the developing countries of the world.

8

Economics and Error

THE TITLE OF THIS CHAPTER, one may surmise, owes something to the title of the famous 1937 paper by Hayek, "Economics and Knowledge."[1] There was, Hayek acknowledged, an intentional ambiguity in the title of that paper: we learned there that the knowledge that economic analysis conveys depends crucially upon propositions about the knowledge possessed by the different members of society. The not-dissimilar ambiguity in the title of this chapter may, I venture to hope, suggest that a good deal of erroneous thought in economics has its source in confusion concerning the nature and role of *error* in the actions of the different members of society. It is my purpose here to dispel at least some portion of this confusion. If, in the course of this attempt, some incidental light can also be thrown on the problems raised by Hayek in his 1937 paper, this will be seen to reflect, once again not accidentally, the symmetrical ambiguities embedded in these two titles.

EFFICIENCY, WASTE, AND ERROR

Economists have traditionally been concerned with issues related to efficiency. Inefficient action occurs when one places oneself in a position one views as less desirable than an equally available alternative state. Inefficiency can therefore not be thought of except as the result of an error, a mistake, an incorrect or wrong move. Much of the work of the modern economist has the declared aim of avoiding errors, of achieving efficiency.

Presented at the Austrian Economics Symposium, held at Windsor, England, September 1976.

At the same time, however, as he directs his energies toward obviating error, the contemporary economist is frequently to be found pursuing his analysis on the assumption that men do not, and will not, ever fall into error. "Waste," declares Stigler in a recent note, "is error within the framework of modern economic analysis, and it will not become a useful concept until we have a theory of error."[2] Modern economic analysis, we are to understand, lacking a theory of error, can and does proceed only by assuming it away: error and waste simply have no place in the world of economic theory. It is this position that I wish to examine critically. Is it really the case, we must ask, that economic theory requires us to abstract completely from the phenomenon of error? As a preliminary step toward the consideration of this question, it is necessary first to review a number of discussions in the economic literature in which the possibility of error has been seriously canvassed.

MISES, MARKSMEN, AND MISTAKES

In a passage in which he is concerned to explain that human action is *always* rational (in the sense of being designed to attain definite ends), Mises considers the objection that men make mistakes. This does not, Mises points out, constitute irrationality. "To make mistakes in pursuing one's ends is a widespread human weakness.... Error, inefficiency, and failure must not be confused with irrationality. He who shoots wants, as a rule, to hit the mark. If he misses it, he is not "irrational"; he is a poor marksman. The doctor who chooses the wrong method to treat a patient is not irrational; he may be an incompetent physician."[3] The implication here is that the incompetent physician and the poor marksman may indeed make mistakes and errors. Rational Misesian human actors *are* human enough to err. But it is clear that these errors are not inconsistent with the position (*excluding* errors) cited earlier as taken by Stigler. In fact, the reason these are not errors in the sense relevant to the Stigler position is entirely similar to the reason why these errors do not, for Mises, constitute irrationality. The mistakes made by the ill-trained doctor do not represent his failure to attain what it is within his power to attain. His failure simply reflects lack of the necessary quality of input. An error, in Stigler's sense, occurs only when an input is used in a way that fails to produce what *that* input can produce. When a poor mathematician makes a mistake in arithmetic[4] he is *not*, therefore, making an error; nor is the failure by a poor marksman to hit the mark an error. It is not an error for a physically weak man to be unable to lift a heavy weight. Nor is it an error, in the relevant sense, when one unschooled in medicine fails to prescribe proper treatment for a patient. To be sure, it may be that the incompetent physician, indifferent mathematician, and poor marksman ought not to waste their time (and their patients' lives) by engaging in tasks for which they are so definitely ill-suited. But, of course, Mises is concerned with the mistakes the physician makes in the course of the practice of medicine, not with the possible error of his attempting medicine at all.

CROCE, TECHNICAL ERROR, AND ECONOMIC ERROR

In the course of his famous correspondence with Pareto at the turn of the century (in the *Giornale degli Economisti*), Benedetto Croce did find a definite place for "economic error." Such an error, Croce explained, must be sharply distinguished from "technical error." Technical error, for Croce, consists in an error of knowledge; it occurs when one is ignorant of the properties of the materials with which one deals (such as when one places a heavy iron girder on a delicate wall too weak to support it). Economic error, on the other hand, occurs, for example, when, yielding to the temptation of the moment, one pursues a transient fancy that is not one's true goal; it is, Croce explains, an *error of will*, "the failure to aim directly at one's own object: To wish this and that, i.e., not really to wish either this or that."[5] Avoiding economic error requires that one aim at one's goal; failure to aim at one's goal constitutes, therefore, a special category of error. This error arises out of the incorrectness not of the pattern of acts taken in pursuing one's immediate aim, since these are, from the point of view of *that* aim, entirely appropriate, but of one's immediate aim itself. To pursue this aim is, from the perspective of one's "true" goals, an aberration. One places one into contradiction with oneself; one aims at what one does *not*, in fact, seek to attain.

Croce's concept of economic error has not found favor among economists. The writer has elsewhere[6] reviewed the careful analysis that Tagliacozzo many years ago made of Croce's position.[7] Briefly, the reason economists have no place for Croce's economic error is that it seems impossible, from the point of view of pure science, to distinguish between "true" goals, and erroneous, transient ones. Once we have accepted the possibility that man can discard yesterday's goals and adopt new ones toward which he will direct today's purposeful actions, we have surrendered the possibility of labeling the pursuit of any end as, on scientific grounds, an erroneous one, no matter how fleeting the "temptation" toward it may be, and no matter how permanent remorse over having yielded to it may turn out to become. Croce's economic error, it then turns out, emerges only as a result of invoking unspecified judgments of value in terms of which to classify, from a man's *own* point of view, those goals of his it is correct to pursue, and those whose pursuit he must consider an error.

Let us digress briefly to note that Mises—in whose writings one finds no room at all for the type of economic error identified by Croce—seems to have consistent scientific grounds for his unwillingness to recognize such error. It is well known that Mises denied the independent existence of a scale of values actuating human choices *apart from the acts of choice themselves*, ("the scale of values . . . manifests itself only in the reality of action").[8] The notion of a given scale of values, Mises is at pains to explain, can therefore not be used to pronounce a real action at variance with that scale irrational. The logical consistency that human action necessarily displays by no means entails *constancy* in the ranking of ends.[9] Mises's insistence on the possibility of changes in adopted preference rankings is closely related to his understanding of choice as *undetermined*. Man does not choose as a *reaction* to given circumstances, on the basis of a previously adopted scale of values; he chooses freely at the time he acts, between different ends and different ways of reaching these ends. It follows that the notion of economic error as perceived by Croce has no place in economic *science*.

ERRONEOUS ACTION AND IMPERFECT KNOWLEDGE

That men frequently act on the basis of imperfect knowledge is, of course, not disputed by writers who exclude error in economic theory. In the passage cited above where Mises defends the rationality of erroneous actions, he mentions an example we have not yet cited. "The farmer who in earlier ages tried to increase his crop by resorting to magic rites acted no less rationally than the modern farmer who applies more fertilizer."[10] Men certainly engage in actions that they may regret when they discover the true facts of the situation. Croce, we have seen, termed this kind of mistake a *technical* error. Erroneous action arising from ignorance is not, however, generally seen as a serious threat to an economics that excludes error. With respect to the *perceived* framework of ends and means, error-free decision making can still be postulated. The very notion of an end-means framework, of preferences and constraints, of indifference curves and budget lines, enables the economist to confine his analysis to choice *within* the given framework. The source of error in such choices, being *outside* that framework, is thus, by the very scope of the analysis, in effect excluded from consideration.

To be sure, it is precisely this aspect of modern economics against which Lachmann and Shackle have, among other matters, so vigorously rebelled. Since action is future oriented, necessarily involving an unknown and unknowable future, men's actions are inevitably attended by what Knight called error in the exercise of judgment.[11] Such error may, if one chooses, be subsumed under Croce's technical error, but the all-pervasive and inescapable character of such errors in judgment does, in the view of these distinguished critics, seriously compromise the usefulness of abstractions depending on given, known ends-means frameworks. I will not pursue further the profound consequences with respect to modern economics that the Lachmann-Shackle critiques imply. Our discussion proceeds, instead, in the context of modes of discourse that do perceive continued relevance in theories of choice dependent on supposedly given known frameworks of preferences and constraints.

It should be pointed out that a good deal of modern theorizing proceeds along a path on which actions based on mistaken knowledge appear *not* to be errors, in a sense deeper than that so far discussed. It is not merely that an action is seen as correct within the framework of the *perceived*, but in fact in the quite wrongly perceived ends-means framework. The action is frequently seen as correct also in that the ignorance on which the mistaken perceptions are to blame, may *itself* be viewed as having been *deliberately* and quite *correctly* cultivated. Economists have long recognized that men must deliberately choose what information they wish to acquire at given prices. One who on a deliberate gamble refrains from acquiring a certain piece of costly knowledge and who then, in consequence of his ignorance, makes a mistake may indeed regret his lack of good fortune in having lost, as a result of his gamble, but he may nonetheless quite possibly feel that the chances he originally confronted when deliberating on whether or not to acquire the costly information rendered his original decision correct. The relevant ends-means framework, within which actions have been pronounced consistently errorless, has now been broadened to embrace the situation within which he chose not to buy the improved information. If Mises's incompetent physician had taken a calculated risk in deliberately not studying with sufficient care the treatment of a rare disease, his subsequent errors may indeed be seen as technical errors; they may also, as we have seen earlier, be seen simply as the entirely to be expected shortcoming in output quality consequent on the less than perfect quality of medical input. But the ignorance responsible for the technical error in medical treatment or, if one prefers, for the less than perfect quality of medical expertise available for deployment, may itself be the consistent result of a correct, deliberate choice. This way of seeing imperfect knowledge—as the correctly planned limitation on input quality—permits one to subsume errors arising out of imperfect knowledge under the general class of errors treated in the section "Mises, Marksmen, and Mistakes"—that is, as not constituting errors at all (in the sense of somehow failing to achieve an available preferred state of affairs). This way of looking at things has gained plausibility as a result of the development during the past fifteen years by Stigler and others, of the the economics of information in which detailed analysis is undertaken of decisions concerning the optimum degree of ignorance to be preserved under different conditions, and of the market consequences of such decisions.

LEIBENSTEIN AND THE LACK OF MOTIVATION

Harvey Leibenstein has written an extensive series of papers developing the concept of X-inefficiency and exploring the extent to which this type of inefficiency has yet to be incorporated into standard economic theory.[12] Here we consider only those aspects of his work that bear directly on the possibility of error within the scope of economic analysis. We briefly note some of the objections raised recently by Stigler against certain aspects of Leibenstein's contribution.

For Leibenstein, X-inefficiency, as contrasted with the more conventional allocative inefficiency, is equivalent to what for others is called technical inefficiency,[13] the failure of producers to achieve, with the inputs they use, the highest level of output technically possible. Among the sources of this kind of inefficiency, in Leibenstein's view, is inadequacy of motivation and effort. "The simple fact is that neither individuals nor firms work as hard, nor do they search for information as effectively, as they could."[14] Stigler has severely criticized Leibenstein for his use of language.[15] For our purposes Stigler's objections can be stated as follows. It is certainly true that greater output could frequently be achieved by greater effort and stronger motivation. But this does not indicate error, in the sense of failing to achieve an available state of affairs more desirable then that actually achieved. If individuals are not sufficiently motivated to work harder, this presumably reflects, deliberately and "correctly," their preference for leisure. If, again, firms have not succeeded in organizing production so as to enhance worker motivation, this constitutes the firm's choice of one technology of production as against the possibility of alternative (more productivity-conscious) technologies. Choice of one technology, yielding lower physical output per week than another, does not, without our knowing all the relevant costs, warrant our asserting the presence of error in the choice of technologies. Stigler's objections are completely convincing. Leibenstein has not, in his exploration of motivational inefficiency, discovered cases of genuine error relevant to our discussion.

ECONOMICS WITHOUT ERROR?

Let us stand back and observe the position to which we have been led. This position might appear to coincide completely with that where there is no place for error in economic analysis, if by error we mean deliberately placing oneself in a situation one prefers less than another equally available situation of which one is aware. We have refused to accept Croce's terminology, in which economic error can occur when one has been temporarily seduced to aim deliberately at a goal that one in fact prefers less than another true goal. We have, with Stigler, refused to accept Leibenstein's apparent perception of inadequately motivated persons, not trying as hard as they really could, as ones who *are* in fact placing themselves in less preferred situations. We have pointed out that errors made by agents whose lack of competence or skill renders such mistakes inevitable clearly do not involve failure to achieve any attainable preferred position, since the inadequate quality of available inputs places such preferred positions out of reach. And where, as a result of imperfect knowledge, an agent achieves a position less preferred than an equally available alternative position, we have seen, too, that he cannot, within the framework of the information he believed to be relevant, be convicted of error. Moreover, we have seen that insofar as this agent deliberately refrained from acquiring more complete or more accurate knowledge, he cannot even be described as having placed himself in a less preferred situation at all, since in his view the cost of acquiring the more accurate knowledge made ignorance the preferred risk.

Our apparent conclusion that error has no place in economics does not depend on any artificial *assumption*, as does, for example, appear to be implied in Stigler. For Stigler, it seems, error is deliberately and artificially excluded by the

economist from his purview on the grounds that we lack a
theory of error.[16] But our own conclusions follow strictly from
the insight that men are purposeful, or rational, as Mises uses
the word. If men pursue purposes, it follows that, of course,
they do not consciously act to place themselves in situations
that are any but the most preferred of those equally available
alternatives of which they are aware. If men turn out to have
failed to achieve the most preferred situations, it must be
either that those situations were in fact *not* available, or that,
possibly as a result of deliberate, purposeful earlier decision,
these agents were not aware of the full range of alternatives.
Not only, that is, have we apparently been led to Stigler's
conclusion that there is no place for error in economics, we
have been led to this conclusion as implied directly in the very
assumption of purposefulness from which we take our point of
departure.[17]

Economics, it thus seems to turn out, is peopled by beings
whose purposefulness ensures that they can never, in retrospect, reproach themselves for having acted in error. They may,
in retrospect, indeed wish that they had been more skillful, or
had commanded more inputs, or had been better informed. But
they can never upbraid themselves for having acted erroneously in failing to command those superior skills or to acquire
more accurate information. They must, at every stage, concede that they had, in the past, acted with flawless precision
insofar as they were able. Any reproaches they may validly
wish to direct at themselves—for example, for not having tried
hard enough or for having succumbed to temptation—arise out
of later judgments of value (concerning the significance of leisure or of the goal represented by the fleeting temptation) with
which they had earlier disagreed. Such self-reproach, as we
now understand, is not for having acted in error, in the sense
relevant to this discussion.[18]

Indeed, the reader might reasonably claim cause for irrita-
tion at the triviality of our conclusion. Given the paramountcy
accorded to purposefulness, and given a definition of error that
excludes "wrong" judgments of value as well as failures as-
cribable to ignorance or inadequacy, whether owing to causes
beyond the control of the agent or to his past purposeful

choices, surely the conclusion that error is excluded is so obviously implicit in our definitions as to be completely uninteresting.

But, as I will attempt to show here, the conclusions to which we have apparently been led by our discussion thus far are not trivial at all; in fact they are not even true. Not only is there nothing, as we shall see, in the assumptions and definitions on which economic analysis is built that rules out error, it can be shown that economic analysis can hardly proceed at all without making very important use of the concept of error, as well as of the concept of the discovery and correction of error. Let us see how all this can possibly be maintained.

IGNORANCE AND IGNORANCE

Much weight was placed, in earlier pages, on our recognition that mistakes made as a result of ignorance do not qualify as errors in the sense relevant to our discussion. A person who acted with complete precision, given the knowledge he thought he possessed, could not, I maintained, be reproached with having acted in error. And where the limits to his stock of knowledge had been deliberately selected, we certainly understood him to have acted, at all times, beyond reproach. That is, the person at no time refrained from exploiting any known opportunity for achieving the most desirable situation possible. Yet surely we must recognize that, valid though these statements are within their own framework, they may *not* fully exhaust our interpretation of the situations to which they refer.

A person walks along a street and sees a store with signs offering to sell apples for one dollar; but, perhaps thinking of other things, he enters a second store where he pays two dollars for identical apples. He may have seen the signs in the first store, but his perception of them was so weak as to mean that, when he paid two dollars in the second store he did not, in fact, know that he was rejecting a preferred opportunity for one less preferred. Within the framework of his knowledge, the two-dollar apples were indeed his best opportunity; he made no error. Yet, surely, in an important sense he will, when he realizes his mistake, reproach himself for having been so absentminded as to pass by the bargain, *which he saw,* for the more expensive purchase. In this sense he *did* commit an error, the error of not acting on the information available to him, on not perceiving fully the opportunity before his very nose. He did, without the excuse of not having the necessary information available to him, consciously place himself in a less preferred position than that available to him. It is true that he was not aware of the superior alternative. But, because the necessary information *was* available to him, it was surely an error on his part to have failed to act upon it (i.e., to have remained unaware of the superior opportunity). His unawareness cannot be excused from conviction of error on the grounds of inadequacy of inputs, since the information inputs were at hand. It cannot be excused on the grounds of an earlier decision to refrain from acquiring information, since no such decision was made. This unawareness cannot be flatly excluded as impossible because of inconsistency with purposeful action because *there is nothing in purposeful action that by itself guarantees that every available opportunity must be instantaneously perceived.*[19]

In the earlier discussion, knowledge was treated as something like an input, a tool. Someone lacking this needed input could not be reproached with error for not achieving that for which this input was needed. And where this input had deliberately and correctly not been acquired because of its cost, this exemption from reproach became even more justified. But we now see that ignorance may mean something other than lack of command over a needed tool; it may be sheer failure to utilize a resource available and ready to hand. Such failure, moreover, is not inconsistent with purposefulness, since an available resource ready to hand may not be noticed; purposefulness is not necessarily inconsistent with tunnel vision. Of course one *might* insist that an agent not blessed with the alertness needed to notice resources available at hand, simply lacks, through no "fault" of his own, *another* "resource" (i.e., "alertness") necessary to take advantage of the resources with which he *has* been blessed. We cannot set down such a use of terms as *wrong.* We simply point out that while decisions can in principle be made by a person lacking any needed resources, including "knowledge," to acquire that resource he lacks, we *cannot* conceive of one who lacks alertness making a decision to acquire it. This is so because, among other reasons,[20] before a decision to acquire anything can be considered, one must *already* assume the alertness necessary for the perception that such an acquisition is needed and possible at all. Or, to put it somewhat differently, one cannot make decisions on how to use alertness, since, to make such a decision about a resource, one must *already* have been alert to its availability. Alertness thus appears to possess a primordial role in decision making that makes it unhelpful to treat it in the analysis of decisions, like any other resource. I therefore claim justification for a terminology that maintains that, where ignorance consists not in lack of available information but in inexplicably failing to see facts staring one in the face, it represents genuine error and genuine inefficiency.[21]

IGNORANCE, ERROR, AND ENTREPRENEURIAL OPPORTUNITIES

We have seen that genuine error is not inconsistent with the fundamental postulates of economics. It remains to be shown that economic analysis *depends* on the presence of this kind of error for its most elementary and far-reaching theorems. Let us consider the theorem that Jevons correctly called "a general law of the utmost importance in economics," which asserts that "in the same open market, at any one moment, there cannot be two prices for the same kind of article."[22] Now Jevons presented this Law of Indifference as valid only where no imperfection of knowledge exists. Yet surely economists ever since Jevons have understood the law as asserting a *tendency* at all times for divergent prices of identical goods to *converge*, ceteris paribus, toward a single price. That is, the law asserts a tendency for imperfect knowledge to be replaced by more perfect knowledge.[23] Now the existence of such a tendency requires some explanation. If the imperfection of knowledge responsible for the initial multiplicity of prices reflected the lack of some resource (as the absence of the means of communication between different parts of a market), then it is difficult, without additional justification, to see how we can postulate universally a process of spontaneous discovery. If, say, imperfection in knowledge resulted from deliberate unwillingness to incur the costs of search, it is not clear how we can be confident that, in the course of the market process, such unwillingness will invariably dissipate, or that the necessary costs of search will invariably fall. Of course, one can construct models in which these costs *may* be supposed to fall. One type of theorizing concerning the nature of the market process has, following on the line of the economics of information, in effect taken this approach.

Surely our justification for asserting the existence of a tendency for the prices of identical articles to converge rests on our understanding that the imperfection of knowledge on which one must rely in order to account for the initial multiplicity of prices reflected, at least in part, sheer error. We understand, that is, that the initial imperfection in knowledge is to be attributed not to lack of some needed resource, but to failure to notice opportunities ready to hand. The multiplicity of prices represented opportunities for pure entrepreneurial profit; that such multiplicity existed means that many market participants (those who sold at the lower prices and those who bought at the higher prices) simply overlooked these opportunities. Since these opportunities were left unexploited, *not* because of unavailable needed resources but because they simply were not noticed, we understand that, as time passes, the lure of available pure profits can be counted upon to alert at least some market participants to the existence of these opportunities. The law of indifference follows from our recognition that error exists, that it consists in available opportunities being overlooked, and that the market process is a process of the systematic discovery and correction of true error. The hypothetical state of equilibrium, it emerges, consists not so much in the perfection of knowledge, since costs of acquiring knowledge may well justify an equilibrium state of ignorance, as in the hypothetical absence of error.

All this permits us to concur, in general terms, if not in detail, with that aspect of Leibenstein's concept of X-inefficiency he identifies with the scope for entrepreneurship.[24] Scope for entrepreneurship, we have discovered, is present whenever error occurs. Pure profit opportunities exist whenever error occurs. Whenever error occurs in the context of production, inputs are being used to achieve less than the optimum quantity and quality of outputs; the producer is operating inside the "outer-bound production possibility surface consistent with [his] resources."[25] X-inefficiency *is* possible; it reflects error and is necessarily reflected in the availability of entrepreneurial discovery and improvement. That our conclusion with respect to this aspect of Leibenstein's contribution apparently differs from that of Stigler, who rejects the notion of X-inefficiency entirely, is fully consistent with our refusal to join Stigler in his insistence on excluding error from economics.

MARSHALL, ROBBINS, AND THE REPRESENTATIVE FIRM

In the course of his critique of Leibenstein, Stigler has valuably recalled our attention to an old issue in the economic literature, the rationale underlying Marshall's concept of the representative firm. It was Lionel (now Lord) Robbins who in 1928[26] explained Marshall's motive in introducing the rather troublesome notion of the representative firm and who showed, with the most effective logic, that there is no need for this awkward construct at all. Our discussion thus far enables us to make several comments on the issue.

Basing his interpretation on the authoritative opinion of Dennis Robertson, Robbins explains that Marshall devised the representative firm "to meet the difficulties occurring in the analysis of supply when there is a disparity of efficiency as between different producers."[27] This disparity means that part of the total supply of each product, the magnitude of which helps determine price, is produced by producers making zero or negative profits. Consequently it appears that "the magnitude of net profit is irrelevant to the determination of...price." For this reason Marshall explained that price is to be understood in terms of the normal costs, including gross earnings of management, associated with the representative firm.[28]

Robbins went to great pains to show that, insofar as concerns those disparities of efficiency between firms that would not disappear in equilibrium, there is no need at all to invoke

the notion of a representative firm. Such disparities in efficiency are to be traced to the presence of entrepreneurs of
varying ability. "Just as units of a given supply may be produced on lands of varying efficiency, so their production may
be supervised by business men of varying ability. What is normal profit for one will not be normal profit for another, that is
all."[29] As Stigler put it, it is inappropriate to use variations in
entrepreneurial ability to account for variations in costs among
firms: "differences in the quality of an input do not lead to
differences in outputs from given inputs.... [When] costs of
firms differed because of quality of entrepreneurs (or other
inputs), the differences in productivity would be reflected in
differences in profits (or other input prices)."[30]

In other words, differences in costs of production arising
from differences in entrepreneurial ability mean that the
equilibrium prices for the various entrepreneurial inputs will
be correspondingly different. When account is taken of the
costs of these entrepreneurial inputs, we will see that, in
equilibrium, there exist *no* cost variations between entrepreneurs. Stigler appears to conclude that Robbins's discussion
justifies the neoclassical practice of viewing each producer as
always at a production frontier. If, as a result of varying quality
of entrepreneurial inputs, output variation occurs, this is simply because, as a result of the variance in entrepreneurial
quality, each producer may have a production frontier above or
below that of others.[31] There is no room, in this scheme of
things, for Leibenstein's X-inefficiency, which implies the possibility that differences in output are a result of genuine differences in sheer efficiency, *not* attributable to differences in
input quality.

What I want to point out here is that the portion of Robbins's
critique of Marshall upon which Stigler draws is confined
explicitly to the state of equilibrium.[32] Under conditions of
equilibrium, we must indeed reject the possibility of genuine
disparities in efficiency among firms that cannot be traced to
differences in input qualities. In equilibrium, such disparities
cannot be traced to sheer error. But under conditions of disequilibrium, when scope exists for entrepreneurial activity,
there is no reason genuine disparities may not exist among

different producers, traceable not to differences in input qualities, since we do not view alertness as an input, but to differences in the degree to which producers have succumbed to
error. Robbins's critique of Marshall does *not*, therefore, imply
any need to reject Leibenstein's X-inefficiency, insofar as such
inefficiency coincides with the existence of a scope for pure
entrepreneurship.

ERROR IN ECONOMICS:
SOME NORMATIVE APPLICATIONS

My concern to defend the possibility of genuine error in
economics is based on more than our wish to show that positive
economic theory cannot proceed without such possibility. In
addition, our concern rests upon important normative grounds.
Allocative inefficiency in a society of errorless individual
maximizers must, it appears on reflection, be accounted for
only by the existence of prohibitive transaction costs.[33] Improvements in social well-being must, in such a world, appear
possible only as a result of unexplained technological break-
throughs.

Surely such a picture of the world, a picture in which no
genuine opportunities for improvement are permitted to exist,
is wholly unsatisfying. Surely we are convinced that enormous
scope exists at all times for genuine economic improvement;
surely we are convinced that the world is chock-full of
inefficiencies. It is most embarrassing to have to grapple with
the grossly inefficient world we know with economic tools that
assume away the essence of the problem with which we wish to
deal.

But as soon as we admit genuine error into our purview, our
embarrassment fades. Our world *is* a grossly inefficient world.
What is inefficient about the world is surely that, at each instant, enormous scope exists for improvements that are in one
way or another ready to hand and yet are simply not noticed. At
each instant, because the market is in a state of disequilibrium, genuine allocative inefficiencies remain to be removed
simply because entrepreneurs have not yet noticed the profit
opportunities these inefficiencies represent. At each instant,
available technological improvements—in some sense already

at hand—remain to be exploited; they remain untapped because entrepreneurs have not yet noticed the profit opportunities embedded in them. We can ascribe many of the world's ills to genuine error, and we need an economics that can recognize this.

Only an economics that recognizes how the profit motive—by which we mean the lure of pure entrepreneurial profits—can harness entrepreneurial activity toward the systematic elimination of error can be of service in pointing the way to those institutional structures necessary for the steady improvement of the lot of mankind.

9

Knowing about Knowledge: A Subjectivist View of the Role of Information

IN RECENT YEARS a good deal of effort has been expended on exploring the role human knowledge plays in the economic process and the degree to which received economic theory takes cognizance of this role.[1] Here I shall argue that, valuable as these explorations have been, they appear in the main not to have exploited the insights that can be derived from an explicitly subjectivist approach to the role of knowledge and information in economic affairs. A consistent emphasis on subjectivism, in this as in other departments of economic theory, yields an understanding of the market process that seems to have escaped notice.

SUBJECTIVISM AND KNOWLEDGE: SOME PARADOXES

The profound importance of subjectivism in identifying human knowledge as central to economic science was perhaps most clearly recognized by Hayek. In his chapter "The Subjective Character of the Social Sciences," Hayek emphasized that "most of the objects of social or human action are not 'objective facts' in the special narrow sense in which this term is used by the Sciences and contrasted to 'opinions,' and they cannot at all be defined in physical terms. So far as human actions are concerned the things *are* what the acting people think they are."[2]

The theory of price, Hayek explains, "has nothing to say about the behavior of the price of iron or wool, of things of such and such physical properties, but only about things about

Presented at a conference on Austrian Economics held at Irving, Texas, December 1976.

which people have certain beliefs and which they want to use in a certain manner."[3] "Only in so far as we can find out what the knowledge and beliefs of the people concerned are in the relevant respects shall we be in a position to predict in what manner a change in the price of the product will affect the prices of the factors."[4] It is the advance of subjectivism in economic theory that has focused attention on "the problem of the compatibility of intentions and expectations of different people, of the division of knowledge between them, and the process by which the relevant knowledge is acquired and expectations formed."[5]

In developing my own thesis concerning the relevance of the subjectivist approach to the economic role of knowledge, I shall argue for what may seem a paradox. Because consideration of this apparent paradox will prove most enlightening, I state it at the outset. Subjectivism teaches us, we have learnt from Hayek, that it is not iron and wool themselves that enter into our economic explanations, but rather the knowledge and beliefs men hold about iron and wool. One might expect, therefore, that in considering economic explanations concerning *knowledge*, a subjectivist approach would emphasize not knowledge itself, but rather what people know about knowledge. What we shall discover, however, is that a subjectivist approach leads to recognition of precisely that kind of knowledge *about which men know nothing at all.* Or the paradox may be put in somewhat different terms. Subjectivism suggests that things about which men are completely ignorant are things that, in the sense relevant to economic theory, *simply do not exist*. Yet, in the case of knowledge itself, consistent pursuit of the subjectivist approach turns out to direct attention precisely to the existence of opportunities for the acquisition of knowledge about which *no* one knows. While in less consistently subjectivist approaches such opportunities are held *not* to exist, it is to the very important and very real existence of these opportunities that subjectivism points.

We shall come to this paradox by considering yet another paradox concerning knowledge, to which several writers have drawn attention. It is now a quarter of a century since Shackle pointed out that knowledge is "a very peculiar commodity."

"All the goods," wrote Shackle, "that serve to educate or entertain us or enable us to communicate with one another, all the books, newspapers, films, theatrical performances, lectures, postal services and television sets, and all the apparatus of scientific research, could have no use or existence if the experiences they will give us could be known for certain beforehand in exact and complete detail.... To admit knowledge and information as ... exchangeable goods is to expose a flank on which the theory of consumers' behaviour, as we find it in our literature is defenceless; for knowledge would not be bought if it were already possessed; and when we buy knowledge we do not know what we are going to get."[6]

More recently, Boulding has noticed this peculiarity of knowledge and has to some extent pointed toward the implications we shall be drawing therefrom. "We have," Boulding observes, "the paradox ... implicit in the very concept of knowledge, that we have to know what we want to know before we can start looking for it. There are things that we ought to know, and which we do not know that we ought to know, that remain largely unknown and unsought for."[7] I contend that the market performs a crucial function in discovering knowledge nobody knows exists; that an understanding of the true character of the market process depends, indeed, on recognizing this crucial function; and, finally, that contemporary economists' unawareness of these insights appears to be the result of otherwise wholly laudable attempts to treat knowledge objectively—that is, as consisting entirely of units of available information that are to be acquired only through calculated expenditure of resources.

KNOWLEDGE AND ACTION

Before turning to the detailed discussion of these contentions, let me clear up possible ambiguities concerning the sense in which I am interested in knowledge. We are, in the subjectivist spirit, concerned with knowledge only insofar as it informs action. We are not, that is, concerned with the extent to which people discover facts or theories that bear no relation to human action. Nor are we concerned with the truth or correctness of the knowledge people possess or of the knowledge they might (if they knew of its availability) wish to possess. We are interested only in the images (to employ Boulding's term) that might become ensconced in people's minds and might, in consequence, motivate and shape their concrete actions.

It follows, of course, that our discussions have nothing to do with the subtleties with which philosophers have invested the theory of knowledge. Knowledge for our purposes includes not only knowledge in the strict philosophical sense, but also beliefs, expectations, and even speculations and guesses, to the extent that people's actions can be recognized as the consistent expression of these beliefs, expectations, and speculation. A subjectivist view of economics sees the world as the outcome of the interplay of deliberate human actions. These actions are the systematic outcomes of the awareness that purposeful human beings have concerning themselves and their environment, in both the present and the future. When we discuss the ways people acquire knowledge, we refer to the ways they acquire the opinions and views, doubts and guesses, as well as certainties, that account for their actions.

On Perfect Knowledge in Economic Theory

All the contributions to the economics of knowledge and information focus uncomplimentary attention on the assumptions made in orthodox microeconomic theory concerning perfect knowledge. These assumptions played, of course, a pivotal role in much of the received theory, especially in the context of perfectly competitive market models. While it was Hayek who apparently first made explicit the place perfect knowledge occupies in the notion of market equilibrium,[8] a host of subsequent economists have worked on the consequences of relaxing this assumption. As we shall see, a good deal of their work has consisted in developing models of search behavior, models that recognize that people are more or less ignorant, and that they are prepared to shoulder the costs of search in order to partially remove their ignorance.

This transition from a world of assumed perfect knowledge to one of consciously accepted search costs has led to a certain revision in the perception of what the earlier perfect knowledge assumption is to mean. Whereas the earlier understanding of the perfect knowledge assumption appears to have been that we are to imagine a world in which people already know everything (without asking ourselves *how* such omniscience might have been arrived at),[9] the more recent perception is that the perfect knowledge assumption postulates the *costless acquisition* of knowledge. If search costs are zero, we are to understand, the perfect knowledge assumption follows as the logical result of the newer theories of search. "In the theory of the competitive market, there is...an...assumption about 'perfect knowledge.' What this means in effect is that the acquisition of knowledge of prices or exchange opportunities in a perfect market is costless, so that knowledge is, as it were, a free good."[10] And one recent attack on the received microeconomic theory of perfect competition rests, in part, on the irrationality of complete acquisition of information in a world in which information is not costless.[11] What is objected to in this critique is not, that is, the assumption of perfect knowledge itself but the implied assumption that market participants go to the pains of acquiring such costly complete information. But we shall see that the assumption of perfect information does not *have* to imply the *deliberate acquisition* of knowledge; nor, on the other hand, does the availability of costless information necessarily imply that people *will* in fact be perfectly informed. Let us consider how knowledge is acquired.

ACQUISITION OF KNOWLEDGE: THE TWO POSSIBLE WAYS

The literature on the economics of information has, at least since Stigler's pioneer article,[12] stressed the role of *deliberate search* for information. This deliberate search is understood to be conducted in exactly the same way as all economic activity. The prospective gross rewards from search are appraised, the relevant costs are carefully calculated, and the appropriate "rational," maximizing decision is taken concerning the extent of search activity to be engaged in. The wealth of literature patterned on this model has tended to suggest that the *only* way knowledge is acquired is through deliberate, cost-conscious search or learning activity. Any ignorance that remains, one is to understand, constitutes the deliberately planned optimal level of ignorance, decided upon in view of the costs of learning. In Stigler's words, "There is no 'imperfection' in a market possessing incomplete knowledge if it would not be remunerative to acquire (produce) complete knowledge: Information costs are the costs of transportation from ignorance to omniscience, and seldom can a trader afford to make the entire trip."[13]

But this view of things is clearly subject, at least to some degree, to the Shackle-Boulding paradox referred to earlier. The theory of search cannot, it is clear, avoid making the assumption that, before undertaking the search, one *already* knows enough about the territory to be able to calculate rewards and costs. So that, if we are to view the acquisition of knowledge as deliberately undertaken, one must postulate some prior knowledge *not* acquired through deliberate search or learning activity. One may, of course, imagine a long sequence of searches for knowledge, each set in motion by the information gathered deliberately from the preceding search. But this cannot free us from the conclusion that at the *start* of the necessarily finite sequence of searches, at least, some knowledge was possessed that was not itself the result of deliberate search. More generally, since economic decision making presupposes some perceived ends-means framework, every decision, including the very first decision to search for more information, must presuppose some given knowledge. The knowledge upon which the first decision to search for knowledge depended was itself *not* acquired deliberately.

The truth surely is that, of the mass of knowledge, beliefs, opinions, expectations, and guesses that one holds at a given moment and that inspire and shape action, only a fraction can be described as being the result of deliberate search or learning activity. Surely a very great volume of one's awareness of one's environment, and of one's expectations concerning the future, is the result of learning experiences that *occurred entirely without having been planned*. The knowledge one obtains from the advertising message thrust before one's eyes was, more likely than not, *not* deliberately searched for; the knowledge one obtains when one is addressed by one's neighbor, or importuned by a beggar, is simply acquired, not at all deliberately. Simply being alive as a human being subjects one to all sorts of sense impressions that continually alter one's awareness of the world. "So far as men are concerned," Shackle has pointed out, "*being* consists in continual and endless fresh *knowing*."[14] To be sure, one is often highly dissatisfied with both the quantity and the quality of information so gained; it is this dissatisfaction, of course, that inspires the search for more and better knowledge. But it would surely be absurd to postulate the complete cessation of flows of knowledge spontaneously acquired. In fact, such spontaneous acquisition of knowledge and information is so pervasive that it is often far too easily taken for granted. It includes not only serendipity in the usual sense, but also spontaneous discovery of the most common and mundane items of daily knowledge. To describe the knowledge so acquired as having been costless or a free good is somewhat misleading. To be sure, the spontaneous learner has incurred no cost or sacrifice through his learning. But this is not so much because the knowledge was costlessly available as because the knowledge was simply not sought deliberately.

It seems reasonable *not* to attribute the prevalence of the assumption of perfect knowledge in so-called neoclassical theories of perfectly competitive equilibrium to an imagined zero-cost availability of knowledge to be acquired. Rather, the perfect knowledge assumption seems to have taken the notion of knowledge spontaneously and undeliberately acquired so much for granted that it imagines *everything* is already known in this way. Now, of course, we should and do protest this monstrous assumption. But we should note that this assumption is not quite the same as to assume that people have taken deliberate advantage of the opportunity to acquire knowledge without cost. So that it is not enough, as Hollis and Nell believe, in order to attack the neoclassical assumption of perfect knowledge, to show that the cost of deliberate acquisition of knowledge is greater than zero. After all, the circumstance that the deliberate acquisition of knowledge may be too costly for a particular individual does not by itself remove the possibility that the knowledge may, *without* any deliberate search decision, already have somehow been spontaneously communicated to him.

So it is necessary for us, it appears, to steer a careful course

between errors that lurk on two sides. On the one hand, we
must avoid the error of imagining that *all* action is inspired
only by knowledge deliberately acquired. This view seems to
be suggested by the literature on the economics of search. This
view suffers, as we shall see, from its neglect of both the positive and the normative implications of information about which
one does not at present know, or whose deliberate acquisition
seems too costly. This view appears to have deflected attention
from the pervasive processes of learning that do *not* depend on
deliberate, costly search.

On the other hand, we must avoid the opposite error of
imagining that action inspired exclusively by *spontaneously* acquired perceptions of one's environment can ever be seriously
thought of as *completely* informed action. Such a view suggests
that any facts in which one might have an interest somehow
slip instantly, without effort of any kind, into one's consciousness. We must avoid this error, not because it underestimates
the costs of deliberate search for knowledge, but because it
blithely assumes such deliberate search, even at zero cost, not
to have been necessary at all.

The Social Significance of Knowledge about Which Nothing Is Known

The emphasis laid here on knowledge not deliberately acquired
is by no means intended to minimize the importance of information purposefully sought. Deliberately learned knowledge
must, of course, fill a critical role in social betterment. And the
economic analysis of the way search is likely to be conducted,
and the institutional framework likely to promote worthwhile
search, must hold great importance for our understanding of
economic development. Here I wish merely to draw attention
to the extent to which social progress depends on a quite different source, in *addition* to deliberate search, for the information that propels and guides human actions. It may be helpful
in this regard to contrast igonrance of knowledge that might be
spontaneously, undeliberately absorbed, with ignorance of
knowledge that might be deliberately sought out or learned.

Ignorance of knowledge or information that might be known
through deliberate search or learning can be explained and

accounted for. Such ignorance is in fact to be defended as justified by the high cost of search or learning. Such ignorance has, then, been deliberately accepted; in a sense it is *optimal*. To know more would mean to sacrifice something more important than the knowledge to be gained. And, again, such ignorance, if it cannot be defended on the grounds of cost-benefit calculations, *must* then clearly be attributed to ignorance concerning the search or learning possibilities that are in fact available. An item of information i_1 may fail to be sought out, that is, simply because knowledge of how to discover i_1 is lacking. The advantages to society that more complete, deliberately sought knowledge may confer may be missing, therefore, either because these advantages are not worthwhile to obtain or because of the lack of a necessary prerequisite, that is, knowledge about knowledge. Each of these possible explanations, while each possibly calling for further levels of explanation, fully responds to our initial surprise as to why available information remained unlearned.

Ignorance of knowledge that might be spontaneously, undeliberately absorbed can, on the other hand, *never be explained in terms of anything other than itself*. Such ignorance is simply there. It cannot be accounted for on the grounds of high search or learning costs, since no searching or learning is needed at all even, to repeat, at zero cost. Such ignorance cannot be accounted for by noting that knowledge concerning the specified knowledge is lacking, since it has been postulated that the specified knowledge can be absorbed quite undeliberately and spontaneously. Ignorance of knowledge that can be absorbed without decision is simply the expression and the evidence of a sheer failure to notice what is there to be seen. It can be given a name—lack of entrepreneurial alertness—but it cannot be explained in terms of the standard economics of microtheory, the theory of deliberate individual decisions.

By the same token, it follows that, whereas in the case of ignorance of knowledge available only through search one must assume that the ignorance must persist until some exogenous change occurs, this does *not* hold for ignorance of knowledge capable of being spontaneously absorbed. Since we can explain why information available through search was deliberately left unlearned, we cannot postulate learning to occur without introducing some change in the circumstances. If search was not worthwhile yesterday, it will not be worthwhile today unless a change has occurred in the value of the expected information or in the costs of search. If worthwhile search was not undertaken yesterday because the opportunity to search was not noticed, it will not be undertaken today unless it has been noticed.

On the other hand, ignorance concerning knowledge that might become spontaneously, undeliberately absorbed *can* be expected to gradually fade. This is so because an item of information that was staring one in the face yesterday, but in some unexplained way remained unnoticed, need *not* necessarily remain unnoticed today. In fact if, as we shall argue, one can assume a tendency to become aware of opportunities that do stare one in the face, then it follows that, as time flows on, men are subject to a spontaneously increasing awareness of information hitherto veiled in ignorance. Of course, this steadily receding tide of ignorance is at all times in opposition to and often overwhelmed by a precisely contrary trend—a continual and spontaneous *widening* of the universe of current facts concerning which knowledge is conceivable but absent. What Shackle calls the kaleidic world[15] is one of continual renewal of ignorance. Constant change constantly turns omniscience into ignorance; but, as we have seen, this continually renewed ignorance is subject to its own relentless erosion through spontaneous discovery.

There is one further important characteristic of ignorance as it relates to knowledge that might be undeliberately discovered, a characteristic that arises from the unexplainable nature of this ignorance. This characteristic is that such ignorance must, in a specific sense, be considered *regrettable*. Since there is no explanation or defense of this ignorance, such ignorance can only be described as a pity, possibly a tragedy. An opportunity stares one in the face; it is inexplicably ignored. Once one has gained the relevant knowledge, one looks back on one's ignorance without having anything to excuse it. One realizes one's earlier error and that is all. Of course, where one's later knowledge shows that the earlier ignorance was unavoidable, as where certain knowledge of the information gained was simply unavailable at the earlier date, one is unable to *condemn* one's earlier ignorance. But nonetheless when, let us say, one discovers that another had guessed the future correctly and had as a result won enormous profits, one must necessarily concede that one made what has turned out to be an error, an understandable error, but an error nonetheless.

Ignorance that *might* have been dispelled by diligent search, but for which the cost of search was too high, cannot be regretted in this way. If the cost calculations were valid, the ignorance was optimal; no error occurred. To regret this ignorance is to regret that the world is not different than it in fact is. But where ignorance was *not* the result of deliberate refusal to learn and has later been shown to have been entirely unnecessary, then one looks back at one's ignorance as upon a deplorable and embarrassing error. From a broader point of view, therefore, it must appear highly desirable to choose among alternative social institutional arrangements those modes of organization that minimize this kind of ignorance—that is, those modes of organization that generate the greatest volume of spontaneous, undeliberate learning. Whether such a choice among institutional arrangements is possible is an issue to which we shall return very shortly. We turn first to remind ourselves briefly that ignorance of spontaneously discoverable information has a special relevance in the decentralized market economy.

IGNORANCE OF OTHER PEOPLE: THE TWO KINDS

It was Hayek who most clearly spelled out the role of knowledge and its absence in the understanding of the market process, and of the wholly fictional state of equilibrium to which that process appears to point. For equilibrium, Hayek taught us, we require a special kind of knowledge, the knowledge of other people's plans. Disequilibrium, it followed, consists of ignorance of other people's plans.[16]

Now, as long as one confines attention to ignorance that is able to disappear only through deliberate, cost-calculating search, it follows that a process of equilibrium necessarily consists of a series of deliberate search efforts on the part of market participants. And it is along this line of analysis that the literature on the economics of information has sought to explicate the market process. A key feature of the market processes so explained, one should notice, is that the speed of the equilibrium process is optimal in the sense that for no participant in the process would it have been desirable, in view of the relevant costs, to have gained knowledge more rapidly.

But we have argued that deliberate search is *not* the only way ignorance is dispelled. And this leads us to recognize that the ignorance that characterizes the market disequilibrium may well include ignorance concerning the plans of other people that is, in principle, entirely unnecessary—ignorance that will tend to disappear spontaneously *without* deliberate search. I will argue for a view that sees the competitive market process as wholly separate and distinct from any systematic, deliberate search adjustment processes that will certainly occur. The market process I will identify will consist, therefore, of a process of *spontaneous discovery* of *the plans of other market participants*. Let us see how this view can be sustained. To do this, we return to the question of whether the pattern of institutional arrangements can have any systematic consequences for the rapidity with which ignorance can be dispelled through spontaneous, undeliberate learning.

ON ENCOURAGING ALERTNESS

I have argued that at least some kinds of ignorance tend to disappear through spontaneous discovery. It would be a mistake to imagine, however, that spontaneous discovery is a wholly unexplainable process, or that it is a process that confers its benefits on all men equally.

The truth is that the ability to learn without deliberate search is a gift individuals enjoy in quite different degrees. It is this gift surely, that we have in mind when we talk of *entrepreneurial alertness*. Entrepreneurial alertness consists, after all, in the ability to notice without search opportunities that have been hitherto overlooked. To be sure, entrepreneurial alertness may also include the ability to notice opportunities for profitable deliberate search. But this opportunity has been discovered by the alert entrepreneur *without* search. Since individuals obviously differ in their entrepreneurial alertness, it is clear that opportunities for social improvement will tend to be exploited most fruitfully if institutional arrangements can be patterned so as to translate such opportunities into opportunities that will be encountered by those whose entrepreneurial alertness is the most acute, the most sensitive, and the most accurate.

Moreover, the process of spontaneous discovery is—admittedly to an as yet very limited degree—a process whose determinants we can at least tentatively discern. It is true that economists and psychologists have a great deal of work to do to explain the forces that influence the pattern of spontaneous learning for different individuals. But surely we are already in a position to identify the more powerful among these forces.

If the advertiser projects his message to the potential consumer in color, or with comic illustration, or accompanied by a certain piece of music, surely this is because the advertiser knows not merely how to lower the cost to the consumer of learning his message, but how to encourage spontaneous learning by the consumer with no deliberate search at all.

And, again, if we know anything at all about the process of spontaneous discovery of information, it is that this process is somehow altogether more rapid when the relevant information will be of benefit to the potential discoverer. Entrepreneurial alertness, that is, is sensitive not so much to information per se as to information that can be deployed to one's advantage.

It follows, then, that for opportunities for social improvement to be more rapidly discovered and exploited, these opportunities must be translated into opportunities that are not merely *encountered* by those whose entrepreneurial alertness is best developed, but into opportunities that are to the advantage of these potential entrepreneurs, and that most effectively excite their interest and alertness. Let us now consider the market process.

THE ROLE OF THE MARKET

Our discussion suggests a view of the market process, both at the level of positive analysis and at that of normative appraisal, that appears not yet to have been clearly enunciated in the economic literature.

We know of various perceptions of the role of the competitive market. The orthodox neoclassical view expressed in the literature of welfare economics sees the market as allocating social resources efficiently. This view suffers both from its concentration on the state of equilibrium and of complete information and from its acceptance of norms of social welfare that rest on illegitimate aggregation of individual preferences. The "catallactic" view espoused by Buchanan sees the market as the set of institutions that facilitate the exploitation of the opportunities for mutually profitable exchange between individuals.[17] Hayek has emphasized the role of the market as a discovery process mobilizing and exploiting the available but scattered scraps of knowledge strewn through the society.[18] Our discussion permits us, I believe, to interpret both the Buchanan and the Hayek positions in a rather novel fashion.

What the market process does is to systematically translate unnoticed opportunities for mutually profitable exchange among individuals into forms that tend to excite the interest and alertness of those most likely to notice what can be spontaneously learned. In this way the opportunities for social improvement via mutually profitable exchanges tend to be most rapidly discovered and exploited.

Where coordination—the mutual recognition of an exchange opportunity by its potential participants—has not occurred, the market translates this into an opportunity for pure entrepreneurial profit available to those with the keenest scent for profit. The ease of calculation provided by money is thus not merely a device lowering transaction costs relevant to deliberate search. It represents a social arrangement with the ability to present existing overlooked opportunities in a form most easily recognized and noticed by spontaneous learners. I have argued at length elsewhere that the competitive-equilibrating process should be understood as an entrepreneurial process, involving continued alertness to shifting opportunities for pure entrepreneurial profit.[19] We now see this process much more deeply, I believe, as a process whereby the general tendency for continued spontaneous discovery of available information is powerfully nudged into its most effective and expeditious channels. This process does *not* consist of deliberate search, it consists of a systematic but wholly unplanned process of undeliberate discovery. The market process disseminates knowledge whose very existence has not been known to its spontaneous learners. The process essentially consists not in a series of deliberate searches for information (although, to be sure, such searches may very well be entailed as by-products of the process). It consists in the spontaneous translation of as yet unexploited exchange opportunities into opportunities for pure profit able to attract the attention of the most alert entrepreneurs. These latter opportunities, noticed and acted upon by entrepreneurs effectively communicate the knowledge needed to ensure consummation of exploitable exchange opportunities.

SUBJECTIVISM AND KNOWLEDGE

Our discussion—billed as a "subjectivist view on the role of information"—has, as promised at the outset, emphasized the role of knowledge about which nothing is known. But the subjectivist approach to social phenomena in general emphasizes that what is important about the objects that surround us is not the objects themselves, but only the knowledge and beliefs about them that inform and shape human actions. It might seem paradoxical, therefore, that I claim that my own emphasis on knowledge about which nothing at all is known is a subjectivist emphasis. But the paradox is easily explained, and the explanation may be of some value in elucidating the meaning of subjectivism.

The foundation of subjectivism in the analysis of social phenomena consists, of course, in the insight that these phenomena are generated by deliberate, purposeful human action. Since action grows out of perceived configurations of ends and means, subjectivism focuses attention on the way these ends and means have been perceived—on knowledge and beliefs concerning them. Now, it might seem that subjectivism then requires us to see action as made possible not only by the availability of the means alone, but by the availability of a more complex package that also includes bundles of information concerning the means and ends. The knowledge and beliefs thus possessed then appear, along with the more narrowly conceived means themselves, as the ingredients of action. The subjectivist view on iron and wool, then, would see not iron alone and wool alone, but iron packaged with information concerning iron, and wool similarly packaged.

A more penetrating understanding of subjectivism surely suggests that the knowledge presupposed by the action postulate is *not* of a character that permits it to be seen as packaged along with the objects or ideas that constitute the means and the ends for action. Instead, subjectivism sees action as inextricably *embedded* in the complex of perceptions and images that make up the consciousness of the human agent at each moment. The means employed in human action can be discussed quite separately from the human agent, but to discuss the knowledge and beliefs that actuate action separately from the human agent would be to imagine away the very notion of a human agent. Consciousness must be treated as primordial to action, so that the knowledge, beliefs, and images that constitute consciousness must for a science of human action be treated as ultimate givens. One must at some point desist from searching for what the agent knows and believes about his knowledge and beliefs. He simply *has* this knowledge and these beliefs.

To be sure, over time the complex of perceptions and images making up consciousness presents a shifting, flexible, and kaleidic scene, and these shifts constitute learning in the broader sense. There is no doubt that a large volume of these shifts are deliberately engineered by the individual, as when he reads a book, listens to a lecture or a harangue, watches a movie, or tours a foreign country. But subjectivism requires us to recognize that, just as man's consciousness itself is an ultimate datum for a science of human action, so also must room be found for spontaneous changes in man's consciousness— changes that are *not* to be viewed as deliberately engineered.

Shackle, as we have seen, pointed out that the knowledge that actuates the deliberate search for knowledge cannot coincide with the knowledge sought. I have argued that the knowledge that propels action of any kind must inevitably embody unsought learning. Our discussion has led us to understand the role of the market process in stimulating undeliberate learning in a socially significant way. I believe this new insight into the market process grows out of applying a consistent subjectivist perspective to the role that knowledge and information play in human action.

10

Alertness, Luck, and Entrepreneurial Profit

ONE OF THE LEADING THEMES running through modern discussions of the nature of and causes for pure entrepreneurial profit is that of unanticipated market conditions.[1] Ignorance and superior knowledge, uncertainty and prescience, are the ideas, intimately bound up with economic change, that have been linked, in a variety of ways, with the notions of opportunities for pure profit, of pure profit captured, and of pure loss suffered. One aspect of this linkage is the subject of this chapter: the relative places to be accorded to "sheer luck" on the one hand, and to superior "entrepreneurial ability"[2] on the other, in the winning of pure profit.

To be sure, this question of luck versus ability is of importance in discussing most other questions likely to be asked concerning profit. Of the fifteen questions that Professor Shackle asks about profit, and that form the framework for his classification of different possible profit concepts, there are very few, it appears, that do not in some degree turn on this basic issue of luck versus ability.[3] My present focus will, however, be upon this issue itself, except for one other closely related question. This other question is that expressed by Shackle, in his fifth question, when he asks whether or not profit can be "imputed to a factor of production through the marginal productivity of that factor."

The significance of the issues we will be examining extends far beyond the analysis of profit itself. Moreover, we will be concerned with certain apparent paradoxes surrounding pure

Presented at a session of the meetings of the American Economic Association, held at Chicago, August 1978.

profit, but the paradoxes relate also to far broader theoretical questions concerning the market process. I have elsewhere been concerned to promote the view of the market that recognizes the central role of the entrepreneur, and especially the uniquely entrepreneurial character of the dynamic processes that make up the market.[4] This view emphasizes as the distinctive aspect of entrepreneurial activity its inability to be compressed within the equilibrium conception of the market. It might then appear that this "entrepreneurial" view of the market process entails that the relationship between entrepreneurial activity, however defined, and pure profit, be altogether different from that which links a factor of production to its equilibrium, marginal-productivity-determined factor share of output. This entrepreneurial view of the market process appears to suggest, therefore, a strong inclination toward a refusal to see pure profit as able to be captured, regularly and systematically, through some endowed entrepreneurial ability.

But this same entrepreneurial view of the market process can be shown to suggest a precisely opposite inclination. If the market process is to be understood as in any sense systematic, it will surely not do to envisage the activities of the entrepreneurs whose activities are the immediate constituents of each new step in the market process as in principle unconstrained by the realities of the underlying market phenomena. It will not do to imagine entrepreneurial activities being carried on without the conscious aim to capture pure profit opportunities embedded in these realities, or to understand that profit is in fact won not by deliberate intent, but by sheer luck. So that the entrepreneurial view of the market process seems to imply a strong inclination toward recognizing entrepreneurial ability as a unique talent systematically capable of locating and pursuing pure profit opportunities.

It is with the paradoxical flavor of these reflections in mind that we take up our inquiry. We shall discover, as it turns out, that this paradoxical flavor is inherent in the very notion of entrepreneurial profit, properly understood. So that, far from being disconcerted by these paradoxical reflections, we shall find ourselves enjoying deeper and clearer insight into the nature of entrepreneurship and of entrepreneurial profit.

Some Elementary Thoughts concerning Profit

It will be helpful, in pursuing our inquiry, to keep firmly in mind certain elementary and well-understood ideas on profit. These will serve to direct our inquiry at the very same time that they might appear to deepen the paradoxical flavor of the foregoing paragraphs.

1. *With complete knowledge, pure profit is impossible.* Suppose item a can be sold to consumers at a price r, while this same item a can be purchased or produced by the seller at a cost s (with $s<r$), when s includes all outlays needed to make a available to consumers. Under these conditions we must, it is obvious, be supposing less than perfect knowledge. Were those selling a at the total cost s (or those selling the inputs the sum of the costs of which are s) aware that other buyers are prepared to pay r (with $r<s$) for a, they would not be selling for as little as s. Again, were those buying at the high price r aware that they could themselves obtain a for a lower price s (with s covering all needed outlays), it is clear that they would not be buying at the higher r price. The opportunity for and the realization of pure profit rests, it is evident, upon imperfect knowledge.

2. *Pure profit tends to be ground down to zero by competition.* Where in fact some entrepreneurs are buying a (or the input services needed to produce and deliver a) at a price below that at which they are selling a, this profit situation will attract other entrepreneurs whose competition will tend both to raise the low cost of acquiring a, and to lower the high price obtained from the final buyers, until the price differential is eliminated. It is upon this insight—that pure profits provide the incentive for market action that results in the elimination of profit—upon which economics depend for Jevons's Law of Indifference. It is upon this insight that economists rely for their understanding of the universal tendency for the "value of the original means of production to attach itself with the faithfulness of a shadow to the value of the product."[5]

In other words, pure profit is the link between imperfect and perfect knowledge: *on one hand, it is generated by ignorance; on the other, it provides the incentive for realizing the truth.*

One who has captured profits has acted in accordance with realities that the market had hitherto failed to recognize. His profit has been won by breaking away from the ignorance that previously prevailed as conventional wisdom. As entrepreneurs attracted by the profits so obtained move to take advantage of their availability, the market in general comes to be pulled and nudged to take proper account of the underlying, and hitherto overlooked, realities.

PROFITS AND THE LAW OF INDIFFERENCE

It is clear, then, that a pure profit possibility can exist only because, and to the extent that, full conformity with the Law of Indifference has not yet been attained. Jevons stated his Law of Indifference as asserting that "in the same open market, at any one moment, there cannot be two prices for the same kind of article."[6] This statement refers, of course, to the state of equilibrium; during the market process tending to generate this equilibrium state, two prices for the same article may indeed exist, and it is the difference between them that is pure profit. Moreover, Jevons stated his Law only in the context of the "same kind of article." But the reasoning upon which Jevons's Law rests clearly applies with equal force to any goods, however physically dissimilar they may be, which the market considers to be completely equivalent. Thus, in particular, if a complex of productive services can together suffice to generate a produced commodity, then economists rely upon an extension of the law of indifference when they assert a tendency for the sum of input prices to equal the price of output.

Thus pure profit of *any* kind can exist only while the tendency toward the fulfillment of Jevons's Law of Indifference, broadly interpreted, has not yet been completed. And, again, it is upon the tendency for pure profit to be eliminated by competition that the tendency toward the fulfillment of Jevons's Law itself depends. The question whether entrepreneurial profit is to be attributed to pure luck or to a special kind of ability turns out, then, to concern the way it is discovered that the market has placed inconsistent valuations upon different samples of what, broadly conceived, amount to the same good.

Should we argue that such discovery of inconsistent market valuations is indeed a matter of pure luck, then the immediate question would raise the difficulty of asserting a tendency toward the fulfillment of Jevons's Law that relies on pure luck for its systematic achievement. On the other hand, should pure profit be seen as the market-determined reward for the exercise of the special ability of discovering inconsistent market valuations, then it seems we will have painted ourselves, once again, into that uncomfortable equilibrium corner from which we had hoped to be freed by recognizing the entrepreneurial character of market processes.

THE INDIVIDUAL AS ENTREPRENEUR

I contend that considerable light can be thrown on these issues by careful analysis of the insight that, in an important sense, each human decision is an entrepreneurial decision. "In any real and living economy," Mises remarked, "every actor is always an entrepreneur."[7] The entrepreneurial element in human action, one may argue,[8] is that element in individual decision making that cannot be pressed into the standard "maximizing" model of the decision. So long as one views the human decision as consisting only in working out the mathematical solution to the problem of allocating *given* scarce means among a multiplicity of ends, each of given relative importance, one has assumed away the entrepreneurial element in human action. To see the individual as entrepreneur one must—as Mises did—see the decision as encompassing also *the very identification of the ends-means configuration itself,* within which action is being conducted.

We shall discover that analysis of individual "entrepreneurship," exercised in situations to which the possibility of winning pure entrepreneurial profits *in the market* is irrelevant, will be helpful in organizing our thinking about the role of entrepreneurs in markets. Let us then consider a series of different cases of economic gain, each of which does not depend on *market* opportunities, and determine for ourselves which, if any, of them constitute a "pure profit" that may be associated with the Misesian element of entrepreneurship asserted to be present in all individual action.

Individual Gain and Pure (Crusonian) Profit

1. Robinson Crusoe has a tree. Without action on his part, the tree yields fruit. Crusoe, who had in the beginning owned only the tree, now has both the tree and the fruit. Crusoe may appear to have "gained" fruit, but clearly this kind of gain has nothing to do with entrepreneurship. In fact, if the yield was correctly anticipated, Crusoe already valued his tree to reflect the full value of the expected fruit. When the fruit finally emerges, then, nothing new has been gained (abstracting, for the present purposes, from all time-preference considerations). Most important, since the fruit is forthcoming without Crusoe's action or decision, it cannot be linked to any entrepreneurial aspects of Crusoe's actions. The unfolding of fully anticipated sequences of events offers nothing new; fully anticipated income derived automatically from capital possessed does not bear the character of entrepreneurial profit. If, on the other hand, the yield was *not* anticipated, then the case belongs to the broader class of cases to be discussed in the next paragraph.

2. Crusoe does not own any tree or, if he owns one, does not realize its fruit-bearing properties, but is suddenly presented by nature with fruit without having undertaken any actions to produce or secure the fruit. This is a windfall gain. Because this gain did not result from any action on his part, this too cannot be linked with any entrepreneurial element in Crusoe's personality. Crusoe has received an unexpected gift from nature; that is all. (A special case belonging under this heading of windfall gain is that in which Crusoe undertakes an action—for example, climbing a tree to look far out to sea—without realizing at all that his action will yield him fruit. Then, even though the gained fruit must be seen as caused by Crusoe's action, it nonetheless clearly still represents, from Crusoe's own perspective, an unexpected gift from nature; no element of entrepreneurial profit is present.)

3. Crusoe has become aware of the certain opportunity to convert a lesser-valued good into a more highly valued good. He can, let us fancifully say, turn one apple into two apples by a costless wave of the hand, or—more plausibly—he can, by laboring in his apple orchard, convert hours of time, valued

cheaply at their worth as leisure, into bushels of highly valued apples. If the possibilities of conversion are indeed assured without shadow of doubt, then no entrepreneurial profit is to be discovered in this kind of case. The efficient deployment of means to achieve given ends is simply a matter of maximizing; it calls for nothing entrepreneurial in Crusoe's character. Indeed, Crusoe will tend to value means so as to reflect precisely the value of the ends to which they are sure to lead. If low-valued means can produce high-valued ends, this itself—as Menger showed so forcefully over a century ago—transforms the low-valued means immediately into high-valued means. If one apple were to be able to produce two apples without delay, then the value attached to any one apple would be that attached to the infinite progeny of apples that each apple can thus instantaneously generate. Precisely because there is no entrepreneurial aspect to Crusoe's strictly allocative decision, that is, because the results aimed at are believed to be completely within reach, the value of the means already fully anticipates the value of the end—leaving no scope at all for any profit differential.

4. A case that to some extent overlaps the preceding one is the following. Crusoe finds himself confronted with the necessity to choose between two packages, one containing a single apple, the second containing two apples. (This case thus differs from the preceding case in that no *physical conversion* of a lower-value package into the more highly valued package is considered here. The preceding case can therefore be reduced to an example of the present case by abstracting from the physical conversion central to the preceding case—for example, by seeing the decision to labor in order to produce apples as simply a choice between one package, of leisure, and a second package containing apples.)

Since we may assume that Crusoe will prefer two apples over one apple, he will of course grasp the two-apple package and is thus better off by one apple than he would have been if he had taken the one-apple package. It might then be argued that this one-apple margin is a gain of sorts. By rejecting the opportunity of enjoying one apple, at the economic cost of one apple, Crusoe is able to enjoy two apples. Crusoe's decision might therefore be described as a profitable decision, yielding two through the sacrifice of only one. But reflection should convince one that no element of entrepreneurial profit is present in this case. Once Crusoe's preference ranking of two apples over one has been accepted as a datum, the decision to select the higher-ranked package is nothing more than a mechanical exercise, calling for no entrepreneurial element at all. And, as we shall see, there is nothing here that might represent a margin of profit generated by inconsistent valuations of the same item. Since in this case there is no conversion of means into ends, there can be no question of the value of means being lower than that of the ends. There is simply one package of lower-valued ends, and a different package of higher-valued ends; this offers no scope for profit.

None of the cases we have considered have qualified as examples of a gain captured by individual entrepreneurship. Where, as in case 2, what was gained was not aimed for, it was certainly not captured; it fell into Crusoe's lap. Where, as in case 3, what was gained had been anticipated with complete confidence and certainty, its capture called for no exercise of entrepreneurial imagination, initiative, or determination. Reflection showed that the other cases considered represent examples of gain—if indeed they display any element of gain—that would be inevitably enjoyed by beings endowed with no entrepreneurial potential at all.

To see how the individual human agent wins entrepreneurial profits, in the Crusoe context, we must introduce the possibility of *erroneous valuation*. Crusoe spends his time uneconomically catching fish, we are told in elementary economics, with his bare hands. One day he begins a net-making or boat-building undertaking. Textbooks focus on the saving-investment aspects of this process of roundabout production. But let us ask why Crusoe begins to build his boat today rather than yesterday, assuming no change in accumulated capital since yesterday. The answer must surely be that it is only today that Crusoe has persuaded himself that building a boat is a better use of his time than catching fish. Nothing has changed since yesterday except that Crusoe has discovered that his time is more valuably spent in building the boat than in catching fish. He has discovered that he had placed an incorrectly low value on his time. His reallocation of his labor time from fishing to boat-building is an entrepreneurial decision, and, assuming his decision to be a correct one, yields pure profit in the form of the additional value discovered to be forthcoming from the labor time applied. This pure profit is not a windfall gain but was deliberately captured, Nor, as in case 3 cited above, was it a gain that could have been captured without the exercise of entrepreneurial alertness. A mechanical, economizing Crusoe who maximized his welfare yesterday, as far as he knew, by allocating his labor time, as he had done since time immemorial, to catching fish with his hands cannot, ceteris paribus, be imagined to do anything different today. To take notice of the possibility that yesterday's welfare maximization be seen today as being a misallocation, one must introduce the possibility of error and of its entrepreneurial discovery.

INDIVIDUAL PROFIT AND MENGER'S LAW

Much of what has been considered in the preceding section can be usefully restated in terms of an insight that we owe chiefly to Carl Menger. Perhaps the central idea running through Menger's *Grundsätze* is that men value goods according to the value of the satisfactions that depend on possession of those goods. More generally, Menger's Law—as we may call this insight—draws attention to man's propensity *to attach the value of ends to the means* needed for their achievement. It is Menger's Law that, in a definite sense, is responsible for the absence of scope for entrepreneurial profit in many of the cases—particularly case 3—discussed in the preceding section. Since the value of ends comes to be attached to means, it follows that, so long as the law operates, no gain in value can be obtained in the course of successful achievement of goals through appropriate deployment of means.

But, clearly, Menger's Law operates only within the context of a given perceived framework of ends and means. During the process by which acting man arrives at his awareness of the ends-means framework within which he is operating, there may be ample scope for the reevaluation of means. It is only after one has settled down to a definite perception of the ends-means environment that Menger's Law comes fully and finally into its own. When Crusoe discovers that his time may be more valuably spent in boat-building than in fishing, he has discovered that the ends achievable with his time have higher value than the ends he had previously sought to achieve. Since Crusoe had valued his means (time) at the lower value of those earlier ends, his new allocation of his time to more valuable goals signifies that Menger's Law is *violated at the instant of entrepreneurial discovery*. The value Crusoe has until now attached to his time is *less* than the value of the ends he now seeks.[9] This discrepancy is, at the level of the individual, pure profit. "The difference between the value of the end attained and that of the means applied for its attainment is profit."[10] To be sure, the very entrepreneurial act of reallocating time for fishing to boat-building implies the reevaluation of the time itself. Once the old ends-means framework has been completely and unquestionably replaced by the new one, of course, it is the value of the new ends that Crusoe comes to attach to his means; Menger's Law ensures this. But, during the instant of an entrepreneurial leap of faith, the instant of daring the new line of production, there is scope for the discovery that, indeed, the ends achieved are more valuable than had hitherto been suspected. *This* is the discovery of pure (Crusonian) entrepreneurial profit.

Although reference has been made to the *instant* of entrepreneurial discovery, it should be clear that in many cases the transition from an old accepted ends-means framework to reasonable confidence in the relevance of a new framework may be far from instantaneous. Thus the final discovery that Crusoe's time is indeed more valuable than hitherto suspected may come with assurance only long after the instant of the initial entrepreneurial decision to switch production. Indeed, during the time when Crusoe's entrepreneurial judgment is being vindicated, Crusoe may come to hold entirely new views concerning the future. So that *each one of his actions* will be taken entrepreneurially; that is, *at no time* will Crusoe have yet fully and confidently adjusted his valuation of means to the ends aimed at by his actions. Individual profit may be a continual phenomenon; Menger's Law may in fact never hold completely; it may represent nothing more than a tendency.

CRUSONIAN PROFIT, ENTREPRENEURSHIP, AND KNOWLEDGE

In considering his actions, whether prospectively or in retrospect, man is very much concerned with the precise relationship between means and ends. He searches for an understanding of how means combine to achieve ends. He seeks to attribute results to causes. It is upon this attribution that, prospectively, he depends, according to Menger's Law, for his valuation of resources. Unless, as in case 2, he has received a gift from nature, Crusoe attributes his consumption enjoyment to his own actions in deploying definite resources that were at his disposal. To what, one may ask, should Crusoe attribute that portion of his successfully achieved ends that corresponds to entrepreneurial profit?

Notice that while Crusoe will in one sense indeed, quite correctly, attribute the results achieved to the physical resources technologically responsible for them, there is another sense in which he may well feel that such attribution will be less than completely justified. Crusoe will, after all, be well aware that, until the moment when he decided to give up fishing to build his boat, the same resources would in fact *not* have yielded the boat. Clearly, to attribute the boat entirely to these resources is to overlook some vital ingredient, other than the services of Crusoe's unchanged physical resources, without which the boat would not have been forthcoming. What is this other ingredient? At first glance this ingredient might appear to be Crusoe's *knowledge*. Before he realized (knew) the possibility and productivity of boat-building, Crusoe lacked the essential ingredient needed to build his boat. After somehow acquiring the relevant knowledge, Crusoe finds himself in a position to build his boat. He may then attribute his boat—and the superior catch of fish the boat eventually makes possible—not only to the physical resources that go into boat-building, but also in part to the information on boat-building technology and on boat productivity in catching fish upon which he based his decision to change his plan of production.[11]

Moreover, our understanding of the way Crusoe's knowledge

may be seen as an essential ingredient in the complex of resources that produced the boat raises a fundamental difficulty for our notion of Crusonian profit. Earlier, we ruled out, as possible examples of pure Crusonian profit, cases in which Crusoe's gain was a simple gift from nature, and also cases in which grasping the gain involved no entrepreneurial judgment or imagination. We ruled out both windfall gains and gains achieved through mechanical resource allocation under certainty. We found true profit only in the case where Crusoe spontaneously discovered a new, superior use for his resources. But, if Crusoe's knowledge is seen as a genuine resource, then it must surely appear that we are, by this very insight, forced to surrender our example of Crusonian profit.

For it must surely appear that, once Crusoe has in fact arrived at his new knowledge, his use of the knowledge in the form of building a boat differs in no respect from his use of the other (physical) resources that went into the boat. So that one might argue that Crusoe's transition from catching fish manually to building his boat came in two separate stages, *each of which fails to display an example of pure profit.* First, one may point out, Crusoe enjoyed a windfall gain in the form of the acquisition (by gift from nature) of a new resource, namely the information, knowledge, and vision needed to build his boat. Second, once having acquired this valuable resource, Crusoe proceeds to put it to deliberate use (in exactly the same way as he deploys his physical resources) in boat-building. The first of these two steps, being the result of no deliberate action on his part, provided, like all cases of windfall gain, no example of profit. The second step, though a deliberate act on his part, was so deliberate as once again to rule out profit. The higher value of the superior catch made possible by the boat is then simply to be attributed to the new knowledge Crusoe now possesses. This higher output value appears, then, to correspond simply to the true Mengerian value of the resources responsible for it at the margin. Without these knowledge resources, output would have been smaller. With the knowledge, output is larger. The knowledge itself was acquired by sheer luck, a windfall gain. No profit seems to be present at any stage of this fish story after all.

The truth is that the difficulty, for the identification of pure

Crusonian profit, discussed in the preceding paragraphs offers, in fact, a valuable opportunity to clarify the entire notion of pure profit. The difficulty is only an apparent one. A discussion of the source of this apparent difficulty can be most helpful in further elucidating the highly elusive and subtle profit concept.

Let us notice that our difficulty arose entirely out of the two stages into which we analyzed the Crusoe boat-building example. And, indeed, if it were always possible, without doing violence to the very nature of the case, to distinguish sharply between Crusoe's acquisition of his new knowledge, and his deliberate deployment of that knowledge, our problem would be insoluble. Crusonian profit would have disappeared.

But such a dissection is not possible without destroying the essence of the situation under analysis. Neither chronologically nor logically may we, in general, separate the deliberate action Crusoe undertakes from the entrepreneurial vision that inspires that action. This assertion requires us to review briefly the notion of human action and its relationship to mechanical maximization (allocation).[12]

It was Lord Robbins[13] who made modern economists familiar with the notion of the allocation of given scarce means among given competing ends. Since, in this concept of Robbinsian economizing—or, in subsequent parlance, maximizing—both ends and means are given, it is clear that the activity of economizing arises only *after* that extra-Robbinsian process has been completed during which ends and means have come to be identified and perceived. In the activity of economizing itself, therefore, there can be no room for flashes of discovery, for sudden illuminations of insight, or realization, or of awareness. While the Robbinsian framework does not preclude a later discovery that the given ends-means framework is incorrect and must be replaced, this process of the discovery of error itself occurs, somehow, *outside* the Robbinsian human laboratory.[14]

Contrasted with this concept of Robbinsian economizing is that of human action, a concept we owe to Mises.[15] The notion of Misesian human action sees the human decision as essentially "entrepreneurial"—that is, *inseparably combining* the allocation aspect of action with the entrepreneurial vision and imagination that inspires action. As Lachmann appears to suggest, this Misesian view of the human decision has much in common with the work of Shackle.[16] In this view, to analyze action purely in terms of maximization-allocation techniques is to rob human decision making of something essential to it. From this Mises-Shackle viewpoint, the notion of purely maximizing activity is at best a limiting case, describing a hypothetical situation from which *all* Knightian uncertainty is imagined to have been exhausted. But human action never does occur in such a vacuum. The analysis of human action must therefore recognize that its allocative aspects express only one side of the human decision. Entrepreneurial vision permeates and suffuses all human action; allocation is itself *embedded* in entrepreneurial vision, initiative, and determination.

From this perspective, Crusoe's action in quitting manual fishing and transferring his labor to boat-building, must be seen as embodying, simultaneously and in an inextricably intertwined manner, both the element of deliberately exploiting an available opportunity and the element of permitting himself, in undeliberate fashion, to follow his entrepreneurial hunch. In following this hunch, rather than sticking to yesterday's time-honored groove, Crusoe may, if his hunch is correct, capture results that were hitherto beyond his reach. To impute this gain simply to his deliberate action—identifying, as a resource within his possession, his vision of the future—is to do violence to Crusoe's decision. The gain he wins is to be linked, surely, with that undeliberate adoption by Crusoe, at the instant of decision making, *not* chronologically before that moment, of the entrepreneurial hunch responsible for his success. In this sense it is quite true that pure Crusonian profit cannot be wholly separated from the element of sheer good fortune. Crusoe's adoption of his hunch is not to be explained as the calculated position taken by the deliberate maximizer-economizer. Crusoe cannot take credit for having correctly calculated his view of the future course of events.[17] But, again, this admittedly undeliberate element in Crusoe's adoption of the fortunate hunch does not qualify the capture of the resulting gain as a windfall gift from nature. A windfall gift occurs when Crusoe gains something without lifting a finger toward it. In our case, Crusoe gains the superior catch, made possible by his boat, because he *acted on his hunch*. Crusonian profit emerges as the result of human action, that is, of deliberate planning to implement the entrepreneurial hunch adopted only at the very instant of action itself.

Menger's Law, as we have called it, operates continually toward wiping out pure Crusonian profit. As the outcome of Crusoe's actions vindicates the hunches on which they were based, Crusoe comes to view these hunches less and less as daring, innovative guesses about an uncertain future, and more and more as the settled knowledge concerning a stable environment. Crusoe's actions, in continuing to exploit his now-established knowledge of his environment, express less and less the entrepreneurial element present in all human action and come more and more to resemble those limiting cases of deliberate action (in the face of *given* ends and means) discussed by Robbins. The results Crusoe continues to enjoy— more fish caught per day—partake less and less of the character of pure Crusonian profit and more and more of that of the deliberately exploited opportunity in a hypothetical world without change and uncertainty.

INFORMATION, HUNCHES, LUCK, AND ABILITY

Our discussion permits us to make some further observations concerning Crusonian entrepreneurship that, like the entire analysis of Crusonian entrepreneurship and profit, will be most helpful in our later analysis of entrepreneurship and profit in the *market* context.

We notice, first, that whether or not Crusoe views his knowledge as simply another resource that must be deployed to achieve a result depends on the degree to which he sees that knowledge as settled or as uncertain information. A piece of technological information about boat-building, about whose correctness Crusoe has no doubts at all, will not be seen as a hunch and will be valued according to Menger's Law.[18] It may be said that Crusoe is well aware that he possesses this kind of information; he will deploy and value it in the same way as he may be imagined to deploy and value other resources he believes are definitely at his disposal. But concerning Crusoe's hunches and his visions in the face of a changing, uncertain environment, it cannot be said at all that Crusoe knows he has a hunch or a vision of the future. He does not act by deliberately utilizing his hunch about the future; instead, he finds that his actions reflect his hunches. One who possess lumber and potential labor time may decide to build a boat with them. It is his hunch about the future that inspires this decision; his hunch is *never* an *ingredient* involved in the deliberations that control action. One does not decide to use or not use one's hunches concerning the exploitation of a pure profit possibility; after all, to decide not to use a hunch would reveal that the hunch simply did not exist. One does not refrain from exploiting a truly perceived opportunity for pure gain.

In other words, it turns out, the essence of entrepreneurial vision, and what sets it apart from knowledge as a resource, is reflected in Crusoe's lack of self-consciousness concerning it. Crusoe does not "know" that he possesses a particular vision, in the sense of being aware that that vision is at his disposal to be used or not. To be sure, Crusoe may, as we have seen, gradually come to be aware of his vision. When he does, that vision ceases to be entrepreneurial and comes to be a resource. Moreover Crusoe's *realization* that he possesses this definite information resource may *itself* be entrepreneurial. As soon as he "knows" that he possesses an item of knowledge, *that* item of knowledge ceases to correspond to entrepreneurial vision; instead, as with all resources, it is Crusoe's belief that he has the resources at his disposal that may now constitute his entrepreneurial hunch.

Further, the element of sheer good fortune we have noticed in Crusonian entrepreneurship should not be misunderstood and should not be emphasized out of proportion. It is true that Crusoe does not arrive at his view of the world merely by deliberate calculation of the solution to a mathematical problem. It is true that we know far too little about the forces—cultural, sociological, or psychological—that go to shape the world view, the entrepreneurial vision, and the awareness of any given individual. But we do know that all human beings—albeit in varying degrees—come to entertain views about their environment and about their future that are not wholly out of line with the facts as they subsequently unfold. Entrepreneurial vision may not be arrived at deliberately, rationally, but neither is it arrived at purely by chance. In fact, as I have argued elsewhere, it is an implication of the purposefulness of human action that tends to ensure, in some degree, that opportunities come to be noticed.[19]

It is not to be denied that different individuals appear to differ in the successfulness with which they become aware of the opportunities available to them. Certainly insofar as Crusoe has been blessed with an alert temperament, he must attribute much of the success in his hunches to his good fortune in enjoying such a temperament. On the other hand, Crusoe's awareness of his temperament will not constitute awareness of a resource at his disposal waiting to be deployed. As we have seen, Crusoe is never aware that he possesses specific entrepreneurial insights.

It follows that while Crusoe's successful entrepreneurial decisions incorporate deliberate action on his part, they also reflect fortunate entrepreneurial hunches, for which he can claim no credit; and yet Crusoe's success is nonetheless far more than sheer luck. The superficially paradoxical flavor of this conclusion mirrors, of course, the paradoxes raised at the outset. Our discussions concerning Crusonian entrepreneurship have, I hope, adequately explored the paradox at Crusoe's level. We are now in a position to transfer our insights into entrepreneurship from the individual to the market. Before doing so, it may be useful to summarize some of our conclusions concerning Crusonian entrepreneurial decisions. I do so by asserting the following propositions:

ENTREPRENEURSHIP: THE CRUSOE CONTEXT

1. The Robbinsian economizing-allocation-maximizing view of the decision is a construct that excludes the entrepreneurial aspect of human action.

2. Real human action, however, in a world of uncertainty, is never purely Robbinsian; every action incorporates, to some degree, the entrepreneurial element.

3. In the limiting case of pure Robbinsian maximizing deci-

sion making, Menger's Law operates fully. No element of value in the results of action remains unimputed to the resources deployed. No Crusonian profit is therefore possible.

4. Because Crusonian entrepreneurship occurs against a background of uncertainty, change, and error, Menger's Law is unlikely to hold completely at any given time. Crusoe, while deciding entrepreneurially to deploy resources towards a hoped-for new result, will not yet have fully valued the resources according to that still very uncertain result. Pure Crusonian profit is present here.

5. The entrepreneurial vision that inspires Crusoe's action is not to be credited to Crusoe's present or earlier success in Robbinsian calculation. The element of sheer good fortune in entrepreneurial success may enter here.

6. Crusoe does not, in the course of making his entrepreneurial decision, consider the entrepreneurial vision that inspires his action as a resource available for deployment. He does not know that he possesses entrepreneurial knowledge.

7. Consequently, Crusoe does not, as would be required by Menger's Law were Crusoe to have regarded his vision as a deployable resource, attach a marginal productivity valuation to his possession of that vision.

8. As experience confirms Crusoe's entrepreneurial hunches, these hunches tend to be viewed as deployable resources; Menger's Law tends to come into fuller application, thus continually grinding away at Crusonian profit, which profit is continually re-created as Crusoe grapples with the possibilities generated by the emergence of continually fresh opportunities.

9. Crusonian profit emerges when Crusoe attaches dual valuations to economically identical or equivalent items, most especially attaching a lower value to a bundle of resources than to the results they are to produce.

10. At any given moment, Crusoe is unaware of the opportunities he is overlooking. Just as Crusoe does not know that he possesses entrepreneurial vision (see point 6), so Crusoe is not aware that he is ignorant of the opportunities he fails to exploit.[20]

11. From the point of view of superior entrepreneurial in-

sight, the wrong decision will appear, in the Robbinsian sense, as an inefficient misallocation of resources.

12. The tendency of purposeful human beings to become aware of available opportunities tends, with greater or lesser rapidity, to eliminate misallocation, error, violations of Menger's Law, and the occurrence of possibilities for pure Crusonian profit (and see point 8).

INDIVIDUAL AND MARKET: THE PARALLELISM

Although we have pursued at some length the Misesian insight that individual human action is entrepreneurial in character, our real purpose in doing so was to shed light on more conventional interpretations of the notion of entrepreneurship. In economics, the term entrepreneur is generally understood, of course, to refer not to an aspect of all human decisions, but rather to a special analytical or actual market role. The entrepreneur is the one who buys in one market in order to resell, possibly at a considerably later date, in a second market. Entrepreneurial profit occurs when the price paid for an item in the first market is lower than that received in the second market. Where the entrepreneur-producer buys resource services and sells their product, we see him as having bought at a low price in one market something that can, without further effort of inputs of any kind, be translated into the output sold at a higher price in a second market.

We shall argue that there is a remarkable parallelism between the entrepreneurial element in individual action, and the role of the entrepreneur in the market.[21] In fact, as we shall discover, each of the twelve summary propositions regarding Crusonian entrepreneurship has its exact counterpart proposition with respect to the market. To perceive this, it will be helpful, as preliminary, to draw attention to certain key ideas at the level of the market that correspond to similar key ideas at the level of individual human action.

1. Corresponding to Robbinsian economizing at the level of the individual, we have market general equilibrium. At both the individual and the market levels, the key idea here is perfect coordination. Robbinsian allocation coordinates activities directed at a variety of goals so as to fit them into a single

overall pattern imposed by the given hierarchy of ends. General equilibrium in the market depends on the successful coordination of all individual market activities so that no single plan need fail to be carried out.

2. Corresponding to what we have called Menger's Law at the level of the individual, we have Jevons's Law of Indifference in the market. Menger's Law tends to ensure that means come to be valued by the individual according to the ends they serve. The Law of Indifference tends to ensure that the market prices for resources reflect accurately and fully the prices of the outputs these resources produce.

3. Corresponding to Crusonian profit at the level of the individual, in markets we have profits made possible by price differentials for the same, or economically equivalent, items.

4. Error, in the case of Crusoe, means overlooking available production or consumption opportunities. At the level of the market, error means, at least in its most superficial sense, that some market participants are buying (selling) at prices higher (lower) than the prices at which others are in fact buying (selling). Price differentials are evidence of market error.

With these correspondences in mind, let us now simply restate each of the twelve propositions in a form that will relate them directly to market rather than to individual situations.

ENTREPRENEURSHIP: THE MARKET CONTEXT

1°. The model of general market equilibrium is a construct that excludes any possibility for market entrepreneurship.

2°. Real markets, however, are never equilibrium markets; every market incorporates entrepreneurial activity.

3°. In the limiting cases of general equilibrium, the Law of Indifference operates fully. No resource complex sells at a price less than the full value of its output. No entrepreneurial profit is possible.

4°. Because markets are not, in fact, in general equilibrium, the Law of Indifference is unlikely to hold completely at any given time. The market will not, at a given moment, have fully valued all units of resources at the value of output these resources are able to yield. Opportunity for pure entrepreneurial (market) profit exists.

erroneously failed to achieve fuller coordination among the preferences of market participants. Or, less precisely, the disequilibrium market may, from the perspective of Pareto optimality, be judged as "misallocating" social resources.

12°. The powerful tendency of the market to discover and eliminate unjustified price differentials tends continually to eliminate the market errors (mentioned in point 11°), departures from compliance with the Law of Indifference, and the possibilities for winning pure entrepreneurial profits in the market (and see point 8°).

More on Market Entrepreneurship and Individual Entrepreneurship

The preceding sections have emphasized the remarkable parallel between the element of entrepreneurship as exercised within the framework of strictly individual human action and entrepreneurship as it manifests itself as a specifically market phenomenon. This parallel raises the following question: To what extent, if any, is it necessary, for the exercise of entrepreneurship (in the *market* sense) and for the capture of entrepreneurial profits (again in the market sense), to depend on the entrepreneurial element in *individual* human action? This question deserves some elaboration; and, as is so often the case, such elaboration will help considerably in arriving at the answer to our question.

We have seen that scope for market entrepreneurship is created by the conditions of market disequilibrium, conditions that consist in the emergence of more than one price for identical, or economically equivalent, items. Entrepreneurs are attracted into the market by the pure profit opportunities reflected in such price discrepancies; they tend to buy where the price is low and sell where the price is high, initiating forces that tend to drive prices together. We inquire whether the economic decision making these market entrepreneurs engage in must necessarily display, in an essential way, those entrepreneurial aspects of all human action to which so much of this chapter has (following the hint of Mises) been devoted. We know that microeconomics has, in its standard presentation, abstracted from the Misesian, entrepreneurial element in

individual decision making. A good deal of microeconomics
has attempted to imagine a market consisting entirely of Robbinsian maximizers. What we ask is whether this kind of
abstraction necessarily fails to come to grips with the
phenomenon of market entrepreneurship. A positive answer to
this question would mean that the phenomenon of market entrepreneurship is not merely *parallel* to the entrepreneurial
element in individual action, but in fact depends on the latter
element for its own existence.

The grounds for thinking that perhaps market entrepreneurship *does* so depend on the entrepreneurial element in individual decision making are fairly easy to see. The opportunity
for the exercise of market entrepreneurship, specifically the
presence of two market prices for equivalent items, reflects the
erroneous expectations of market participants. Were market
participants to have anticipated the price discrepancy, it would
already have been grasped at by eager profit-seekers, whose
competition would soon have eliminated it. For market participants to replace an erroneous perception of market prices
by a more correct one, one must depend, surely, on their
capacity to become aware of the errors in their earlier perceptions. One must, that is, depend on something other than
man's propensity to maximize and to allocate against the
background of given perceptions; one must depend on the entrepreneurial aspect of individual human action—on man's
capacity to become alerted to changed conditions. Certainly
our understanding of man's entrepreneurial potential enables
us to understand the systematic process by which the market
operates through entrepreneurs' continual grasping of opportunities for market profit.[22] But it is not quite enough to show
that the entrepreneurial element in individual human action
may be sufficient to generate examples of market entrepreneurship; we must still ask whether this element is necessary
for this purpose. Perhaps market entrepreneurship may occur
without special dependence on the entrepreneurial aspect of
human action? Two possibilities may be considered.

1. Let us take up the first possibility that a market participant has somehow already become aware with certainty of the
existence of a price discrepancy, of the opportunity to grasp

pure profit. Any subsequent action by him to grasp the profit opportunity would not be considered entrepreneurial. Since his action consists simply in grasping an *already* perceived opportunity, it would fit entirely into the Robbinsian model of maximizing man. And yet, from the market perspective, his activity would be truly entrepreneurial, consisting in taking advantage of the multiple-price situation created by the errors of others.

This possibility cannot be dissolved merely by pointing out that from the Mises-Shackle viewpoint the very notion of man acting without any element of entrepreneurship is ruled out, so that even one "convinced" of the existence of a price differential must be seen as being sufficiently uncertain about his convictions, at least, to render his profit-grasping action entrepreneurial in the Crusoe sense. This way of treating this possibility will not do because the question raised inquires whether market entrepreneurship depends *in an essential way* upon the individual entrepreneurial element. Showing that the possibility here considered does find room for such an element does not yet convince us that this element is essential to the market entrepreneurship the possibility sets forth.

But this possibility can surely not be sustained. Let us consider the market participant at the instant of his arbitrage. We must ask why he has not undertaken this profitable activity earlier, since we were told that, even before his profit-grasping action, our participant had become certain that it was worthwhile.[23] The only explanation must be that our participant was, up to the present, *not* completely convinced of the profitability of the situation. The possibility cannot, then, be considered valid. Entrepreneurial activity in the market has not yet been shown to be possible without invoking the capacity of individual market participants to perceive things differently from the way they had previously seen them. A second possibility, however, cannot be dismissed so easily.

2. This possibility is that a market participant, having no inkling of a future rise in price, buys when the price is low. At a later date he finds himself able to sell at a substantial profit. Surely this case is one of true entrepreneurial profit in the market sense. Yet the profit cannot be attributed to the market

participant's entrepreneurial perception of the higher price that will eventually be available in the second market. From his individual perspective, his gain can appear as nothing but a windfall. And we saw earlier that a windfall gain, not attributable to the individual's purposeful activity, is not entrepreneurial profit in the individual sense.

Now it *may*, of course, happen that while our market participant had no inkling that the price would rise, he nonetheless realized that it *might* rise. And his action in buying may have reflected his judgment that the price would not fall. So his act of purchase *may* perhaps be seen as entrepreneurial in character, with any resulting gain qualifying as entrepreneurial profit, not only from the market perspective, but also from that of the individual himself. Presumably this is what Shackle had in mind when he declared that he inclined to the view "that any windfall realized receipts to which any degree of potential surprise less than the absolute maximum...was attached, ought not to be classified as due to pure luck."[24]

But this does not rule out the possibility of cases in which our market participant is astonished by the price rise. In such cases, as Shackle observes, where the windfall receipts carried the "absolute maximum potential surprise," they ought surely to be classified as due to pure luck.

Here, then, we have indeed discovered a class of cases in which profit in the market sense does *not* coincide with profit and entrepreneurship in the individual sense. Without individual entrepreneurship, market profits *may* yet be captured. What should be emphasized, in spite of the validity of these cases, is that this kind of "lucky" market entrepreneurship cannot be relied upon systematically to grind away profit margins, to bring about the tendency toward the full application of the Law of Indifference, or to tend to eliminate lacunae in social coordination. So that while individual entrepreneurship is not absolutely necessary for entrepreneurship to be exercised in markets, it is upon individual entrepreneurship that we must necessarily rely for any systematic process of market equilibration.

Now it cannot be denied that pure luck plays a most significant role in determining the fortunes of market participants in general and of market entrepreneurs in particular. For this reason it becomes easy to see all market profits as generated fortuitously by unanticipated change. This, in essence, was Knight's view of the world. But our discussion will have made it clear that *besides* those entrepreneurial profits won by sheer luck, the market displays entrepreneurial profits captured by the deliberate exploitation of opportunities glimpsed by individual entrepreneurs. Let us now return to the fundamental questions concerning pure profit raised at the beginning of this chapter; in this I will confine myself to those market profits that qualify, at the same time, to be classified as entrepreneurial profits also from the perspective of individual acting man.

LUCK AND ABILITY

In examining Crusonian profit, we found it expressed an intertwining of apparent good fortune and of ability. Crusoe's profit, we discovered, was deliberately grasped at, so that it could not be treated as a simple windfall gift from nature. Yet, at the same time, Crusoe's deliberate grasping after Crusonian profit could not be seen as merely the natural product obtained by the use of available resources. The product of Crusoe's labor, under settled conditions, may be seen as the outcome of his ability as a laborer. But the profit won by Crusoe in a changing world, we saw, came to him as a result of an inextricable combination of deliberate planning and undeliberately adopted hunch. It was incorrect, we found, to categorize all kinds of gain as falling exhaustively into two classes: gains flowing naturally and inevitably from the deliberate application of resources already possessed, and pure windfall gifts from nature. Human action, we found, undertaken in the face of the uncertainty of a changing world, achieves results that fit into neither of these categories.

It follows, therefore, insofar as market profits are derived from the entrepreneurial aspects of the individual human agent capturing these profits, that market profits, too, will not fit into either of these two categories. Market profits of the kind under discussion will not be attributable to sheer luck, since they resulted from the exercise of deliberate profit-seeking individual action. On the other hand, market profits will not be able to be linked absolutely with some special assured ability possessed by the entrepreneur. Entrepreneurs, as discussed earlier, do not see themselves as deliberately deploying their vision and alertness in the same way as they deploy their other resources. Nor does the market identify any specific ability to discover and profit from price discrepancies. The essence of entrepreneurship, we found, amounted to unawareness both by the entrepreneur himself and by the market in general that he in fact possesses the resources of vision at all.

All this should help us understand why the capture of pure entrepreneurial profits in the market will appear, paradoxically, to the outside observer, to reflect *both* sheer luck, *and* some apparent human capital element unique to successful entrepreneurs. Sheer luck will appear to play a significant role because market profits may indeed result, without exercise of the entrepreneurial element in individual human action, from fortuitous change. The link between the capture of market profit and some apparent entrepreneurial ability is to be understood because different individuals certainly differ in their ability to perceive opportunities entrepreneurially. What we must insist on is only that the *entrepreneurial* character of the vision under consideration here, renders it incorrect to see profit as the inevitable gain flowing naturally from the application of a possessed resource. The apparent paradoxes cited at the outset, we now see, are derived from the very nature of the entrepreneurial element with which we are attempting to grapple.

SHOULD MARKET PROFITS BE SEEN AS A FACTOR RETURN?

This is, of course, an old question. Schumpeter discussed the advisability of treating market entrepreneurship as a special category of productive factor.[25] Shackle raised the corresponding question concerning market profits: May they be seen as the marginal productivity return to a factor? This chapter should have provided grounds for refusing to recognize entrepreneurship as a factor and, therefore, for refusing to see market profit as a marginal productivity return. Both at the Crusoe level and at the market level, it should now be clear, entrepreneurship is not to be treated as a resource.

At the individual, Crusoe level, we have seen, the human agent does not "deliberately deploy" his entrepreneurial hunches; he simply has them, and they propel him into action. Menger's Law, therefore, never gets a chance to be applied; Crusoe never sees his hunches as means that can be applied to achieving given ends.

At the market level, we have seen, the market never recognizes entrepreneurial ability in the sense of an available useful resource. Were it to do so, there would be markets in which this factor service was hired, with its price rising to reflect its full productivity, ruling out scope for pure market profit.

The essence of individual entrepreneurship is that it consists of an alertness in which the decision is *embedded* rather than being one of the ingredients *deployed* in the course of decision making. This sets it altogether apart from being a class of productive factor.

Quite analogously, and consistent with the parallelism that was seen to exist between individual and market entrepreneurship, the market does not "demand" the services of entrepreneurs. Market entrepreneurship reveals to the market what the market did not realize was available or, indeed, needed at all. It is essential, in this context, that what is won by market entrepreneurship cannot be construed as a marginal productivity return *either* from the perspective of the market *or* from that of the individual human agent who acts to capture market profits.

Part Four

ENTREPRENEURSHIP, JUSTICE, AND FREEDOM

11

Producer, Entrepreneur, and the Right to Property

"THE INSTITUTION OF PROPERTY," John Stuart Mill remarked, "when limited to its essential elements, consists in the recognition, in each person, of a right to the exclusive disposal of what he or she have produced by their own exertions, or received either by gift or by fair agreement, without force or fraud, from those who produced it. The foundation of the whole is the right of producers to what they themselves have produced."[1] My purpose is to point out the ambiguity of the phrase "what a man has produced" and to draw attention, in particular, to one significant, economically valid meaning of the term, a meaning involving the concept of entrepreneurship, which seems to have been overlooked almost entirely.

Precision in applying the term "what a man has produced" seems to be of considerable importance. The ethical views associated with widely disparate ideologies, relating both to the justifiability of private rights to property and to the problem of justice in the distribution of incomes, appear to involve in some form the notion of "what a man has produced." Thus the Lockean theory of private property, which came to serve as the source of the moral case for capitalism,[2] has been understood as depending on the view that man has the right to the "fruits of his work."[3] As Milton Friedman has pointed out, the capitalist ethic (which he identifies as holding that "a man deserves what he produces"[4]) is shared by Marx, since Marx's view on the exploitation of labor, resting on the premise that

Presented at a Symposium on Property Rights, held at San Francisco, January 1973.

labor produces the whole product, is valid "only if labor is entitled to what it produces."[5]

Without necessarily accepting, therefore, any one of these ethical positions, it seems worthwhile to achieve clarity by seeking to understand exactly what the notion "what a man has produced" is to mean. The literature seems to have perceived production *insofar as it flows from factors of production,* so that the statement "what a man has produced" has been intended to mean "what has been produced by those factors of production identified with the man with whom we are concerned." Briefly, a man is a producer insofar as he is himself considered a factor of production, or as he is the owner of factors viewed as responsible for output. Thus, Friedman seems to further identify the capitalist ethic with the view that "an individual deserves what is produced by the resources he owns."[6] J. B. Clark rested "the right of society to exist in its present form" on his marginal productivity theory of distribution, seeing it as satisfying the requirement that each man gets what he produces.[7] Locke's labor theory of property begins from the premise that "every man has a property in his own person.... The labor of his body and the work of his hands we may say are properly his."[8] Production is made possible only by the ownership of agents of production.

It follows that if we perceive production as flowing from factors of production, and if we correspondingly relate the ethical implication of "what a man has produced" strictly to that which derives from the factors of production that man owns including, of course, his own labor capacity, then the exercise of pure entrepreneurship in production (i.e., seen as involving no element of factor ownership) carries with it none of the favorable ethical connotations attached to "that which a man has produced." This conclusion requires some elaboration.

FACTOR OWNERSHIP AND ENTREPRENEURSHIP

It is well known that economic literature suffers from insufficient attention paid to the entrepreneurial role, so that we find few careful attempts to define precisely what this role consists of. In the more sophisticated discussions of entrepreneurship, a fairly sharp distinction has emerged between the factors of production, on the one hand, and entrepreneurship on the other. In Schumpeter's classic discussion, for example, the means of production include *all* agents required to produce the product in the state of circular flow (equilibrium). In equilibrium there is the tendency "for the entrepreneur to make neither profit nor loss . . . he has no function of a special kind there, he simply does not exist."[9] In disequilibrium, on the other hand, innovations in product quality and in methods of production are attributable to the initiative of pioneering Schumpeterian entrepreneurs. Although, that is to say, the new products or the new productive techniques require *no* resources beyond those consistent with the state of equilibrium, these new products and techniques would not have appeared at all in the first place had it not been for entrepreneurial daring and drive.

It follows that there is a built-in ambiguity, therefore, concerning the sense in which pure entrepreneurship can be considered a resource necessary for the emergence of the product. And this ambiguity is no doubt partly responsible for the disagreement among economists whether to treat entrepreneurship as a factor of production.[10]

However, until a product or technique has been introduced, possession of all necessary means of production (including relevant knowledge) guarantees nothing without the presence of entrepreneurial initiative. So even Schumpeter recognizes that entrepreneurship "may be conceived as a means of production."[11] On the other hand, if a would-be producer asks the question: "Supposing I decide to produce product X (or to utilize production technique Y), what means of production will it be necessary for me to obtain?" then it is clear that the answer will not include "the decision to produce product X (or to use technique Y)." And this is undoubtedly why Schumpeter stated that "ordinarily" he did *not* conceive of entrepreneurship as a factor of production.[12]

Clearly a sharp distinction must be drawn between means of production ordinarily conceived and entrepreneurship. The latter is *not* similar to factors of production insofar as concerns the theory of marginal productivity.[13] More fundamentally, entrepreneurship, even if considered a means of production, *cannot be purchased or hired by the entrepreneur*; that is, it is never perceived by the potential entrepreneur as either an available or a necessary productive factor. Either the entrepreneur is prepared to take the initiative or he is not.[14] If he is not prepared to take the initiative, the would-be entrepreneur simply sees the project as, on balance, not worth undertaking. He does not see it as a project for which a needed resource is unavailable. If he is determined to take the initiative again, then all he needs to obtain are the factors that would be required in the entrepreneurless state of equilibrium. Or, to put the matter in a slightly different form, the engineer asked to identify the productive agents to which a product is to be attributed, may indeed include intangibles such as "knowledge," but will *not* list "initiative," since the very notion of attribution presupposes the decision to produce. Accordingly, since the entire product can be attributed to the "other" means of production, it follows that entrepreneurship is not a means of production at all and cannot be credited with having contributed anything to the product.

To sum up, the literature revolving around the ethical implications of "what a man has produced," is concerned with what has been produced by the factors of production a man owns or even more narrowly, by the man himself seen as a factor of production. If one perceives pure entrepreneurship as not being a productive factor, it follows that it cannot share in the favorable ethical implications of being responsible for the product. On the other hand, if one views entrepreneurship as a productive factor, attributing some portion of the product's value to the initiative of the entrepreneur, parallel with the contributions made by the other factors, then that portion, however calculated or evaluated—*but no more than that portion*—may be considered as having been produced by the entrepreneur and as relevant, therefore, to the corresponding ethical implications.

In the following pages I will draw attention to the possibility of a position almost precisely opposite in all respects to that just presented. In this position, the favorable implications of the phrase "what a man has produced" *do not apply at all to factors of production*. Rather, pure entrepreneurship is responsible—in the sense relevant to the ethical connotations of "what a man has produced"—to the *entire* product. Moreover, this way of seeing matters is only helped by insight into the sense in which entrepreneurship is *not* to be considered a factor of production. In other words, paradoxically enough, the entrepreneur is to be considered the sole "producer" of the entire product—in the ethically relevant sense—precisely because he makes *no* contribution to production in the sense relevant to the theory of marginal productivity. A sentence from Knight presents, I believe, the essence of this argument. Much of it can be viewed as a commentary on the following: "Under the enterprise system, a special social class, the businessmen, direct economic activity: *they are in the strict sense the producers, while the great mass of the population merely furnish them with productive services, placing their persons and their property at the disposal of this class;* the entrepreneurs *also* guarantee to those who furnish productive services a fixed remuneration."[15]

SOME OBSERVATIONS ON THE LOCKEAN THEORY OF PROPERTY

A philosopher-critic of Locke's theory of property has summed up the theory as follows: (1) every man has a (moral) right to own his person; therefore (2) every man has a (moral) right to own the labor of his person; therefore (3) every man has a (moral) right to own that which he has mixed the labor of his person with.[16] This summary will serve us conveniently.

Apparently Locke took it for granted that, since a man has a moral right to his own labor in the sense of "working," he also has a moral right to that which his labor produces. This view, which we call proposition 3*a*, (and which we have cited above as an example of the ethical values attached to the notion of "what a man has produced"), seems implicit in proposition 3.[17] However proposition 3 goes beyond the view that what a man has produced is morally his own. Proposition 3 asserts that when a man mixes his labor with unowned natural resources, in the natural state in which there is "still enough and as good left,"[18] he is to be considered as the natural private owner of what results from the mixing. Clearly, it is the ambitious prop-osition 3 that is of the greatest importance for Locke's own thesis. It is, however, with the more modest proposition 3a that I am concerned.

That in proposition 3a Locke has in mind labor-as-factor-of-production seems clear from his often cited extension of his proposition 3 to include hired labor. "Thus...the turfs my servant has cut, and the ore I have dug in any place where I have a right to them in common with others, become my prop-erty without the assignation or consent of anybody."[19] A man's own labor is his own in a sense no different from that in which the labor of his servant is an employer's. What has been pro-duced by a man's own labor is his own in the same sense in which what has been produced by an employee's labor is the employer's.

It is true that Day is sharply critical of Locke, denying that one can talk significantly of owning labor in the sense of "working". Laboring, Day contends, is an activity, "and al-though activities can be engaged in, performed or done, they cannot be owned."[20] However, economists will find Locke's use of terms quite familiar and acceptable. Economists speak of agents of production (in the sense of *stocks*), and of the "services" of agents of production (in the flow sense). A man who "owns" an agent of production is considered by economists to own, by that token, also the services flowing from that agent. Again, by hiring the services of a productive agent, a producer is considered by economists to have ac-quired ownership of the service flow, by purchase from the previous owner of that flow (that is, the owner of the agent "itself"). In speaking of owning the services of an employee, therefore, the economist does not in fact have in mind the ownership of the *activity* of working, nor the ownership of that which the activity of working produces, nor even the ownership of the *capacity* for working.[21] Rather the economist is per-ceiving the employee as a stock of human capital, capable of generating a flow of services. So that, to the various different meanings Day discovers to be attached to the word labor should be added labor viewed as the flow of abstract productive service generated by a human being.

Viewed in this economist's sense, therefore, Locke's theory seems to say, quite understandably: (1°) Every man has a (moral) right to own the human capital represented by his person; therefore (2°) every man has a (moral) right to own the flow of labor services associated with his person; therefore (3a°) every man has a right to the product produced by these labor services—just as he has the right to the product produced by the labor services he has hired from an employee.

Clearly, therefore, proposition 3a°, with which we are ourselves concerned, relates to labor viewed as a physical factor of production. It appears, moreover, that even the notion of labor as *sacrifice*—a notion that might permit one to regard the product as being deserved by the laborer in the sense of reward for sacrifice—is foreign to Locke's theory. Thus, as Myrdal has pointed out, Locke's view "that labor is the source of property has nothing to do with pain and sacrifice but follows from the idea of labor as a natural property of the worker and as the cause and creator of value."[22] So Locke, at any rate, is not arguing his proposition (3a°) on the basis of any ethically merited *reward* for the pain or sacrifice of labor. Instead, it appears, Locke's proposition (3a°) rests on the ethical view that the product *physically derived from a man's property* should belong to him in the same sense that the natural growth from a man's property may be deemed to belong to him naturally.[23] This is entirely consistent with the usual interpretation of Lockean ethical arguments, as presented by modern economists, in terms of the language of the theory of marginal productivity.[24] We shall see that there are grounds for discovering, however, elements of an alternative perception of the ethical meaningfulness of production in Locke.

HUMAN WILL AND THE ACQUISITION OF PROPERTY

Contrasted with the notion of the product as *physically* produced by man, with or without the use of other productive resources, is the perception of the product as resulting from the *human will*. As discussed briefly above, I shall be arguing that for the purposes of ethically justifying property in products, it may be relevant to draw attention to the sense in which the product finds its source in entrepreneurial decision making rather than to the sense in which it is derived from factor ownership. While explicit recognition of this insight is almost entirely absent from the literature, it is possible to discover a number of remarks and views that suggest an "entrepreneurial" approach to a justification for property.

Thus, in Locke's own century, Pufendorf emphasized the distinction between an action that is forced and one that is performed freely. Only the latter is properly a *human* action, involving "an element of subjective spontaneity" and a "free project of the self."[25] A century later, Kant's theory of the acquisition of property through labor saw the labor itself as almost irrelevant to the act of acquisition. "When it is a question of the first acquisition of a thing, the cultivation or modification of it by labour forms nothing more than an external sign of the fact that it has been taken into possession."[26] It is not the mixing of labor with an object that makes it one's own, but "the transcendental operation of directing [one's] will upon [it]."[27] Hegel, too, saw in the human will the true source of property rights and moreover saw it as providing a justification for the acquisition of natural resources superior to that depending upon the mixing of labor.[28]

Moreover, it has seemed to some writers that Locke's labor theory of property, too, as well as the labor theory of value of the later classical economists,[29] cannot be properly understood unless one recognizes the special character of labor, the *human* factor, as compared with other factors of production. So, if one accepts their view, it turns out to be not quite correct to interpret Locke's theory of property as depending on the view that the product arises physically from an owned factor of production that happens to be labor. Thus Weisskopf, in his psychological analysis of classical economics, viewed as deriving from Locke, emphasizes labor as *an activity of the person*. Following on Myrdal,[30] Weisskopf points out that in the classical view nature is seen as dead, with only human labor seen as the *active* agent. Petty's dictum comparing labor to the father, the active principle of wealth, with land seen as the mother, is used by Weisskopf to explain the Locke-classical treatment of labor as the sole origin of wealth for purposes of justifying property rights and of explaining the determination of value.[31]

If Weisskopf's view of the matter is correct, then Locke's labor theory does not relate to that aspect of labor in which it is seen merely as a physical source of the product, but rather to the aspect of labor in which it is seen as inseparable from the active human will of the laborer. Plausible though Weisskopf's view may be for an understanding of the classical preoccupation with labor, it seems difficult to reconcile it with Locke's treatment of hired labor as being as complete a justification for property rights in the product as one's own labor. If Locke's treatment of hired labor envisages the employer as hiring not only the physical labor services of the employee, but also the active, spontaneous, human elements associated with these services, then of course he is not understanding these elements in their purely entrepreneurial sense in which, by definition, they cannot be hired at all.[32]

Finally, we notice that, more recently, Oliver, in drawing attention to the inadequacy of Marxian labor theory for a doctrine of "earned-income," in which a man is entitled to what he has produced, argues that Marx leaves no room for the role of the free will exercised by the laborer in his work, when such a role is essential for the very concept of "earning."[33] We thus have an example of the recognition of the role of the human will in ethical evaluation of "what a man has produced."

PRODUCTION: AUTOMATIC GROWTH OR HUMAN CREATION?

From the foregoing discussion, it will be apparent that we are confronted with two quite different views on the nature of production. I turn now to spell out explicitly what these two views are and to consider briefly their plausibility as foundations for the ethical view that what a man has produced ought to be his.

1. *Production as automatic growth from the factors of production.* The one view sees production as it would occur in the state of equilibrium. In such a state, each producing firm has already been fully adjusted to the conditions of the market. The services of necessary inputs (including the services of managers) flow smoothly into the firm in synchronized fashion,

with the corresponding output flow emerging with equal smoothness. The market value of the input flow corresponds exactly to that of the output flow; alternative uses for input services offer no higher factor prices, alternative sources of input supply promise no saving. Certainly one can say that the output has been produced by the productive input services. But because there has, in such a state, been no room for entrepreneurship, output must be seen as emerging *automatically*, as it were, from the combined input flow, exactly as fruit might grow from a tree without direction from the owner of the tree. To rest an ethical case for ownership in a product on the circumstance that a man's productive resources have produced it, in *this* sense, is to claim that the product is his not on the grounds that *he* has permitted the factors to create the product, but on the grounds that the product has grown—as it were automatically—from the factor services he owns.

2. *Production as a human creation.* The alternative view refuses to see the product as emerging automatically from a given combination of factor services. In this view, the product has come into being only because some human being has *decided* to bring together the necessary productive factors. In deciding to initiate the process of production, this human being has *created* the product. In his creation of the product this entrepreneur producer has *used* the factors of production his vision has brought together. He has not cooperated jointly with these factors, so that this view does not see the entrepreneur's contribution as consisting of a portion of the value of the product, with the remaining portion being the contributions of "other" productive agents. He has produced *the whole product entirely on his own,* being able to do so by his initiative, daring, and drive in identifying and taking advantage of the available productive factors. In this view, an ethical case for ownership in a product, based on one's having created it, depends strictly on one's *not* having been the owner of one of the cooperating input factors. To the extent that an entrepreneur was also a factor owner, he is credited with the creation of the product only in the sense that he purchases his factor services from himself, so to speak, rather than permitting them to serve alternative purposes.

If one uses the first of these two views on production as the

5°. The superior entrepreneurial vision, alertness, and drive that inspires the capture of market profits has not, (as have, for example, produced means of production, or other resources) been deliberately supplied in the market in response to market demand.

6°. The market has not, in fact, in any given case of market profit, recognized either the very existence of or the need for these qualities of vision, alertness, and drive. Were the market to have recognized the need for and the availability of these qualities, the market would have treated these qualities as simple factor services, in a manner fully consistent with general equilibrium. Services that have been hired, must be presumed not to be entrepreneurial.

7°. The market does not, therefore, attach marginal productivity prices to the uniquely entrepreneurial human qualities able to spot gaps in the fabric of market prices. Profits are not a factor income.

8°. As successful market entrepreneurship reveals the disequilibrium in market prices, prices are pushed toward the general equilibrium pattern; the Law of Indifference tends to come into fuller application, grinding away at pure entrepreneurial (market) profits. On the other hand, in a continually changing world, disequilibrium continually reasserts itself, creating anew a continual series of price differentials, with consequent pure profit possibilities.

9°. Market entrepreneurial profits emerge when the market displays more than a single price for the same or economically equivalent items, especially when the market values a complex of resources at a sum below what the market is paying for what these resources can produce.

10°. During disequilibrium there is no market demand for the entrepreneurial qualities needed to spot and eliminate pure price differentials. Were the market to know that such a need existed and how it could be filled, it would already have wiped out those price differentials. (See also point 6°.)

11°. From the perspective of the model of full general market equilibrium, the disequilibrium market may be seen as falling short of fulfilling some postulated relevant social norm. For example, the disequilibrium market may be seen as having basis for an ethical case for property in the product, or in the distribution of income, it is entirely relevant to use a Clarkian marginal productivity approach. The contribution of a factor of production must somehow be disentangled from the contributions of other factors, and the theory of marginal productivity may, with greater or lesser success, be called upon for this purpose. But if it is the second (creation) view that is to be used, then marginal productivity is entirely irrelevant except in a sense to be discussed below. On this second view, the necessarily indivisible entrepreneur is responsible for the entire product. The contributions of the factor inputs, being without any entrepreneurial component, are irrelevant for the ethical position being taken.

Of course, it is true that also on this second view, the entrepreneur producer must, in order to create the product, acquire the services of the necessary productive factors. (And, in fact, competition may force him to compensate them to the full extent of their respective marginal products.) However, it should be plain that this view does not claim rights in the product for the entrepreneur on the grounds that, since he has fairly purchased these factor services, production has now been carried on with *his* factor services. In this view, the entrepreneur's rights rest strictly on the vision and initiative with which, at the time when he owned *no* productive resources, he undertook to marshal them for his purposes.

It is not my purpose to choose between these two interpretations of the ethical implications of producing. Rather, I want to draw attention to the existence of the second view and to emphasize that it is diametrically opposed to the first view. In choosing which of these views to endorse (if, indeed, one wishes to endorse either of them at all) or which of them to ascribe to particular writers, it is necessary to consider carefully whether it is the active human *creativity* of the producer that is to be underlined and recognized or the ownership of the physical or other *ingredients of production*.

FINDERS, KEEPERS, AND SPECULATIVE PROFITS

The points made in the preceding section may perhaps throw light on certain matters raised in discussions concerning the ethics of property and income distribution. Oliver[34] has noted

that sometimes writers presenting ethical positions based on
"what a man has produced," introduce the notion of finders-
keepers. "The man...that first discovers and claims title to
natural resources thereby gains ownership." Oliver points out
that Locke's position bases ownership in natural resources
(with which one has mixed one's labor) partly on discovery. For
Oliver, finders-keepers is a rule that bears no relation at all to
the ethical deservingness associated with having produced
something. Our insight into the entrepreneurial view of production may perhaps be of some help in this respect.

Briefly, it seems that Locke's labor theory of property rights
is best understood as involving a combination, possibly a confusion, of *both* the factorial and the entrepreneurial views of
production. We recall our earlier reference to Myrdal's and
Weisskopf's understanding of Locke in terms of the contrast
between active, live labor, and passive, dead nature. This
certainly supports the theory that Locke viewed labor not
merely as a factor of production, but as also involving the
uniquely human element we have identified with entrepreneurship. Again, the initially puzzling view Locke presents, in
which title to natural resources is acquired by the mixing of
labor, becomes understandable when the mixing of labor with
the natural resource is perceived as the grasping of the entrepreneurial opportunity offered by the available but as yet unap-
propriated resources. The finders-keepers rule that Oliver discovers in Locke thus represents essentially the same ethical
view as that underlying the entrepreneurial view of production.
In this view, a producer is entitled to what he has produced not
because he has contributed anything to its physical fabrication,
but because *he perceived and grasped the opportunity* for its
fabrication by utilizing the resources available in the market.
This is clearly an example of finding and keeping.

These insights appear relevant to some comments by
Samuelson on the normative aspects of speculative profits.
Where a crop failure generates speculative profits, Samuelson
points out that the successful speculator need only be a trifle
quicker than his rivals in order to make his fortune. In his
absence, the socially advantageous consequences of his
speculation (i.e., the curtailment of relatively less urgently

needed consumption at earlier dates, making possible some more urgently needed consumption at later dates) would occur seconds later through the activities of other speculators. Even if one accepts "a Clarkian naive-productivity theory of ethical deservingness," Samuelson remarks, one can hardly justify the capture of all the profits by the successful speculator who saved society from no more than a few seconds of unwise consumption. Without commenting on the substance of Samuelson's normative criticism of speculative profits,[35] it seems useful to remark that, as we have seen, a Clarkian ethical approach is wholly inappropriate anyway in dealing with entrepreneurial profits. What *might* be of greater relevance would be the entrepreneurial view that, as we have seen, consists essentially in precisely a finders-keepers ethic. According to such an ethic, an opportunity perceived and grasped confers ethical deservingness. Necessarily, this perceives the gain from grasping the opportunity as having been deserved, despite the possibility or even the likelihood that others might have perceived and grasped the same opportunity seconds later. No one is bound, of course, to subscribe to this entrepreneurial ethic; in fact one may reject it precisely on Samuelson's grounds, if one chooses. But it does seem appropriate to judge the deservingness of one particular example of entrepreneurial profit on the approach relevant to a defense of the deservingness of entrepreneurial profits in general.[36]

THE ENTREPRENEURIAL ELEMENT IN FACTOR OWNERS' DECISIONS

Although I have emphasized the distinction between the factor-of-production view on the one hand and the creation-entrepreneurial view on the other, it seems wise to point out a circumstance that operates to blur, to some extent, the sharp line we have drawn between these views. This circumstance is the presence of an entrepreneurial element in *every* human action and decision, including, especially for our purposes, the decisions of factor owners.

The isolation of a purely entrepreneurial element in production is, of course, an analytical device. Human action in its totality is made up of an entrepreneurial element (to which is attributable the decision maker's awareness of the ends-means framework within which he is free to operate), *and* an economizing element (to which we attribute the efficiency, with respect to the perceived ends-means framework, of the decision taken).[37] Analytically, we conceive of factor owners as pure economizers operating within an already-perceived market framework. Entrepreneurs, on the other hand, we perceive as becoming aware (with no resources of their own at all) of changed patterns of resource availability, of technological possibilities, and of possibilities for new products that will be attractive to consumers. But flesh and blood resource owners are, of course, also to *some* extent, their own entrepreneurs, just as flesh and blood entrepreneurs are likely to be owners of some factor services themselves.

It follows that when a producer hires the services of productive agents, entrepreneurship has, in fact, been exercised not only by "the" entrepreneur, but also by the factor owners in deciding to sell. While productive services may be viewed as flowing passively from the productive agent, it is the factor owner's decision (from which all elements of entrepreneurship cannot be entirely absent) that permits the flow to proceed in the adopted channel, rather than in alternative processes of production. In the case of labor in particular, the factor owner's decision to permit the service flow is required at every minute of his service. So that when we say, in an apparently "factor-of-production" view of the matter, that a factor has produced a product, we are, *in real-world cases*, referring *both* to the factor as producer and to the factor owner as, at least to some extent, entrepreneur. Now, it seems of great importance to emphasize the two quite different senses of production so involved. It seems, at the same time, helpful to notice how easily the two views on production can become combined or confused. This will perhaps account not only for the view my interpretation has ascribed to Locke, but also for the circumstance that the literature has failed almost entirely to notice explicitly the possibility of an entrepreneurial, factorless view of the ethical implications of producing. The single but outstanding exception is the sentence in Knight cited earlier, in which it is the entrepreneurs who are seen in the strict sense as the producers, with the factor owners merely furnishing them with productive services.

12

Entrepreneurship, Entitlement, and Economic Justice

NOZICK'S ENTITLEMENT THEORY of justice plays a crucial role in his carefully and brilliantly crafted case for the minimal state. Accepting the theory, it appears, sweeps away with one stroke all those demands for state interference with the market that rest on the claims of distributive justice. The persuasive elegance with which Nozick develops his position can leave few thoughtful, moralist critics of uncurbed capitalism unimpressed, at least, by the strong claims that Nozick advances, precisely on the grounds of economic justice, for the free market. It is the thesis of this chapter, however, that Nozick's theory of entitlement, important though it undoubtedly is for any defense of the morality of laissez-faire, does not—at least without significant reformulation—solve all the difficulties that exist in respect to the justice of the market. Pursuing this theme, I will offer a suggestion for supplementing, or perhaps reformulating, Nozick's theory that may not only equip it to handle the difficulties to which I will draw attention, but may, in fact, render its defense of the morality of the market even more straightforward and subject to fewer qualifications than Nozick apparently believes justified.

Nozick's theory depends largely, in its application to the market, on the view that with few definite exceptions, the market adheres to the principles of justice both in the *original acquisition of holdings* from the natural state and in subsequent *transfers of holdings* in market transactions. The difficulties to which I draw attention here pertain to the claim

Presented at a meeting of the Austrian Economic Seminar, New York, May 1978.

that the market is fully consistent with the principles of justice in transfer. This claim carries conviction only if we are prepared to incorporate into our entitlement theory certain somewhat novel views concerning the morality of the entrepreneurial role. Recognizing this aspect of the entrepreneuial role makes it no longer useful to distinguish as sharply as Nozick does between justice in original acquisition, on the one hand, and justice in transfer. So that, while the entitlement theory may indeed be deployed to defend the morality of the market—and with fewer reservations, perhaps, than in Nozick's own statement—this will have been achieved only through a fairly substantial reformulation of that theory.

JUSTICE IN TRANSFER, VOLUNTARINESS, AND ERROR

For now, I accept Nozick's entitlement theory of justice without reservation. If an object was originally acquired justly from nature, and if all subsequent transfers of the object have been justly accomplished, then, we will say, the present holder of that object holds it justly, and no aesthetic or moral considerations concerning desirable distribution patterns can, without injustice, permit the state to tamper with the rights of the present holder. The issue that concerns us is whether this theory, when applied to the results of the free market, can certify these results as being in accord with just principles. Let us, for the time being, accept Nozick's own conclusion[1] that the free operation of the market system is consistent with past acquisition of initial holdings. Our concern will be with the justice of market transfers.

Now Nozick has not, he explains,[2] attempted in his book the task of specifying the details of the principles of justice in transfer. The general outlines of his position on the justice of market transfers are, however, clearly implied: What has been acquired through market transaction has been justly acquired for the simple reason that such transactions are *voluntary*. The money a professional athlete receives from spectators eager to watch his performance is justly his because those who paid have done so willingly. They preferred to watch the athlete at the given money price rather than to retain the money without witnessing the performance.[3] Because a property system excludes taking anyone's goods or money without his consent, whether by theft or fraud, because such a system permits transfer only by gift or voluntary market exchange, it follows that such a system has room only for transfers that are just.

The view assigning so critical a role to voluntariness in just transfers is surely highly appealing, and we will accept it fully as the basis for our discussion. Involuntary transfers, I have said, are ruled out in the market by definition; only voluntary exchanges qualify as market transactions. The question I wish to raise has to do with the extent to which *error*, in the decisions of market participants to engage in exchange, erodes the voluntariness—and hence the justice—of the transfers effected by such exchange. Now it might appear that consistent application of our definition of market transactions as being voluntary avoids any difficulty for the justice of market transfer arising out of error. If, say, a seller sells an item in error, then either the error was so serious as to definitely impair the voluntariness of the sale, or it was not. That is, either the error on the part of the seller was so fundamental that we are compelled to say he did not *really* wish to sell at all (i.e., that his consent to sell was utterly erroneous and was thus no consent at all) or else it was not serious enough to impair the voluntariness of the sale. If the error *was* serious enough to render the sale involuntary, then we should simply pronounce the exchange a total mistake and thus not a permissible market transaction at all. Unjust though we must consider the purchase to have been, it was, we should say, not a market transaction but simply an involuntary transfer. If, on the other hand, the voluntariness of the sale was *not* undermined by the error, then the transfer remains a just one. Either way, it seems, the possibility of error presents no problems for the justice of market transfers. Defenders of the market have, after all, always made it clear that fraudulent transactions are a form of theft and are—with or without state action—to be expunged from the market system.[4] But surely a fairly persuasive case can be made for a less comfortable view of the matter. Such a case may perhaps gain plausibility from a consideration, first, of the degree to which the market process *depends*, in fact, on the profitability of entrepreneurial trading with market participants who have, at least to some extent, erred.

Equilibrium, Disequilibrium, and Error

For the economist's model of market equilibrium it is not only possible, but indeed necessary, to imagine a world without error. As Hayek explained forty years ago, equilibrium is defined as the state of correct foresight.[5] Were, then, a market economy to be continuously in equilibrium, it would be indeed easy to defend the voluntariness—and hence the justice—of all market transfers, since every one of them would reflect decisions made with complete awareness of market conditions. In no way could it be claimed that any exchanges were entered into out of ignorance.

But it is now well understood that the function of equilibrium models is hardly to portray the real world. Rather, such a model serves to illuminate the nature of the equilibrating market forces that are at work during the states of disequilibrium that, in fact, prevail at all times.[6] And it is the essence of states of disequilibrium that the decisions being made are quite different from those that would have been made in an errorless world. It is, further, the case that insight into the equilibrating forces of the market generated by the conditions of disequilibrium reveals them to operate through entrepreneurial discovery and exploitation of the errors characteristic of disequilibrium. A simple example illustrates the matter effectively.

It is one of the features of models of competitive equilibrium that, in the market for a given good, no more than one price can prevail during the same period. Before equilibrium has been attained, however, many prices for the same goods may be simultaneously paid and accepted by different buyers and sellers. The disequilibrium situation in which many prices prevail in this way generates a spontaneous equilibrating tendency toward the elimination of such gratuitous price differentials. The existence of a price differential constitutes an attractive opportunity for entrepreneurial profit. Eager seekers of profit will tend to grasp these opportunities until their competitive activity has squeezed out all such opportunities, that is, until prices have become uniform throughout the market.

Consideration of this simple example immediately shows how heavily the equilibrating process rests on the profitability of acting to take advantage of the errors of others. We notice at the very outset that the multiprice situation characteristic of disequilibrium reflects widespread ignorance on the part of buyers and sellers. Those who paid the higher prices were clearly unaware of the sellers who were prepared to accept, and in fact did accept, lower prices; and those sellers who accepted the lower prices were obviously unaware of the buyers who offered and paid the higher prices. The entrepreneur who discovers and moves to exploit the profit opportunities presented by the multiprice situation is buying at low prices from those who are unaware of the possibility of selling at higher prices. He, on the other hand, is buying at the low prices in order to sell at higher prices to those who are, in turn, unaware of the possibility of buying at lower prices. The equilibrative aspects of the market process depend, in an essential way, upon the lure of the profits made possible by the errors of those with whom the entrepreneur deals. In fact, the insights gained from the simple illustrative example we have used apply not only to this simple case but to the most complicated of markets, involving production in any number of stages, inputs in any number and any variety, and outputs of any degree of multiplicity and heterogeneity. The coordination and allocative properties of competitive markets depend entirely on the attractiveness of pure entrepreneurial profit opportunities; such opportunities arise only out of the less-than-perfect omniscience of those from whom entrepreneurs buy, and of those to whom they sell.

The questions I wish to raise concerning the justice of market transfers thus emerge fairly clearly. If the market depends heavily on the exploitation of profit opportunities made possible only by the errors of others, and if goods purchased from sellers who sold only as a result of error and money received from buyers who bought only as a result of error are considered unjustly acquired, then surely the justice of the market has been fatally compromised. It will not do to declare that transactions entered into in error—being "involuntary"—are excluded by definition from the class of market transactions, since a market process without "erroneous" transactions is unthinkable. The only logical possibility for defending the general morality of market transactions must be to maintain that the errors that characterize disequilibrium markets do *not* affect the voluntariness of the transactions completed. The profits won by entrepreneurs taking advantage of the errors of others are, one would have to maintain, not unjust, as measured by Nozick's "voluntarism" yardstick of justice in transfer. Can such a position, we must ask, in fact be maintained?

THE MORALITY OF ENTREPRENEURIAL PROFIT: A BRIEF DIGRESSION

It will be seen that the question I have raised about the justice of market transfers generally has led us to question, in particular, the justice of pure entrepreneurial profit.[7] The form in which this last question is posed makes it rather different from other challenges to the morality of profits. It may be useful to digress very briefly in order to explain this difference. The roots of the matter lie, in the first place, in the theory of profit one chooses to embrace, and, in the second place, in the theory of justice one wishes to apply.

Most criticisms of capitalism made on moral grounds have denounced profit as unjust. Usually such criticism has rested on one or another of the theories of economic justice that Nozick has, persuasively, rejected in favor of the entitlement theory. Entrepreneurial profits are likely to violate many of the patterns of distributive justice one might wish to promote. In addition, the critics saw profits as generated by, say, the exploitation of labor or the unfair exercise of economic power; or else what they were criticizing as profit was not pure entrepreneurial profit at all, but the interest on capital.[8]

The question that I, on the other hand, have raised about entrepreneurial profit and, indeed, about all market transfers rests on what has been described as an *arbitrage theory of pure profit*;[9] and it has been raised against the specific background of Nozick's entitlement theory. The arbitrage theory sees profit as generated by the existence of different prices in different parts of the market for what are, economically if not physically, identical goods. Such differentials can arise only as the result of imperfection in knowledge. It is this theory of profit that, in the context of Nozick's "voluntariness" criterion of justice in transfer, is responsible for the question raised here.

Optimum Ignorance, Deliberate Mistakes, and Genuine Error

We return to consider the possible challenge to the justice of market transfers, arising out of the errors on the basis of which market transactions are completed. Here I discuss and reject one possible way of dismissing this challenge altogether. In subsequent sections the question itself is examined.

One way that one might reject the challenge of injustice based on error is to deny altogether the possibility of genuine error. One might, that is, maintain that while market transactions are indeed frequently entered into as a result of incorrect knowledge or expectations, this *never* involves genuine error. After all, one who knows his vacation may be ruined by bad weather and nonetheless travels to the resort and occupies his hotel room cannot, when bad weather indeed arrives, be said to have really erred in the sense of having consented to do something which he did not "really" wish to do. After all, he deliberately erred; he deliberately risked his money; he gladly took his chances; every transaction he entered was a wholly voluntary one. To the extent that *every* decision made in error is made either through deliberately accepting an uncertainty (such as bad weather) concerning which accurate knowledge is simply unavailable, or through deliberately choosing not to spend the resources necessary to remove the possibility of error,[10] every decision has been deliberately and hence voluntarily made. A deliberate decision not to acquire costly knowledge is, after all, made voluntarily. If we rule out deception, where, for example, an entrepreneur misleads a seller into thinking no one else is prepared to pay a higher price,[11] the fact that someone sells to an entrepreneur at a low price (knowing full well that diligent search *might* yield the possibility of selling at a higher price) can surely not raise doubt concerning the voluntariness of the sale (even though it is true that, had the seller known that higher prices were being paid, he would not have sold at the lower price).

This line of argument denies that *genuine* error (in the sense of a decision's being made in unwitting ignorance of pertinent information) can be made at all. *All* mistakes are seen as the result of deliberately assumed risk. No mistakes can raise questions concerning the voluntariness of decisions made.

I have elsewhere argued at length that genuine error can and does indeed occur.[12] Without repeating that discussion here, I will simply point out that decisions are often made in ignorance of the very need or possibility of acquiring information that might be freely available. It is one thing to know that one is ignorant and to deliberately maintain one's ignorance because of the high cost of gaining knowledge. It is quite another to be ignorant simply because one has no inkling that one is ignorant, because one has no idea that information exists, or indeed that any such thing is imaginable, in the relevant context, as information. Surely the latter kind of ignorance is abundantly present; genuine error is alive and well. We cannot rule out the possibility that market decisions have been made not out of deliberately accepted ignorance, but out of genuine error. The "voluntariness" of such decisions still calls for examination.[13]

MISTAKES: LAW AND MORALITY

The question of erroneously made decisions has, of course, been treated thoroughly by jurists in regard to the law of contracts. And the kinds of error occurring during disequilibrium that have given us concern—where, say, sellers would not have sold at the price they accepted had they known the true eagerness of buyers elsewhere in the market—are, in the legal literature, *not* seen as affecting the validity of transactions completed. Providing the entrepreneur-buyer did not explicitly deceive the seller concerning the facts—extrinsic to the goods sold—about which he has been misinformed (and providing no fiduciary type of relationship between them exists that might render the buyer's silence concerning the truth a form of implied deception), the law finds no grounds to invalidate market transactions into which one of the parties has entered under mistaken assumptions concerning present or future market conditions. "Tacit acquiescence in the self-delusion of another, if nothing is said or done to mislead, or silence which does not make that which is stated false, draws with it no legal liability,"[14] we are told. And the kinds of self-delusion referred to include that of the landowner who sells his land for the price of grazing land when in fact it contains valuable minerals, or who is ignorant of the fact known to the buyer that a railroad is intended to pass through it. "If the parties are at arms' length, neither of them is under any obligation to call the attention of the opposite party to facts or circumstances which lie properly within his knowledge, although he may see that they are not actually within his knowledge."[15] The law thus takes a hard-boiled view of commercial transactions—an attitude often loosely and imprecisely identified as caveat emptor—that does not see a mistake (except where it is *induced* by one's trading partner) as legitimate cause for the invalidation of a completed transaction or commitment. Apparently the law does occupy a position close to that (rejected in the preceding section) which sees a mistake merely as a deliberately assumed gamble that failed, rather than as representing lack of true will to participate in the transaction as it turned out.[16]

But the *legal* validity of entrepreneurial transactions in disequilibrium markets is not at all what is of concern to us and was never in question. Of course the legal system within which the capitalist economy operates recognizes the validity of the market transactions that make up the system. We have been concerned with possible challenges to the morality of that very legal system that sustains capitalism. What answer, we have been asking, can one give those who might contend that market transfers violate Nozick's canons of justice in that error (which invariably characterizes market transactions) introduces an ineradicable moral stain of *involuntariness* into the very fabric of these transactions? It is noteworthy that the jurists expounding the hard-boiled attitude of the law toward mistake go out of their way *not* to defend the morality of those who benefit by the law's tough-mindedness. "No doubt" we are in fact told, "such dealings would be repugnant to a man of high honor and delicacy."[17] The view of fraud taken by the law is carefully distinguished from the view of moralists.[18] It will not do simply to denounce moralists who fail to include, in their assessment of the morality of market transactions, the enormous social benefits these transactions generate. To be sure, these benefits ought not to be overlooked by the moralist.[19] But Nozick's demonstration of the justice of the free market cannot, surely, be pronounced complete if the *voluntariness* of market transfers, upon which Nozick's case depends, can possibly remain under a cloud. What does one say to the critic who argues that the law permits the gullible to be *cheated*? ("Fraud is difficult to prove" is a repeated refrain;[20] and, anyway, what is not *technically* fraud may, to men of honor, be seen as cheating all the same.) And, in the broadest of senses, can it not be said that the market process *depends* on at least a mild form of "cheating"?

ON CHEATING AND THE JUST PRICE

No examination of the possibility of injustice in market transfers can avoid some reference to recent discussions of the medieval doctrines of just price. Earlier scholars understood the medieval writers to have seen *cost of production* as the criterion for justice in pricing. An unjust price for a good was one that diverged from its true value as defined by production costs, with the latter "determined by a fixed standard of living on the part of the producers and ... not to include any element of *interest*."[21] An unjust price was thus seen as unjust not primarily because it involved deceit by the one party (or at least an error on the part of the second), but simply because justice requires that each party to an exchange receive the true value of what he has given up. If divergence from the true value is described as involving "cheating," this must then mean either merely that without deceit it would presumably be impossible to secure more than the true value of what one gives up, or that to cheat is to be *defined* purely in terms of divergence from true value. (Compare the phrase Nozick used in describing the old question about the possibility of profits: "How can there be profits if everything gets its full value, if no *cheating* goes on?"[22]) For decades after 1870, economists found it necessary to explain how inadequate such a conception of justice in transfer, ignoring all demand considerations, must be considered. And in Nozick's entitlement theory little room seems to be assigned for divergence from production costs as a criterion for injustice in transfer. (In referring to the possibility of "gouging," Nozick seems quite content to leave to buyers the responsibility of looking out for themselves.[23])

More recently, however, historians of medieval economic thought have emphasized references in the scholastic writings to market price as the criterion for justice.[24] And such references are occasionally couched in language suggesting that to take advantage of imperfect knowledge of market conditions on the part of one's trading partner is to violate the canons of the just price.[25] But it appears to be incorrect to ascribe to the medieval writers the concern for the possible injustice of disequilibrium market transfers I have expressed here. Whether, with Schumpeter and De Roover, one is prepared to credit Aquinas and the medieval writers with a sophisticated understanding of the relationship between cost of production and long-run equilibrium price, or whether, with Hollander, one is not prepared to do so, it seems fairly clear that for Aquinas actual market price is understood as being always the equilibrium price. It was because the market price was therefore seen as expressing the true value of a good, reflecting "the entire set of objective and subjective elements which forms the community estimate,"[26] that it was considered unjust to take advantage of a buyer's ignorance of the market price. It is true that pure profits were, as Hollander has explained, generally frowned upon by Aquinas, but this was clearly on grounds other than the taking advantage of the ignorance of one's trading partners. In other contexts it was clearly not considered unjust to take advantage of another's ignorance. A number of writers have drawn attention to Aquinas's view that a seller may charge a high price for grain in a place where it is dear, even though he knows that others are following with more supplies—a fact that, if known to the buyers, would have led them to refuse to pay the present higher price.[27] Clearly a price paid only out of ignorance of the true facts does not, in this view, by itself mark it as unjust.

Aquinas's justification for this permissive position clearly implies that the market price at a given instant is the true equilibrium price relevant to questions of justice. The present high value of the grain is its true present value. The anticipated arrival of additional supplies of grain can be expected to lower the market price *in the future,* so that a seller who sells at today's price does not act unjustly in failing to disclose what will happen in the future.[28] One can understand that if the market price is considered the just price because it reflects the current "community estimate" of value, then information concerning the future possessed by a single market participant may not be seen as altering the present community estimate; and his exploitation of his superior information need not, therefore, be seen as unjust according to the criterion adopted. But if one questions the justice of market exchange precisely because it occurs under conditions one of the parties is ignorant about (so that his consent to the deal might be said to hinge on a wholly erroneous perception of the relevant circumstances) then the scholastic insight into the justice of market price has not helped us answer our question. Our awareness that market prices are never equilibrium prices does not encourage us to accept the market prices as just because they are somehow expressive of *all* relevant circumstances. These prices, we must recognize, necessarily reflect the very errors that have occasioned our concern.

The Base for the Justice of the Market: The Ethical and Economic Building Blocks

I will argue that the difficulties raised concerning the justice of disequilibrium market transactions can be resolved definitively by (1) accepting a particular *ethical judgment,* and consistently applying it in conjunction with (2) the acceptance of a particular economic insight into the nature of disequilibrium market transactions. The ethical judgment referred to has been called the "finders-keepers" ethic.[29] The economic insight is that which permits us to perceive the discovery of a hitherto unknown market use for an already-owned resource or commodity as the discovery of (and consequently the spontaneous establishment of ownership in) a hitherto *unowned* element associated with that resource or commodity. I will argue that acceptance of the morality and justice of a market system does imply the acceptance of these ethical and economic ways of seeing things. Many who consider a market system just may not perhaps have explicitly articulated their own position to themselves in precisely these terms, but upon reflection they will probably recognize my exposition as faithful to their own view. It should be noted that it is not my purpose to insist on the *acceptance* of these views. My purpose is only to show that there exist plausible (and, at least implicitly, apparently widely accepted) moral and economic insights upon which a consistent defense of the justice of the market can be constructed. These insights, we will discover, remove the difficulties we have encountered so far. Moreover, they can easily be grafted onto a suitably reformulated entitlement-theoretic interpretation of market justice. Let us consider separately and more carefully each of these ethical and economic insights, building blocks for constructing the case for the justice of the free market.

FINDERS, CREATORS, AND KEEPERS

The finders-keepers ethic has been discussed only slightly in the literature on the ethics of private property.[30] In fact, it seems fair to conclude that most writers on the justice of private acquisition from nature of hitherto unheld resources, do *not* accept it. The mere fact that an individual has stumbled on a rich deposit of a valuable natural resource does not (without at least some effort on his part, say, some mixing of his labor with the resource) entitle the discoverer, according to this view, to claim title to it merely on the grounds that he found the resource. Mere discovery has not placed the discoverer in any kind of privileged position with respect to the hitherto unheld resources. If the rest of mankind were seen, up to the present, as enjoying rights of access to and common use of these hitherto unheld resources, then these rights are seen as in no way dislodged by the mere event of the discovery.

To introduce plausibility into the notion of finders-keepers,[31] it appears necessary to adopt the view that, until a resource has been discovered, *it has not,* in the sense relevant to the rights of access and common use, *existed at all.* By this view it seems plausible to consider the discoverer of the hitherto "nonexistent" resource as, in the relevant sense, the *creator* of what he has found.[32] It becomes, then, fairly easy to understand how the finder can be held justly entitled to keep that which he has "created."

It should be noted that ownership-by-creation is quite different from ownership-by-just-acquisition-from-nature, as the latter is spelled out in, say, Nozick's entitlement theory. Ownership by acquisition occurs against the prior background of *given* unheld resources even if no one is aware of their existence. Acquisition is, in fact, a kind of "transfer" from nature to the first holder. Ownership by creation, on the other hand, involves no notion of transfer at all. The finder-creator has spontaneously generated hitherto nonexistent resources and is seen, therefore, as their natural owner.

The adoption of a finders-keepers ethic does not, of course, rule out scope for acquisition from nature in the usual (Nozick's) sense.[33] The first man to land on Mars can hardly claim title to it as its "creator." To establish just ownership in an unheld resource whose existence everyone is fully aware of, it is certainly necessary to follow the criteria considered appropriate to just acquisition from nature.

Moreover (and this will be of some importance later), it does not seem necessary to choose between adopting the finders-keepers ethic absolutely and not accepting it at all. It seems possible to view some kinds of creation-by-discovery as conferring just natural ownership, while in other circumstances (perhaps those in which discovery was *wholly* accidental, or those in which discovery by one person came on the heels of years of exhausting search by another), one may not be so prepared to recognize the actual discoverer as the sole just keeper of his find. Certainly the cases in which we might invoke the ethics of finders' remaining keepers call for systematic analysis and classification. My purpose has merely been to emphasize the possible role a finder-creator view of discovery can play in a theory of justice.

ENTREPRENEURIAL DISCOVERY AND CREATIVITY

We turn to the second of the building blocks referred to earlier: the economic insight that the discovery of a hitherto unknown market use for an already-owned resource or commodity constitutes the discovery of a hitherto *unowned* element associated with that resource or commodity. In the conventional view (apparently shared by Nozick), once a unit of resource has been acquired, ownership has been established in it with respect to *all* its properties and powers, whether or not these have been known or imagined. In the view now being considered, on the other hand, those aspects of a thing that are unknown remain, so to speak, nonexistent. Their discovery constitutes the discovery of a hitherto unknown, nonexistent, and hence unowned dimension of the thing. An owner owns only those aspects of his property of which he is aware. Acceptance of this way of viewing the matter has far-reaching implications for the perception of the entrepreneurial role in the market.

The entrepreneur perceives and exploits opportunities in the market that others have not noticed. He discovers, for example, that a quantity of oranges is being sold, for eating, throughout the market at $5, while consumers would gladly pay a total of $12 for these same oranges converted to orange juice and marmalade, at a total manufacturing cost, above that of the oranges, of $4. Entrepreneurial discovery of the $3 profit opportunity—of buying oranges for $5 and selling them for $8 (i.e., the $12 obtainable from the sale of juice and marmalade less the other costs of $4)—represents, in the view being discussed, the discovery of $3 value in the oranges that did not previously exist. Up to the moment when the entrepreneur's vision "saw" the juice and marmalade the oranges represent, oranges had value only for eating, a value the market set at $5. The entrepreneur has discovered $3 additional value in the oranges. He may, then, be held to have created this additional value in these oranges.[34] It is as if the entrepreneur found orange juice and marmalade in nature, where no one had perceived their existence; he has created the orange resource that can provide juice and marmalade.

Pursuing the matter further, it may be held that *any* price differential discovered and exploited by the entrepreneur constitutes the discovery of hitherto unknown and nonexistent value (even where no new, physically different, use is entailed). If orange juice can be bought at $3 (in one market) and sold at $4 (with no additional costs involved) in a second market, this means that those who were buying and selling at $3 did not know of the presence of those sufficiently eager for juice to be willing to pay $4 for it. Entrepreneurial discovery of this may, then, be seen as the discovery in the first market of a hitherto unsuspected intensity of potential value in orange juice. The entrepreneur may be held to have created this additional value by introducing these oranges to the second market.

It should be observed that this view of entrepreneurial discovery and creativity arises out of an understanding of the entrepreneurial role in a strictly arbitrage sense.[35] According to this view, the entrepreneur adds nothing to the production process other than his alertness to the production possibilities already existing. He provides no services, managerial or other; he simply notices that inputs can be obtained at a total outlay less than the sales revenue obtainable from output. We see the entrepreneur as creator not in the sense of the physical producer, but strictly in the sense of his being the discoverer of an available opportunity.

ENTREPRENEURSHIP AND THE EXPLOITATION OF ERROR

Acceptance of the finders-keepers ethic and of the economic insight into entrepreneurial discovery discussed in the preceding sections clears away the difficulties surrounding the justice of disequilibrium market transactions to which attention has been drawn. The central feature that distinguishes the market in disequilibrium from the model of market equilibrium can, after all, be stated in terms of the scope open for entrepreneurship. In the equilibrium model, all profitable opportunities have already been discovered and exploited. Nothing remains for entrepreneurs to discover and to create. In the disequilibrium market, it is precisely the changes introduced by entrepreneurial discovery of existing errors (and the consequent opportunities for profit), that constitute the market process and that are, in fact, the *meaning* of the label describing the market as in disequilibrium.[36]

It follows that entrepreneurial profits captured during the disequilibrium market process can be defended as new value that entrepreneurs have discovered and thus created. The equilibrating market process is thus perceived not simply as economic theory has traditionally shown, as a process tending to correct the misallocation of resources, but as a process of the continued net *creation of values*, as it were ex nihilo, as goods tend to move from lower-valued to higher-valued uses.

But what of the difficulty that such entrepreneurial activity in disequilibrium has involved transactions with trading partners who would never have bought or sold (at prices they accepted) had they known the true state of the market? What of the possibility that these transactions, having been made in error, lack the critical element of true voluntariness, that the consent given to these sales and purchases was in reality no consent at all? Reflection shows that, given the basis of the views discussed, these difficulties no longer obtrude.

If a man sells oranges, knowing full well their usefulness for marmalade and juice, because of some serious misunderstanding on his part, we may wish to say that the sale really lacked consent and is thus invalid. The oranges, including their potential in producing juice and marmalade, were his; without genuine consent they cannot justly become owned by another. But consider the man who sells oranges for $5 because he is unaware that, as potential raw material in producing juice and marmalade, they are worth $8 to the entrepreneur to whom he sells. The shadow clouding his consent arises from the existence of the $3 of additional value about which he is ignorant. But we have seen that this additional $3 value may well be held *never to have been possessed by the seller at all*. This $3 value was discovered (indeed *created*) by the entrepreneur's purchase and subsequent sale. So the error on the part of the seller (on the basis of which we sought to invalidate the sale) can, by the present view of things, hardly be held to affect the conclusiveness of the consent of the seller to the sale of what was his to sell in the first place.

It thus turns out, not at all accidentally, that the reasoning that justifies pure entrepreneurial profit on the grounds that the entrepreneur has "created" previously nonexistent value is at the same time able to protect one who purchases or sells any good at a disequilibrium price from the charge that it was sold to him or purchased by him only on the basis of error and hence of flawed consent. Market transfers are, according to this view, just because no one consents voluntarily to a transaction except insofar as it gives him a satisfactory exchange for what he sees himself as giving up. And until someone discovers that what is given up is more than the owner sees, no more than that exists, in the sense relevant to this view of economic justice.

It should be observed that this justification of entrepreneurial alertness to the errors made by others does *not* extend to the justification of fraud, properly defined. Nor does it necessarily rule out the possible view that at least some cases of nonfraudulent exploitation of error be considered morally questionable. Fraud is not covered by the reasoning that justifies market transfers because fraud involves the deceitful *inducement* of error, either positively or—where a fiduciary type of relationship exists—tacitly, on the basis of which consent is fraudulently obtained. And even some cases of nonfraudulent exploitation of error may be condemned, despite an otherwise general acceptance of the justification of disequilibrium market transfer we have discussed. It seems entirely possible to restrict one's adoption of the "finders-creators-keepers" ethic to only some kinds of entrepreneurial finds and creations. Perhaps it may seem that to take advantage of prior knowledge of information that will be commonly known in five years' time is justified, but that exploiting the knowledge that everyone will surely know in five minutes is going too far.[37] The point has not been to show that all possible forms of entrepreneurial exploitation of error sanctioned by the law are rendered immediately morally acceptable by application of the finders-keepers ethic. The purpose has been to show that this ethic can plausibly be deployed to rebut possible blanket condemnation of market processes on grounds of error and consequent lack of genuine consent.[38]

MODIFICATIONS IN THE ENTITLEMENT THEORY

We are now in a position to spell out how Nozick's entitlement theory needs modification if it is to effectively demonstrate the possible justice of the market system. The entitlement theory maintains the following definitions: (1) a distribution of holdings is just if all those are entitled to the holdings they possess under the distribution; (2) one is entitled to a holding only if he has acquired it from the unheld state in accordance with the principle of justice in acquisition, or if he has acquired it in accordance with the principle of justice in transfer from someone else entitled to the holding.[39] Our discussion calls for modification of Nozick's view that these latter definitions under (2) "exhaustively cover the subject of justice in holdings."[40]

For Nozick, the justice of holdings depends "historically" on the justice of the original acquisition from the unheld state, and on the justice of each of the subsequent transfers of the holding. Our discussion of the finders-keepers ethic, and its application in the justice of entrepreneurial creation, indicates first that Nozick's definitions have not definitively covered all cases of holdings that may be considered just, and, again, that the lines Nozick draws between original acquisition and acquisition by transfer are not as sharp as his discussion suggests.

The framework of Nozick's definitions sees things as being held either as the result of original acquisition from an unheld state or else as the result of acquisition by transfer from a previous holder. Our discussion has pointed out a third possibility: a thing may be held as the result of the holder having, in the relevant sense, created it ex nihilo, by finding it.[41] To be sure, the possibility that a thing has been, at one level of discourse, created from the state of nonexistence, does not preclude its having been acquired (either originally or by transfer) from what, at a different level of discussion, is treated as an earlier state of existence. Oil discovered in an unsuspected location may, at one level, be treated as not having existed before; at another level, it did already exist. Nozick's schema is certainly an exhaustive one at this latter level; but our discussion has shown that discourse may be fruitful when the third possibility we have mentioned enters as an important additional class of holdings.[42]

Recognition of this possibility, the holding of a thing as a result not of its acquisition from the unheld state, or from a previous holder, but of its having been created, introduces a certain fuzziness in the line Nozick draws between holdings resulting from original acquisition and those resulting from acquisition by transfer. In his schema, transfer involves only the acquisition of a previously held thing. For us, transfer may well involve, besides the acquisition of what was already held, the creation of an entirely new dimension of the holding, something not only not previously held, but something that did not, in the relevant sense, exist previously at all.[43] Recognizing this complexity in transfers, especially in market transfer, has enabled us to perceive the possible justice of the entrepreneurial discoveries that may be expressed in disequilibrium market purchases and sales.

Another implication in the entitlement theory relates to the justice of original acquisition. As we will see in the following section, it appears that some of Nozick's views that flow from his treatment of the justice of original acquisition arise from his decided lack of enthusiasm for the possibility that many cases of original acquisitions may qualify, at least in part, for justification under the finder-creator-keepers ethic. To the implications of this possibility we now turn.

Nozick and the Lockean Proviso

Nozick has not attempted to spell out in detail the proper principles of justice in original acquisition or in acquisition by transfer. Nonetheless, he has devoted a good deal of attention to what he has termed the "Lockean Proviso." And, while Locke himself enumerated the proviso in relation to the original acquisition from nature, Nozick has pursued its implications insofar as it introduces complications into the justice of acquisition by transfer.

Locke's theory of justice in original acquisition, requiring only that the would-be expropriator of an unowned object mix his labor with it, was qualified by the proviso that there be "enough and as good left in common for others."[44] Nozick explains that, by this qualification, Locke meant "to ensure that the situation of others is not worsened."[45] While Nozick sharply limits the scope of the Lockean proviso as it enters into his own entitlement theory of justice,[46] he does, without hesitation, strongly accept the principle that justice in original acquisition requires that such acquisitions shall leave no one else in a worse situation than he would have been in without it. In fact, Nozick seems almost relieved to be able to invoke this principle in cases involving appropriation of the entire stock of a limited, life-giving resource, to which critics of the private property system have traditionally pointed as exemplifying the injustice of the system. The case of "someone who comes upon the only water in the desert several miles ahead of others who also will come to it and appropriates it all"[47] is a violation of the proviso circumventing original acquisition. And even, Nozick argues, where one appropriates only one of many water holes in the desert, but it subsequently happens that all the other holes dry up, the Lockean proviso stringently limits what he can do with "his" hole.[48]

My emphasis on the role of discovery and creation in justifying title to a holding enables us to question the rather sweeping scope that Nozick, at least in principle, assigns to the Lockean proviso. (Nozick believes that, in practice, "the free operation of a market system will not actually run afoul of the Lockean proviso.")[49] Clearly, once we admit that the discovery of an unknown thing justifies its finder's holding it on the grounds that, in the relevant sense, he created it, as it were, ex nihilo, the entire basis of the Lockean proviso becomes vulnerable to challenge. Is it really true that, where a discoverer appropriates all of a limited deposit of resource, he is worsening the situation of others for whom this deposit was completely unknown and nonexistent? This question seems so obviously to call for a negative answer that, indeed, Nozick finds himself forced by it to accept, in effect, a limited finders-keepers ethic. Nozick circumscribes the Lockean proviso by observing that where a researcher synthesizes a new substance out of easily available raw materials he may justly refuse to sell except on his terms since by so doing he does not harm others, who are free to do what he had done. Moreover, Nozick adds, one who appropriates the total supply of a new substance by finding it "in an out-of-the-way place" has not worsened the situation of others: "If he did not stumble upon the substance no one else would have." But Nozick immediately qualifies this by pointing out that in the latter case, "as time passes, the likelihood increases that others would have come across the substance," justifying, Nozick suggests, possible limitation on bequest by the first discoverer.[50]

Nozick's limited recognition of the exemption of discovery from the Lockean proviso does not appear to go nearly far enough. For Nozick, even appropriation of an object after its discovery may be considered to worsen the situation of those (possibly in later generations) who would have found the object for themselves. But our insight into the creative aspect of discovery suggests a different view of the matter on two separate grounds. First, we must maintain that one who *might* at a given date have created an object ex nihilo has hardly been hurt because a second individual in fact did create the object first. It was the latter individual who was the creator, not the former. A finders-creators-keepers ethic cannot, it must be maintained, confer any claim on those who *might have*, but did not in fact, create. Nozick's concern for the harm done to those who would have themselves discovered the new substance is based on the view that, whether discovered or not, the new substance *has* always existed, for both present and future generations. So that the basis of Locke's proviso—that others have some claim on unowned objects, requiring that they therefore not be harmed by appropriation—applies also to undiscovered substances. But if we recognize that an undiscovered substance does not, in the relevant sense, exist for those who are not aware of it, then Nozick's concern loses its justification.

But perhaps even more important is a second reason we cannot share Nozick's view that the discoverer of a new substance is justified to hold it only to the extent that it would not have been discovered by others. For Nozick, Lockean acquisition of an unowned object from nature seems to be justified only in the negative sense that such appropriation (where, of course, it does not violate the proviso) has not harmed others. That is, one who has mixed his labor with the unowned resource, of which ample supply is left for others, has not acquired just title on the basis of any powerful positive moral claim. He has acquired title because mixing one's labor with the resource *is* the act of appropriation, and compliance with the Lockean proviso ensures that no *in*justice is involved in this acquisition. But acceptance of a finders-creators-keepers ethic confers just title on the discoverer-creator not in the negative sense that such title involves no injustice to others, but in the positive sense that justice requires that the creator be recognized as the owner of what he has created: to deny the creator title would be to inflict injustice on him. From this view of the ethics of creation, it is by no means clear that Locke's proviso has necessary relevance to discovery at all. If justice requires that the creator of an object be recognized as its owner, then this *may* remain true even if it might be shown that others who might, say, have otherwise discovered the object for themselves can be considered as having been rendered worse off by the creation.

The consideration advanced tends to exempt from the Lockean proviso a substantial proportion of the cases—all those involving discovery—that Nozick includes under the heading of "original acquisition from the unheld state." On this basis, the troublesome water hole in the desert cases must, where they have involved discovery, be viewed as indeed involving no violation of strict justice, despite whatever other moral stricture one may invoke to criticize selfish behavior by a just owner, especially in situations involving threat to life. Moreover, it should be pointed out that consistent application of the reasoning developed earlier suggests that the Lockean proviso cannot claim necessary relevance even for cases in which discovery does not seem obviously to be involved. I have argued that genuine entrepreneurial discovery and creation may occur even with respect to objects whose existence is known to all.

Consider the case (referred to only by implication in Nozick's discussion) of the unheld sole water hole in the desert which *everyone* in a group of travelers knows about, which one of the travelers, by racing ahead of the others, succeeds in appropriating. For Nozick this case, involving as it does no discovery at all, clearly and unjustly violates the Lockean proviso: the other travelers who, in the absence of appropriation by their fellow, would all have enjoyed some water without cost, are now forced to pay a price (even a monopoly price) for that same water. For us, however, this view is by no means the only one possible. We notice that the energetic traveler who appropriated all the water was not doing anything that (always ignoring of course, prohibitions resting on the Lockean proviso itself) the other travelers were not equally free to do. The other travelers, too, could have raced ahead. Assuming, for simplicity, that all the travelers were of equal strength and speed, there would have ensued a gold rush in which each would have, let us say, captured *some* water. As it happened, the other travelers did not bother to race for the water. May it not be that they were less alert, entrepreneurially, to the possibility that someone else might indeed appropriate all the water than the energetic traveler? Should we not, then, say that the latter was the first to discover the true market value of the unheld water? For the others, the water was indeed known, but the worthwhileness of its application was not known. Perhaps they mistakenly thought there was more water available than could possibly be drunk; perhaps they mistakenly thought that no one would or could race across the desert faster than they were traveling, or perhaps they gave the water no thought at all. It does not seem obvious that these other travelers can claim that they were *hurt* by an action they could themselves have easily taken had they been as alert as the successful appropriator. What, one must ask, even under conditions involving the appropriation of known substances, is so obviously acceptable about the Lockean proviso, as interpreted by Nozick?

THE JUSTICE OF THE MARKET

It turns out, then, that the insight into entrepreneurial discovery, coupled with the possibility of a finders-keepers ethic, has not only solved the difficulties raised earlier, but has enabled us to perceive possible justification for the free operation of a market system with fewer qualifications than those that Nozick, on the basis of the Lockean proviso, was impelled to introduce.

A finders-keepers ethic, we have observed, may *not* be found compelling. Even if the basic idea is accepted, there remains ample room for moral reservations concerning particular cases of application of the ethic. Nonetheless there does seem to be a certain plausibility in the notion of ownership through creativity. This plausibility may help explain how so many observers of the market appear to find it consistent with economic justice in the face of the denunciations of the moralist critics of capitalism. We have explored the sources of this apparent plausibility and have scrutinized its ability to serve as possible support for the morality of the market. For this purpose, Nozick's entitlement theory has served as a crucial framework. That our discussion has suggested certain modifications in the framework itself has, I hope, been a positive contribution.

13

Entrepreneurship, Choice, and Freedom

THE CONCEPT OF FREEDOM is notoriously difficult to pin down. Philosophers and social scientists have exercised extraordinary ingenuity and subtlety in identifying the slight variations in meaning separating the many writers who have attempted to define freedom. Economists, perhaps more than others, have been subject to strong temptation to altogether overlook what should surely be considered an important, if not the essential, aspect of human freedom. The task of pointing out the source of this possible confusion presents, it will turn out, an opportunity worthwhile not only for its own sake, but also for its help in understanding the role of freedom in achieving social efficiency and in assessing the consequences for society of its curtailment. Stigler has recently challenged those who see the growth of the modern state as a danger to liberty to specify concretely the liberties that have been, in fact, impaired by this growth.[1] I shall argue that a proper understanding of liberty suggests that, in the very nature of things, such specification cannot be expected; moreover such proper understanding, it can be shown, reveals the loss of liberty that results from the growth of government in a manner so convincing as to render such specification hardly necessary.

FREEDOM, CHOICE, AND ECONOMICS

Among the multitude of meanings attached to the notion of freedom, it is widely held to pertain to some or other aspect of choice. And this circumstance seems responsible for what I

Presented at a meeting of the Southern Economic Association, Washington, D.C., November 1978.

shall argue to be the overly narrow perception of individual freedom that holds peculiar temptation for economists. Choice is, after all, very much a matter of concern to the economist. Efficiency—the norm for economic discussion—has everything to do with correct choice; rationality in choice is the assumption basic to the main body of economic theory, and economics itself is defined in terms of the choices people make concerning the allocation of scarce means to satisfy multiple competing ends. But this preoccupation by the economist with choice, one may argue, is responsible for the incomplete appreciation of freedom that seems to pervade much economic literature.

The problem is easily presented. Choice, for the economist, has come to mean the solution of a maximization problem. The economist sees the decision maker, whether consumer, producer, or resource owner, as allocating given means in such a way as to maximize the value of ends attained, with the relative rankings of the various ends seen as given. Freedom of choice refers to agent's liberty to select those courses of action he sees as maximizing his utility (or profit, or whatever else is seen as being maximized). Limitations on freedom take the form of prohibitions or constraints that prevent one's attaining goals that might otherwise be selected.

Basic to choice for the economist, then, is the *given* character of both ends and means.[2] The hierarchy of ends worthy of attainment is given; the constellation of means capable of achieving the various ends is also given. The act of choice is seen as occurring within the framework of this given ranking of ends and constellation of means. Freedom of choice, as well as limitations on such freedom, then, is viewed only as it impinges on the situation of the economizing individual *facing his given ends-means framework*. No matter what constraints, limitations, or prohibitions may be imposed on the economizing individual, they touch his freedom of choice not at all, for the economist, so long as they do not affect his ability to achieve the optimum position *relevant to and implicit in the given ends-means environment*.

It is here that confusion is found. No matter how important the problem of efficient decision making against the background of given ends and means may be, it represents only one narrow aspect of the human condition. As Mises,[3] Shackle,[4] and Lachmann[5] have again and again reminded us, the economist's view of the decision abstracts from elements that are crucial to the true character of human choice. The notion of given ends and means may be useful for certain purposes, but it does serious violence to the full reality of choice. The acting person never approaches the moment of decision *already* equipped with a clear, given picture of the relevant ends and means. It is only *at the moment of decision itself* that man is compelled to bring to some kind of focus all his doubts and conjectures concerning what goals are worth pursuing and what resources and technologies are available. The choices of people subject to unexplainable whims and taste changes— operating in a world whose realities are by no means immediately apparent and moreover characterized by continuous, kaleidic change—can hardly be subsumed, without serious strain, under the heading of maximizing calculations.

Once this broader view of choice is recognized, the notion of freedom of choice is surely seen to mean far more than the ability to realize a calculated optimum position. Freedom of choice can now be seen to encompass the liberty *to make up one's own mind as to the ranking of the ends to be pursued and the means judged available for the purpose*. Once a given ends-means framework has been adopted, freedom can only mean the freedom to achieve what one has already announced that one wishes to achieve. It is this narrow view of freedom that many economists seem to have adopted. But, with the acting man seen as approaching choice without having firmly adopted any one framework of ends and means, freedom of choice is at once seen as freedom to announce (i.e., to choose) what it is one wishes to achieve.

We may, to put it more bluntly, say that the narrow view of freedom we have attributed to the standard economist's conception of choice turns out to involve no choice at all. One has, in this conception of choice, in effect already chosen *before* the moment of decision. With given ranking of ends and with given means, the optimum position is fully implied in the data. Freedom, as well as its curtailment, can in such assumed circumstances refer only to the ability to achieve a given goal (or to its curtailment).[6] On the other hand, the wider view of freedom recognizes that, when people refer to the freedom to choose, they have in mind liberty to select among a wide range of moral and value frameworks, of ethical systems, of tastes; to make their own guesses concerning present realities and future uncertainties; to determine for themselves what opportunities they are in fact confronted with.

The above discussion can be stated concisely using the contrast I have elsewhere drawn between the Robbinsian allocation, maximizing view of the economizing decision and the Misesian entrepreneurial view of human action.[7] For the Robbinsian decision maker freedom means freedom to proceed to where one (already) wishes to be; for the Misesian entrepreneurial human agent, freedom means freedom to discover and to determine for oneself where it is that one wishes to be.[8]

FREEDOM AND POWER

The foregoing may throw light on the much-discussed confusion between *freedom* and *power*. Economists have tended to succumb to the temptation to define freedom so as to make it indistinguishable from power. For these writers, freedom means simply the ability to attain what one wishes to attain.[9] A small number of writers, among economists notably Hayek[10] and Machlup,[11] have emphatically denounced the blurring of the distinction between freedom and power. A number of writers (perhaps Knight is the most notable)[12] while recognizing that freedom is not the same as power, have somehow offered formulations of the concept of freedom that turn out to substantially identify it with power after all. Our earlier discussion can be helpful in clarifying the issues. Let us consider what has changed when a particular option, hitherto available to a decision maker, is somehow removed from the list of possibilities. In particular, let us ask what this change may possibily have done to the freedom of choice of that decision maker.

Now, from a Robbinsian point of view—that is, seeing the decision maker as having *already*, before the act of choice, become fully aware of the options available to him, and having *already* determined his ranking of conceivable outcomes—it should be apparent that the removal of an option that had hitherto been available may mean one of two things. If the option in question was one the Robbinsian decision maker would *not* have adopted, then its removal has no effect whatsoever. Since, even before his moment of decision, the decision maker had already adopted a well-defined ends-means framework, courses of action dominated by the optimal solution are simply irrelevant; they have been inexorably declared irrelevant by the structure of the ends-means framework taken as a datum. On the other hand, should the option that has been removed be the optimal one, then of course its removal affects our decision maker in a very significant way. But it is important for us not to misinterpret in what this effect consists. What has occurred is that a course of action the decision maker wished to adopt has been denied him. He may well be bitterly disappointed at having an anticipated desirable experience pulled out of his reach. If this option was removed by human design, he may well be outraged by its loss. He may denounce the loss as a violation of a commitment made to him, or as a violation of a right he possessed, or as sheer robbery, *but he will not be able to describe it as having affected his freedom to choose*. To be sure, his maximizing decision must now be recalculated from among those other courses of action he had hitherto rejected as suboptimal. The second-best solution now steps up into first place. But this does not constitute a restriction on freedom of choice. If there is a line of standby passengers, ranged in order of priority, hoping to get onto a particular flight, and only one seat is available, the person at the head of the line will get on the plane. If, just before he is permitted to enter the aircraft this individual is suddenly removed from the line, for whatever reason, the passenger second in line now steps up to the head of the line. The relative positions of the individuals in line has *already* marked out their priority ranking, and no selection needs to be made of who is to be admitted. The removal of the first passenger does not, therefore, create any new need to choose. It would not be correct to say that the removal of the first passenger has restricted freedom of choice with respect to who is permitted on the plane, because the line of hopeful passengers is now shorter. So, for Robbinsian decision making, the removal of a preferred option does not interfere with the decision maker's freedom of choice. In fact, the Robbinsian decision maker never does have to choose, in the true sense of the word. If, nonetheless, the removal of a preferred option does, in some crude use of language, come to be described as somehow cramping the freedom of choice of the decision maker, this can be understood only as consisting in the restriction imposed on the decision maker's ability to achieve definite goals. *Freedom has, in the Robbinsian framework, come inevitably to be merged with the concept of power to achieve goals.*

On the other hand, from the perspective of the acting person as an entrepreneur for whom the task of deciding embraces the very identification and ranking of ends and recognition of means, the matter seems altogether different. From this perspective, the removal of an option does indeed interfere with the decision maker's freedom of choice. For the human agent, seen as entrepreneur, *each* available course of action is, quite possibly, the optimal one. In fact, it is the essence of choice, in this context, *to choose* the optimal course of action, not in the sense of figuring out the solution to a maximization problem where the solution is already determined by the rankings assumed in the data, but in the sense of choosing the ranking itself. So the removal of an option does indeed affect freedom of choice. This is so not because its removal denies the decision maker something he wishes to attain; before the act of choice it has not yet been determined which option he does in fact wish to attain. The removal of an option restrictively alters the range from which choice may be made. Even if the lost option would, in some not well-defined sense, have been a *rejected* course of action, its removal nonetheless still constitutes an interference with freedom of choice. At the moment of choice, this option *was a possible option;* it had not yet been rejected either explicitly through choice, or implicitly through the given structure of some already-adopted ends-means framework.

FREEDOM AND THE RANGE OF ALTERNATIVES
Is freedom increased by the addition of options that the decision maker will not adopt because he prefers one of the existing

options? Is freedom restricted by the removal of options the decision maker would have rejected anyway? The preceding discussion can throw light on these questions that have been raised from time to time in the literature on freedom.

Locke maintained that even if a prisoner does not wish to leave his cell, he is nonetheless not a free man because the option of leaving his cell is not available to him. If the action voluntarily taken by a man is the only one available to him, "he is not free, though perhaps the action is voluntary."[13] Knight, on the other hand, argued that a fence along the edge of a ravine does not restrict the freedom of hikers, since they would not wish to fall over the edge anyway.[14] As we have seen, the issue appears to revolve around the distinction between Robbinsian maximizing decisions and Misesian entrepreneurial choice.

If Locke's prisoner, who loves his cell beyond any other place he can imagine, is to be seen as not free, this can only mean that one considers what the prisoner would be at liberty to do *were he to change his mind*. Clearly, this is relevant only if one admits the possibility of escaping from a given Robbinsian framework in which one has one's mind already fully made up except for the chore of calculation. Knight's fence may be declared innocent of interfering with the freedom of hikers only because one views them as having already adopted a framework of ends that, however tentative and fluid, is yet seen as definitely ranking suicide below all other conceivable options.

Machlup, who insists strongly on maintaining the sharp distinction between freedom and power, has drawn attention to the possibility that an increment of freedom may itself inspire the acquisition of power. "In other words, certain freedoms may be of great importance for individuals and for society when no knowledge, no opportunity, and no power exist as yet to make use of presumably 'empty' freedoms. Their importance lies in the aspirations and ambitions which they arouse and which may lead to the search for the knowledge, opportunity, and power that are required to exercise the previously unused freedoms."[15] Machlup has in mind a potential option that the decision maker lacks the physical power to attain. So long as he is barred by human restrictions from exercising this option, even if he *had* the physical power to do so, he will not expend the effort or search for the knowledge required to win this physical power. The acquisition of freedom from human restrictions may inspire him to discover ways of overcoming the physical obstacles to exercising the option. This very interesting possibility provides an excellent example to illustrate my position.

On the face of it Machlup's case appears difficult to understand. There is, we take it, some course of action whose implementation requires certain inputs. These inputs may be physical, or they may take the form of knowledge or services of various kinds. Now, either the individual under consideration already has these inputs—or other inputs able to produce these inputs—available to him, or he does not. If he already had them available to him, then it is not clear how the acquisition of the freedom to pursue this particular course of action can be credited with inspiring the power to do so; this power was already possessed. On the other hand, if the inputs were not available until the moment when this freedom was acquired, then it is not clear how, merely through acquiring this freedom, our individual suddenly becomes endowed with inputs previously unavailable to him. Machlup uses the example of a bicycle rider able to pedal at no more than 20 mph who did not find it worthwhile to work harder to earn money to buy a car because of a law limiting all vehicles to a maximum of 25 mph. The abolition of the legal speed limit increases his desire for a car, and he works harder to earn the money to buy it. Thus the freedom to drive at 60 mph, while ineffective to one not owning a car, is effective, nonetheless, in arousing the ambition to achieve the power to exercise the previously unused freedom (to acquire a car).

But surely this example is one in which the *power* to acquire a car (and to drive at 60 mph) *was* possessed all the time. This individual always had open to him, physically, the option of working harder to earn money to buy the car; he did not exercise this option because of the existence of the speed limit which made this option not worthwhile. Machlup uses this example to show that actual capacity may be "created only after the freedom is established." It is true that the individual, until the lifting of the speed limit, had no car and thus lacked the "actual capacity" to drive at 60 mph immediately, but he certainly did not lack the actual capacity to acquire the car and thus, indirectly, to drive at 60 mph. It is true that the freedom acquired to drive at 60 mph converted the potential of owning a car into a reality. It is not, however, clear how this constitutes an expansion of power in any sense relevant to economic discussion.

What Machlup has noticed for us, it appears, is something highly significant, though his example, or his exposition of it, does not seem sufficiently clear. The point concerns the acquisition of freedom to pursue a particular course of action for which the individual indeed possessed the necessary inputs, but the very possibility of which has escaped his entrepreneurial attention. So long as the law limits all vehicles to 25 mph, a worker *may not see the acquisition of a car as being within his reach at all*. Opportunities one is unable to take advantage of tend not to be noticed at all. It is only when the speed limit has been lifted that an already feasible course of action comes into the decision maker's field of vision. The acquisition of freedom may indeed be credited with inspiring the determination to achieve a specific goal. As Machlup has noticed, freedom is fertile in creating actual (perceived) opportunities. A potential opportunity not yet noticed, may, through the addition of an increment of freedom, become an actual one. The process by which potential opportunities can, in this sense, be converted into actual ones is certainly of utmost importance for economists.

What I wish to point out here is that this *fertility of freedom*, to which Machlup has so valuably drawn our attention, can be discussed only within the context of what we have called the broader, entrepreneurial concept of freedom. An increment of freedom, in this sense, may be responsible for a decision maker's identifying a perceived ends-means framework otherwise hidden from him. This fertility of freedom is completely excluded from the purview of the narrower, "Robbinsian" conception of freedom. Within the Robbinsian given ends-means framework, freedom means the freedom to pursue perceived, chosen courses of action. The essence of this concept of freedom is that all opportunities have already been given to the decision maker in a manner that ensures his awareness of them. Under such conditions, an increment of freedom can hardly inspire new opportunities. Opportunities that may be physically possible *with* this increment of freedom are opportunities that would have been equally physically feasible without it. All opportunities of which the decision maker will be aware *after* acquiring an increment of freedom were opportunities of which, by the rules of the Robbinsian framework, he was aware *before* the increment of freedom was acquired. There is no room, within this framework, for any fertility in freedom.

On Not Knowing What One Lacks

So long as freedom is perceived from what we call the Robbinsian perspective, it becomes inevitable for it to become identified with the power to achieve chosen goals. Loss of freedom quite similarly, comes to be identified with thwarted desires. Freedom comes, from such a perspective, to be something whose curtailment triggers immediate pain. One cannot lose freedom, in this view, without feeling its loss. The matter is seen quite differently from the entrepreneurial perspective on freedom.

The entrepreneurial view of freedom permits us to see how freedom to choose may inspire the discovery of opportunities that may be invisible to those to whom this freedom is denied. Those to whom the freedom to choose has been denied will, in such cases, have no inkling that they are being denied an otherwise attainable goal. One denied the right to choose to enter college may never realize that he possesses the intellectual potential to be admitted to college. Denial of freedom to choose, from this perspective, does not necessarily inflict the pain of thwarted desires. In fact, *one may lack freedom and be convinced that one's well-being is wholly unaffected by its lack*.

All this appears directly relevant to Stigler's challenge. He asked for concrete specification of what liberties have, in fact, been impaired by the growth of the modern state. If "we canvass the population," Stigler claims, "we shall find few people who feel that their range of actions is seriously curtailed by the state."[16] Such a challenge takes it for granted that each impairment of liberty removes out of the reach of an individual some perceived and desired opportunity. To speak vaguely about loss of liberty without being able to specify precisely what opportunities have been closed off would, by such an understanding, indeed raise serious questions concerning the reality of the loss. But a broader understanding of the meaning of freedom, and of its loss, makes it entirely plausible that abrogations of freedom may indeed affect individuals without their being aware or for that matter without the awareness of anyone else, observing social scientists included, that their welfare has been damaged by this abrogation. It is no longer a necessary condition for the existence of loss of freedom that the loss be a felt one. It is true that Stigler himself seems not entirely unaware of the point here being made. He recognizes that "the most exploited of individuals probably does not feel the least bit exploited," citing the example of the complaisant slave. But the point as Stigler sees it appears to rest on naive ignorance of the very existence of limitations of freedom, and clearly assumes only the slightest importance in his view. For us, the point arises peculiarly from the entrepreneurial perspective on freedom, and is of much greater significance. I shall return later to the further implications of this insight.

THE PARADOX OF FREEDOM

Our discussion of the entrepreneurial view of the nature of freedom may throw some light on the riddle to which philosophers have drawn our attention in their discussions of the relation between freedom and reason. On the one hand, human choice is declared to be free, at least in the sense that people *feel* free to choose what they may. On the other hand, in the very exercise of their free choice, people discover themselves to be searching for the "correct" course of action, so that in fact their choice is in some sense *dictated* by that "correct" option. From this perspective, "when people...understand that in moral questions they are free to form their own opinions, they feel this freedom not as an emancipation but as a burden."[17] At least some philosophers have argued that no inconsistency is involved in this apparent paradox. "For a moral agent to choose that good which in the light of reflection approves itself as intrinsically greatest is to exercise the only freedom worth having. . . . To choose most responsibly is to see alternative goods with full clearness and to find the greatest of them tipping the beam."[18] No doubt these classic philosophic issues entail considerations far more profound than those raised here. Nonetheless our discussion does appear to hold some relevance for these issues.

In the course of arriving at a decision on any question, people *simultaneously* (1) fix the ends-means framework relevant to their situation, and (2) calculate the optimal course of action relevant to that framework. The latter task is one to which freedom of choice is, in a definite sense, irrelevant; the correct answer is given; one is merely searching for it. Freedom to choose, at this level, consists entirely of the burden of calculating correctly, of avoiding mistakes. Nonetheless, because this second task of calculation is never in fact divorced from the first step—that of identifying the ends-means framework—acts of choice are never possible without a genuine sense of freedom, without the unconstrained freedom to select whatever ranking of ends one may wish to uphold or whatever set of means one may wish to recognize as available. Now there may well be deeper levels of rationality that moral philosophers may wish to consider relevant to the very selection of a ranking of ends, but, at least at the superficial level appropriate to the economist, one source of the apparent paradox between one's sense of freedom and one's sense of the burden imposed by the rationality postulate seems to be illuminated by this discussion.

We now realize that in the course of the act of choice people freely identify the *criteria* for what will *now* be considered correct calculation of the optimal course of action. Ex post, one understands the course of action chosen by an individual as having been *constrained* by these criteria. In the calculations that are part of their actions, individuals seek the answer dictated by these criteria. But, at the same time, the very act of choice that encompasses these calculations encompasses also the free, undictated identification of what criteria are to be considered relevant. The sense of emancipation and the sense of burden and responsibility thus simultaneously have their places in free choice.

THE SOCIAL IMPORTANCE OF FREEDOM

The insights provided by the entrepreneurial view of freedom enable us to understand the social implications of individual freedom in a manner more profound than otherwise possible. Moreover, these insights enable us to understand how such a limited view of the social significance of freedom has in fact come to be adopted by so many economists.

For most economists, individual freedom is held to carry social significance, if indeed it is so held at all, only insofar as it permits the simultaneous achievement by each market participant of an optimal course of action within a framework of given ends and means. With given technological opportunity sets, with given resource endowments, and with given consumer preference functions, individual freedom allows market participants under specified assumptions to achieve the Paretian optimum embodied in the relevant general equilibrium solution. Restrictions on freedom by the state are therefore seen as bringing about suboptimal market outcomes, from the standpoint of the data. A free market in housing, it is understood, generates an equilibrium configuration of construction and of housing prices that may be, in some sense, optimal. Rent control, it is therefore shown, by restricting individual choices, generates suboptimal levels of prices and production. And so forth.

All this is no doubt correct and important. But it should be clear that it fails entirely to exhaust the full significance for society of an environment of freedom. This view rests entirely on the assumption that available opportunities are somehow instantaneously and costlessly known to market participants. But in the real world this is not the case. It is here that the full significance of freedom can be glimpsed. A free society is one in which individuals are free *to discover for themselves the available range of alternatives*. In his masterly critiques of the theory of central planning, Hayek directed attention to the circumstance that the information available in an economy is always scattered among countless individuals, never concentrated in the mind of a single central planner. Hayek pointed to the need for a social institutional structure capable of organizing the scattered scraps of available information so they can be used for the efficient allocation of society's resources.[19] The competitive market, Hayek showed us, is a discovery process, one in which society discovers what options are feasible and how important they are. Freedom, Hayek has shown in his more recent work, is of social significance precisely because no single mind can know in advance what will be discovered by social cooperation within a free environment. The "case for freedom," Hayek pointed out, "rests chiefly on the recognition of the inevitable ignorance of all of us concerning a great many of the factors on which the achievement of our ends and welfare depends. . . . Liberty is essential in order to leave room for the unforseeable and unpredictable. . . . It is . . . because we rarely know which of us knows best that we trust the independent and competitive efforts of many to induce the emergence of what we shall want when we see it."[20] "If we knew how freedom would be used, the case for it would largely disappear."[21] Our discussion approaches very similar conclusions from a somewhat different angle.

For us, individual freedom emerges as significant for society because it inspires each individual to discover what opportunities confront him. It is not only the case, that is, that society—or its central planners—do not know all the scattered information held by individuals in a society. In addition, at any given moment each individual does not know the information costlessly available to him. An environment of freedom encourages individuals to discover what opportunities each of them faces. If a market economy is believed to possess powerful equilibrating tendencies, these tendencies depend on freedom not only to permit, as Hayek showed, the social deployment of existing information, but also to permit (through the very same Hayekian market processes) the discovery by individuals of those opportunities made available by the attitudes and the knowledge of fellow market participants as well as by the technological possibilities existing in nature, the grasping of which constitutes the steps in the equilibrating process.

Restrictions on economic freedom hurt society, therefore, in ways far more serious than recognized by most economists. I have drawn attention to the circumstance that, from the entrepreneurial view of freedom, an individual may suffer loss of freedom without realizing any loss in his welfare. We now see that an analogous situation pertains to society as a whole. Restriction of economic freedom restrains society from reaching what would have been Pareto-optimal equilibrium situations. As Hayek showed, this in effect means that society would not know what losses in social welfare have been suffered as a result of the restricted freedom, since no one can know what the market might have discovered. Our own discussion shows us that restriction of economic freedom restrains society from achieving its full potential in yet another sense, again a sense in which it may never be known that any loss of welfare has occurred. As we have seen in our discussion (following Machlup) of the fertility of freedom, the restriction of economic freedom may inhibit individuals from discovering opportunities they might have noticed had they been free to exploit them. Loss of freedom may thus lower individual and social achievement without anyone's realizing what has been lost or not achieved. A free society is fertile and creative in the sense that its freedom generates alertness to possibilities that may be of use to society; a restriction on the freedom of a society numbs such alertness and blinds society to possibilities of social improvement. By the very nature of the damage such restriction wreaks, its harmful effects on social welfare may not be able to be noticed, measured, or specified. For the understanding of these profoundly important social consequences of economic freedom, I have argued, economists must in turn deepen their understanding of the nature of freedom itself.

Notes

CHAPTER ONE

1. For an elaboration of a number of issues raised here, see Israel M. Kirzner, *Competition and Entrepreneurship* (Chicago: University of Chicago Press, 1973).

2. Joseph A. Schumpeter, *Capitalism, Socialism, and Democracy* (New York: Harper and Row, 1942), pp. 81–106.

3. Oscar Morgenstern, "Thirteen Critical Points in Contemporary Economic Theory: An Interpretation," *Journal of Economic Literature* 10 (December 1972): 1163–89.

4. Ludwig M. Lachmann, "Methodological Individualism and the Market Economy," in *Roads to Freedom: Essays in Honour of Friedrich A. von Hayek*, ed. Erich Streissler et al. (London: Routledge and Kegan Paul, 1969), p. 89.

5. Alfred Marshall, *Principles of Economics*, ed. C. W. Guillebaud, 2 vols. (London: Macmillan, 1961), 1:345–48; Marshall sometimes used the Walrasian approach (ibid., pp. 333–36).

6. Lionel Robbins, *An Essay on the Nature and Significance of Economic Science* (London: Macmillan, 1962), pp. 1–23.

7. Ludwig von Mises, *Human Action: A Treatise on Economics* (New Haven: Yale University Press, 1949), pp. 11–142; on the comparison of Misesian and Robbinsian notions, see Israel M. Kirzner, *The Economic Point of View* (Princeton: Van Nostrand, 1960), pp. 108–85.

8. In the preface to the first edition of his book, Robbins acknowledged his debt to Mises (*On the Nature*, pp. xv–xvi).

9. Kirzner, *Competition and Entrepreneurship*, pp. 75–87.

10. Edward Hastings Chamberlin, *The Theory of Monopolistic Competition*, 7th ed. (Cambridge: Harvard University Press, 1962), pp. 123–29.

11. See the literature cited in Kirzner, *Competition and Entrepreneurship*, pp. 141–69.

CHAPTER TWO

1. See especially A. Leijonhufvud, *On Keynesian Economics and the Economics of Keynes* (New York: Oxford University Press, 1968), p. 401;

241

K. E. Boulding, "The Economics of Knowledge and the Knowledge of Economics," *American Economic Review* 56 (May 1966): 1; "Economics as a Moral Science," *American Economic Review* 59 (March 1969): 4; P. J. McNulty, "A Note on the History of Perfect Competition," *Journal of Political Economy* 75 (August 1967): 402; and "The Meaning of Competition," *Quarterly Journal of Economics* 82 (November 1968): 649; J. M. Buchanan, *Cost and Choice* (Chicago: Markham, 1969), p. 24; G. S. Becker, *Economic Theory* (New York: Alfred A. Knopf, 1971), p. 214; G. L. S. Shackle, *Epistemics and Economics* (Cambridge: Cambridge University Press, 1972), p. 124; F. Machlup, "Friedrich Von Hayek's Contribution to Economics," *Swedish Journal of Economics* 76 (1974): 514 ff.

2. F. A. Hayek, "Economics and Knowledge," *Economica,* vol. 4 (February 1937); reprinted in *Individualism and Economic Order* (London: Routledge and Kegan Paul, 1949), p. 42. All page references to this article will be from this reprint.

3. Ibid., p. 46.

4. Ibid., p. 45.

5. F. A. Hayek, "The Use of Knowledge in Society," *American Economic Review,* vol. 35 (September 1945); reprinted in *Individualism and Economic Order,* pp. 77 ff. All page references to this article will be to this reprint.

6. Ibid., p. 77.

7. Ibid., p. 78.

8. Ibid., p. 79.

9. Ibid., p. 87.

10. F. A. Hayek, *The Constitution of Liberty* (Chicago: University of Chicago Press, 1960), pp. 3 ff.

11. Ibid., p. 25.

12. Ibid., p. 29.

13. For earlier expressions of concern see K. Arrow, "Toward a Theory of Price Adjustment," in *The Allocation of Economic Resources,* ed. Abramovitz et al. (Stanford: Stanford University Press, 1959); G. B. Richardson, *Information and Investment* (London: Oxford University Press, 1960), pp. 23 ff.; D. Bodenhorn, *Intermediate Price Theory* (New York: McGraw-Hill, 1961), p. 185.

14. D. Patinkin, *Money, Interest and Prices,* 2d ed. (New York: Harper and Row, 1965), pp. 531–40, note B. See also N. Kaldor, "The Determinateness of Static Equilibrium," *Review of Economic Studies,* vol. 1 (February 1934).

15. See J. R. Hicks, *Value and Capital,* 2d ed. (Oxford: Clarendon Press, 1946), p. 336.

16. See P. A. Samuelson, *Foundations of Economic Analysis* (Cambridge: Harvard University Press, 1947), chap. 9 and the cited literature.

17. On this see Arrow, "Theory of Price Adjustment," p. 143. See also Patinkin, *Money,* pp. 539 ff.

18. F. H. Hahn, *On the Notion of Equilibrium in Economics: An Inaugural Lecture* (Cambridge: Cambridge University Press, 1973), p. 7.

19. See also I. M. Kirzner, "Rejoinder," *Journal of Political Economy* 71 (February 1963): 84, note 3.

e, e.g., L. Mises, *Human Action* (New Haven: Yale University
P.   1949), pp. 353, 707.

21. Hayek, "Economics and Knowledge," p. 45.

22. F. A. Hayek, "The Meaning of Competition," in *Individualism and Economic Order*, p. 94.

23. For a critical comment on the historical validity of this label, see Samuelson, *Foundations of Economic Analysis*, p. 264 n.

24. Ibid., p. 263.

25. See D. F. Gordon and H. Hynes, "On the Theory of Price Dynamics," in E. S. Phelps et al., *Microeconomic Foundations of Employment and Inflation Theory* (New York: W. W. Norton, 1970), pp. 371 ff.; M. Rothschild, "Models of Market Organization with Imperfect Information: A Survey," *Journal of Political Economy* 81 (November/December 1973): 1285; K. J. Arrow and F. H. Hahn, *General Competitive Analysis* (San Francisco: Holden-Day; Edinburgh: Oliver and Boyd, 1971), pp. 266, 322; for an earlier reference see the article by Arrow, "Toward a Theory of Price Adjustment," p. 43. See also J. M. Ostroy, "The Informational Efficiency of Monetary Exchange," *American Economic Review* 63 (September 1973): 597 and note 2.

26. Gordon and Hynes, "Theory of Price Dynamics," p. 371.

27. R. J. Barro and H. L. Grossman, "A General Disequilibrium Model of Income and Employment," *American Economic Review* 61 (March 1971): 85 n; Gordon and Hynes, "Theory of Price Dynamics," p. 372, note 7; see also M. Rothschild, "Models of Market Organization," p. 1291.

28. Arrow and Hahn, *General Competitive Analysis*, p. 322.

29. It was the phenomenon of price dispersion that was central to G. J. Stigler, "The Economics of Information," *Journal of Political Economy* 69 (June 1961): 213–25. See M. Rothschild, "Models of Market Organization," sec. 5, for models in which equilibrium itself consists of a distribution of prices.

30. F. A. Hayek, "Economics and Knowledge," p. 45.

31. F. A. Hayek, "The Meaning of Competition," p. 94.

32. Ibid.

33. Ibid., p. 96.

34. For a detailed analysis of the kinds of error buyers and sellers can make in disequilibrium, and the kinds of learning processes generated by these mistakes, see I. M. Kirzner, *Market Theory and the Price System* (New York: Van Nostrand, 1963), chap. 7.

35. Hayek, "Economics and Knowledge," p. 44 (italics supplied).

36. Ibid., p. 45.

37. Ibid., p. 33.

38. Ibid., p. 46.

39. Ibid., p. 47.

40. See, e.g., J. M. Buchanan, "Is Economics the Science of Choice?" in *Roads to Freedom*, ed. E. Streissler (London: Routledge and Kegan Paul, 1969), p. 52; see also Buchanan, *Cost and Choice*, p. 24.

41. For an excellent discussion of this issue, see J. M. Buchanan, "Is Economics the Science of Choice?"

42. See I. M. Kirzner, *Competition and Entrepreneurship* (Chicago: University of Chicago Press, 1973), pp. 32–37.

43. Ibid., pp. 33 ff.

44. Ibid., p. 36.

45. Ibid., pp. 33 ff.

46. Mises, *Human Action*, p. 253.

47. Kirzner, *Competition and Entrepreneurship*, p. 72.

48. Hayek, "Economics and Knowledge," p. 46.

49. Ibid., p. 47.

50. Mises, *Human Action*, p. 325.

51. For further discussion on this point see Kirzner, *Competition and Entrepreneurship*, pp. 228 ff.

52. "It seems that that skeleton in our cupboard, the 'economic man,' whom we have exorcised with prayer and fasting, has returned through the back door in the form of a quasi-omniscient individual." Hayek, "Economics and Knowledge," p. 46.

53. For an example of this approach, see Kirzner, *Market Theory and the Price System*.

CHAPTER THREE

1. L. Mises, *Human Action* (New Haven: Yale University Press, 1949), p. 532.

2. M. Dobb, *Capitalist Enterprise and Social Progress* (London: Routledge and Sons, 1925), p. 17.

3. F. Redlich, "The Origin of the Concepts of 'Entrepreneur' and 'Creative Entrepreneur,'" *Explorations in Entrepreneurial History* 1, no. 2 (February 1949): 3 ff.

4. Ibid.

5. B. F. Hoselitz, "The Early History of Entrepreneurial Theory," *Explorations in Entrepreneurial History* 3, no. 4 (April 1951): 196 n.

6. Mill did use the term undertaker (*Principles of Political Economy*, Ashley ed. [London, 1909], p. 406), but he regretted the unfamiliarity of the term and the unavailability of a counterpart for the French entrepreneur. Cannan remarked that Mill was probably writing with Say's criticism of the lack in English of a "name for the *entrepreneur d'industrie*" in mind. Cannan believed Say was "ignorant or forgetful of the word 'undertaker'" (E. Cannan, *A Review of Economic Theory*, London, 1929, p. 308). See also Hoselitz, "Early History of Entrepreneurial Theory," p. 200 n.

7. A. Smith, *The Wealth of Nations*, Cannan ed. (New York: Modern Library, 1937), p. 48. Hoselitz ("Early History of Entrepreneurial Theory," p. 204) cites Smith's use of the phrase "undertaker of a great manufacture" in *Wealth of Nations*, p. 438.

8. A. Smith, *Wealth of Nations*, p. 114.

9. Ibid., p. 115. On p. 339 Smith contrasts "prodigals and projectors" with "sober people."

10. Hoselitz, "Early History of Entrepreneurial Theory," pp. 194 ff.

11. Redlich has remarked that with Cantillon "the word entrepreneur first assumed the role of a technical term" ("Origin of the Concepts," p. 2).

12. See Hoselitz, "Early History of Entrepreneurial Theory," pp. 198 ff., 207, 210. See also C. A. Tuttle, "The Entrepreneur Function in Economic Literature," *Journal of Political Economy* 35, no. 4 (August 1927): 503–4.

13. F. B. Hawley, *Enterprise and the Productive Process* (New York: Putnam, 1907), pp. 153 ff., 340 f.

14. Tuttle, "Entrepreneur Function," thus appears incorrect in asserting the contrary.

15. Ibid.

16. F. H. Knight, *Risk, Uncertainty and Profit* (New York: Houghton Mifflin, 1921), p. 24; see also M. Blaug, *Economic Theory in Retrospect*, 1st ed. (Homewood, Ill.: Irwin, 1962) p. 86 n.

17. In a recent paper Nathan Rosenberg expressed his surprise at discovering that *Wealth of Nations*—"a book that shook the world by recommending a maximum degree of freedom for business enterprise"—assigns no major role to the entrepreneur (N. Rosenberg, "Adam Smith on Profits: Paradox Lost and Regained," *Journal of Political Economy* [November/ December 1974], p. 1177).

18. Smith, *Wealth of Nations*, pp. 52, 97.

19. Ibid., p. 48.

20. Ibid.

21. J. Marchal, "The Construction of a New Theory of Profit," *American Economic Review* 41, no. 4 (September 1951): 549. For a sharply different appraisal of Smith, exculpating him from the "post-Smith classical treatment of interest as identical with profits," see J. W. Conard, *An Introduction to the Theory of Interest* (Berkeley: University of California Press, 1959), p. 12.

22. Redlich, "Origin of the Concepts," p. 7.

23. J. B. Say, *Traité d'économie politique*, 6th ed. (Paris: Guillaumin, impression of 1876), p. 84 n (cited by Cannan, *Review of Economic Theory*, p. 308).

24. M. Blaug, *Ricardian Economics: A Historical Study* (New Haven: Yale University Press, 1958), pp. 153 ff.

25. Smith, *Wealth of Nations*, p. 51.

26. E. Cannan, *A History of the Theories of Production and Distribution in English Political Economy from 1776 to 1848*, 3d ed. (London, 1917), pp. 201 ff.

27. R. Cantillon, *Essai sur la nature du commerce en general*, ed. with an English translation, etc., by H. Higgs (London: Royal Economic Society, 1931), p. 53.

28. Ibid., p. 55.

29. Note that Cannan, in commenting on Cantillon's discussion of the independent worker, writes that "ordinary people in Cantillon's times and ours would not say he made a profit unless he had to pay out money" for the materials needed for production (E. Cannan, *A Review of Economic Theory* [London, 1929], p. 303).

30. Knight, *Risk, Uncertainty and Profit*, p. 25.

31. J. A. Schumpeter, "Economic Theory and Entrepreneurial History," in *Explorations in Enterprise*, ed. H. G. Aitken (Cambridge: Harvard University Press, 1965), p. 46.

32. Hoselitz, "Early History of Entrepreneurial Theory," p. 212.

33. "The concept of profit in the eighteenth century was complicated by the fact that capitalist and manager-entrepreneur were, so often, the one person" (R. M. Hartwell, "Business Management in England during the Period of Early Industrialization: Inducements and Obstacles," in *The Industrial Revolution*, ed. R. M. Hartwell [New York: Barnes and Noble, 1970]). See also N. Rosenberg, "Adam Smith on Profits," p. 1177.

34. M. Blaug, *Ricardian Economics*, pp. 153 ff.

35. Schumpeter, "Economic Theory and Entrepreneurial History," p. 48. See also Tuttle, "Entrepreneur Function," pp. 507–8; Knight, *Risk, Uncertainty and Profit*, p. 23.

36. Sidney Sherwood, "The Function of the Undertaker," *Yale Review* 6 (November 1897): 244; Hawley, *Enterprise and the Productive Process*, p. 10.

37. L. Haney, *History of Economic Thought*, 4th ed. (New York: Macmillan, 1949), p. 563.

38. Ibid., p. 564. For further comments on the relation between the classical economists' notions concerning capital and the business environment of their day, see J. R. Hicks, "Capital Controversies: Ancient and Modern," *American Economic Review* 64 (May 1974): 310. It is of further interest to note, in passing, that the view that explains classical neglect of the entrepreneur by reference to the infrequency of joint stock firms, contrasts, as well, with the thrust of the Galbraithian view that the mature corporate form of business organization is responsible for the eclipse of the entrepreneur in contemporary capitalism (J. K. Galbraith, *The New Industrial State* [New York: Houghton Mifflin, 1967], chap. 8).

39. Cannan, *Review of Economic Theory*, p. 309.

40. Ibid., p. 310.

41. Ibid., p. 356.

42. Ibid., p. 309.

43. R. L. Meek, "The Physiocratic Concept of Profit," *Economica*, vol. 26 (February 1959); reprinted in *The Economics of Physiocracy* (Cambridge: Harvard University Press, 1963), p. 297. Meek notes that Smith "was careful to distinguish profit from wages of management."

44. Hawley, *Enterprise and the Productive Process*, pp. 153 ff.; see also pp. 340 ff.

45. Schumpeter, "Economic Theory and Entrepreneurial History," p. 47.

46. R. E. Kuenne, *Eugen von Böhm-Bawerk*, Columbia Essays on Great Economists, no. 2 (London and New York: Columbia University Press, 1971), p. 2.

47. R. V. Eagly, *The Structure of Classical Economic Theory* (New York: Oxford University Press, 1974), chap. 8.

48. J. A. Schumpeter, *History of Economic Analysis* (New York: Oxford University Press, 1954), p. 556.

49. Schumpeter, "Economic Theory and Entrepreneurial History," p. 47.

50. Blaug, *Ricardian Economics*, p. 154.

51. Cannan, *History of the Theories of Production and Distribution*, p. 398.

52. See also ibid., pp. 313 ff., where Cannan refers to entrepreneur as displacing the capitalist as the most active element in economic theory.

53. Ibid., p. 119.

54. Ibid., p. 398.

55. Knight, *Risk, Uncertainty and Profit*, pp. 23 ff.

56. Smith, *Wealth of Nations*, p. 114.

CHAPTER FOUR

1. For an example see W. J. Baumol, "Entrepreneurship in Economic Theory," *American Economic Review* 58 (May 1968): 72.

2. Important exceptions were two monographs on profits: V. Mataja, *Der Unternehmergewinn* (Vienna, 1884), and G. Gross, *Lehre vom Unternehmergewinn* (Leipzig, 1884). Hayek describes both Mataja and Gross as "immediate pupils" of Menger (F. A. Hayek, "Carl Menger," in *The Collected Works of Carl Menger* [London: London School of Economics and Political Science, 1934], vol. 1).

3. F. H. Knight, "Introduction" to Carl Menger, *Principles of Economics*, trans. and ed. J. Dingwall and Bert F. Hoselitz (Glencoe, Ill.: Free Press, 1950), p. 30. Knight presumably meant by this not that Menger altogether ignored these questions, or that he exerted no influence on later writers, but that he and his followers pursued an approach that Knight in his own work on the matter (*Risk, Uncertainty and Profit* [New York: Houghton Mifflin], 1921) found unhelpful. This interpretation would fit in with what seems to be Knight's grossly inadequate references, in his latter book, to the work of Schumpeter, presumably one of the "successors" to Menger, whom Knight had in mind in the citation in the text.

4. E. Streissler, "To What Extent Was the Austrian School Marginalist?" *History of Political Economy* 4 (fall 1972): 432 ff.

5. J. A. Schumpeter, *The Theory of Economic Development*, trans. R. Opie (Cambridge: Harvard University Press, 1934), p. 76.

6. Ibid., p. 32.

7. J. A. Schumpeter, *History of Economic Analysis* (New York: Oxford University Press, 1954), p. 893.

8. Hayek's remark is well known: "The reputation of the [Austrian] School in the outside world . . . [is] due to the efforts of his brilliant followers, Eugen von Böhm-Bawerk and Friedrich von Wieser. But it is not unduly to detract from the merits of these writers to say that its fundamental ideas belong fully and wholly to Carl Menger" (Hayek, "Carl Menger," p. v).

9. E. Streissler, "Structural Economic Thought: On the Significance of the Austrian School Today," *Zeitschrift für Nationalökonomie* 29 (1969): 237–66;

idem, "To What Extent Was the Austrian School Marginalist?"; idem, "Menger's Theories of Money and Uncertainty: A Modern Interpretation," in *Carl Menger and the Austrian School of Economics*, ed. J. R. Hicks and W. Weber (Oxford: Clarendon Press, 1973).

10. Hayek, "Carl Menger"; G. J. Stigler, "The Economics of Carl Menger," *Journal of Political Economy* 45 (April 1937): 229–50 (also in G. J. Stigler, *Production and Distribution Theories* [New York: Macmillan, 1944], chap. 6); Knight, "Introduction" to C. Menger, *Principles of Economics*.

11. These passages appear in the English translation (C. Menger, *Principles of Economics*, trans. and ed. J. Dingwell and Bert F. Hoselitz, Glencoe, Ill.: Free Press, 1950), on pp. 160, 172. The passage appearing in the English text on p. 160 was a footnote in the original German edition, *Grundsätze der Volkwirtschaftslehre*, 1871.

12. Nonetheless, Menger at one point talks of the "entrepreneur himself" requiring "helpers" to assist him in his entrepreneurial activities, if the firm is large (*Principles of Economics*, p. 160).

13. Ibid., p. 172.

14. Ibid., p. 160. In this citation I have omitted the word "obtaining" (which appears in the English translation under (*a*) before the word "information." Streissler has valuably pointed out that "the German text does not make it clear whether [entrepreneurs] have to inform others or themselves" ("To What Extent Was the Austrian School Marginalist?" p. 432, n. 24).

15. Ibid., p. 161.

16. Ibid.

17. A. Marshall, *Principles of Economics*, 8th ed. (London: Macmillan, 1920), book 6, chaps. 7, 8.

18. E. Streissler, "To What Extent Was the Austrian School Marginalist?" pp. 431 ff.

19. Ibid., p. 433; "Structural Economic Thought: On the Significance of the Austrian School Today," p. 249, and p. 250, n. 44; "Menger's Theories of Money and Uncertainty: A Modern Interpretation," passim.

20. Streissler, "To What Extent Was the Austrian School Marginalist?" p. 341. The citation from Menger is from *Principles of Economics*, p. 74.

21. Menger, *Principles of Economics*, pp. 52 ff.; 115.

22. Ibid., p. 148.

23. Ibid., pp. 68, 80, 89.

24. Ibid., pp. 71–74.

25. Ibid., p. 160.

26. Ibid., pp. 179 ff., 188 ff., 195.

27. Ibid., p. 282, n. 9.

28. Ibid., pp. 260–61.

29. Ibid., p. 95.

30. Ibid., p. 90. The entire section, pp. 80–94, is relevant to this level of discussion.

31. Ibid., pp. 92–93.

32. Ibid., p. 91.

33. In an important sense, Menger treated uncertainty simply as an aspect of the consequences of error. See, for example, his section (pp. 67–71) entitled "Time and Error," which in fact deals with uncertainty.

34. Ibid., p. 120.

35. Ibid., p. 188.

36. W. Jaffé, "Menger, Jevons and Walras De-Homogenized," *Economic Inquiry* 14 (December 1976): 521. Jaffé's reference to the "lightning calculator" is, of course, cited from Veblen.

37. "The term entrepreneur as used by catallactic theory means: Acting man exclusively seen from the aspect of the uncertainty inherent in every action" (L. Mises, *Human Action* [New Haven: Yale University Press, 1949], p. 254).

38. Knight, "Introduction," p. 16.

39. Ibid., p. 21.

40. In fact, in the translator's note to Menger's "Preface"—in the very edition to which Knight was providing his "Introduction"—it is carefully explained that Menger's economizing man is not a reference "to 'the profit motive' or to 'the pursuit of self-interest,' but to the act of economizing" (Menger, *Principles of Economics*, p. 48, n. 4). For the classic reply to those ridiculing the role of economic man in economics, see L. Robbins, *An Essay on the Nature and Significance of Economic Science*, 2d ed. (London: Macmillan, 1935), pp. 94 ff. Robbins (p. 16 n) cites Menger as the earliest source for his own conception of economics as dealing with "human behavior as a relationship between ends and scarce means which have alternative uses"—i.e., with economizing. As is evident from the earlier discussion of the role of knowledge in economizing activity, there is ample scope, as Jaffé believes, for interpreting imperfect knowledge in Menger as a context within which economizing activity may be carried on. Menger's reference, at one point, to "economizing individuals aware of their advantage" (*Principles of Economics*, p. 213) must therefore be understood to refer to economizing individuals whom, for the sake of a particular problem in hand, we *choose to imagine* to happen to be so aware.

41. Hayek, "Carl Menger," p. xvii. For a view diametrically opposed to that of Hayek on this point, see Jaffé, "Menger, Jevons, and Walras," p. 519.

42. Menger, *Principles of Economics*, p. 216.

43. Ibid., p. 224.

44. Streissler, "To What Extent Was the Austrian School Marginalist?" pp. 438 ff.; idem, "Menger's Theories of Money and Uncertainty," p. 167.

45. Jaffé, "Menger, Jevons, and Walras," p. 520.

46. Schumpeter, *History of Economic Analysis*, p. 918.

47. F. A. Hayek, "The Place of Menger's *Grundsätze* in the History of Economic Thought," in *Carl Menger and the Austrian School of Economics*, ed. J. R. Hicks and W. Weber (Oxford: Clarendon Press, 1973), p. 10.

48. Streissler, "Structural Economic Thought," p. 254.

49. Streissler, "To What Extent Was the Austrian School Marginalist?" p. 436 (italics in original). See also Streissler, "Menger's Theories of Money and Uncertainty," pp. 169 ff.

50. Streissler, "Structural Economic Thought," p. 254.

51. Jaffé, "Menger, Jevons, and Walras," p. 520.

52. Streissler, "To What Extent Was the Austrian School Marginalist?" pp. 439 ff.

53. Ibid., p. 430.

54. Menger, *Principles of Economics*, p. 218, n. 7.

55. Ibid., p. 219.

56. Ibid., p. 249.

57. Ibid. It is worthwhile to cite at length Menger's discussion of the character of "economic prices," in his 1883 treatise on methodology. "There is scarcely need to remark that . . . as a rule *real* prices deviate more or less from *economic* ones (those corresponding to the economic situation). In the practice of economy people in fact endeavor only rarely to protect their economic interests *completely*. Many sorts of considerations, above all, indifference to economic interests of lesser significance, good will toward others, etc., cause them in their economic activity not to protect their economic interests at all in some cases, in some cases incompletely. They are, furthermore, vague and in error concerning the economic means to attain their economic goals; indeed, they are often vague and in error concerning these goals themselves. Also the economic situation, on the basis of which they develop their economic activity, is often insufficiently or incompletely known to them. Finally their economic freedom is not infrequently impaired by various kinds of relationships. A definite economic situation brings to light precisely *economic* prices of goods only in the rarest cases. *Real* prices are, rather more or less different from economic" (C. Menger, *Problems of Economics and Sociology*, ed. L. Schneider [Urbana: University of Illinois Press, 1963], p. 69).

58. Menger, *Principles of Economics*, pp. 173–74.

59. F. A. Hayek, "The Use of Knowledge in Society," in *Individualism and Economic Order* (London: Routledge and Kegan Paul, 1949), p. 90. Hayek's citation from Schumpeter is from *Capitalism, Socialism and Democracy* (New York: Harper and Bros., 1942), p. 175.

60. Ibid., pp. 90 ff.

61. Ibid., p. 91.

62. I. M. Kirzner, *Competition and Entrepreneurship* (Chicago: University of Chicago Press, 1973), chaps. 3 and 4.

63. Streissler, "Menger's Theories of Money and Uncertainty," pp. 168 ff.

64. Ibid., p. 169; Streissler, "To What Extent Was the Austrian School Marginalist?" p. 435. See also Streissler, "Menger's Theories," pp. 230 ff.

65. Streissler, "Structural Economic Thought," p. 249; see also idem, "To What Extent Was the Austrian School Marginalist?" pp. 427, 430 ff.

66. This is the passage cited by Streissler as the source for his assertion.

67. Menger, *Principles of Economics*, pp. 73 ff.

68. On this see S. Peterson, "Antitrust and the Classical Model," *American Economic Review* 47 (March 1957): 60–78.

69. Streissler, "Structural Economic Thought," pp. 275 ff.; and see relevant notes.

70. Ibid., p. 259.

71. Ibid., pp. 244–47.

72. Ibid., p. 248.

73. F. X. Weiss, "Zur zweiten Auflage von Carl Mengers 'Grundsätzen,'" *Zeitschrift für Volkswirtschaft und Sozialpolitik*, N.F., 4 (1924): 154.

74. Ibid.

CHAPTER FIVE

1. Ludwig von Mises, *Nationalökonomie: Theorie des Handelns und Wirtschaftens* (Geneva: Editions Union, 1940).

2. Frank H. Knight, "Professor Mises and the Theory of Capital," *Economica* 8 (November 1941): 410.

3. Friedrich A. Hayek, "Time-Preference and Productivity: A Reconsideration," *Economica* 12 (February 1945): 22.

4. Friedrich A. Hayek, *Pure Theory of Capital* (London: Routledge and Kegan Paul, 1941), p. 45.

5. Ludwig von Mises, "Das festangelegte Kapital," in *Economische Opstelen: Aangeboden aan Prof. Dr. C. A. Verrijn Stuart* (Haarlem: De Erven F. Bohn N. V., 1931), pp. 214–28; also in *Epistemological Problems of Economics*, trans. George Reisman (Princeton: Van Nostrand, 1960), pp. 217–310. For bibliographical information on Mises's works I am indebted to Bettina Bien [Greaves], *The Works of Ludwig von Mises* (Irvington-on-Hudson, N.Y.: Foundation for Economic Education, 1969).

6. Ludwig von Mises, *Socialism: An Economic and Sociological Analysis* (New Haven: Yale University Press, 1959), pp. 142–43.

7. Ludwig von Mises, *The Theory of Money and Credit* (New Haven: Yale University Press, 1959), p. 339, and esp. p. 24.

8. Ludwig von Mises, *Human Action: A Treatise on Economics* (Chicago: Henry Regnery, 1966), p. 524.

9. Ibid., p. 526.

10. Ibid., p. 493.

11. Knight, "Professor Mises," p. 409.

12. See Joseph A. Schumpeter, *History of Economic Analysis* (New York: Oxford University Press, 1954), p. 847. See also Erich Streissler and W. Weber, "The Menger Tradition," in *Carl Menger and the Austrian School of Economics*, ed. J. R. Hicks (Oxford: Clarendon Press, 1973), p. 231.

13. Hayek, *Pure Theory of Capital*, p. 46 n. For Hayek's criticisms of Böhm-Bawerk's work, see ibid., pp. 414–23. A critique of Böhm-Bawerk by an "Austrian" theorist may be found in Ludwig M. Lachmann, *Capital and Its Structure* (London: London School of Economics and Political Science, 1956).

14. Knight, "Professor Mises," pp. 422.

15. Friedrich A. Hayek, *The Counter-Revolution of Science: Studies on the Abuse of Reason* (Glencoe, Ill.: Free Press, 1955), p. 31.

16. Ibid., p. 210, note 24.

17. Mises, *Human Action*, p. 488. See also Ludwig von Mises, *Epistemological Problems of Economics*, trans. George Reisman (Princeton: Van Nostrand, 1960), p. 31.

18. Mises, *Human Action*, pp. 488–89.

19. See I. M. Kirzner, *An Essay on Capital* (New York: Augustus Kelly, 1966), pp. 79, 99.

20. Frank A. Fetter, "The 'Roundabout Process' in the Interest Theory," *Quarterly Journal of Economics* 17 (November 1902): 177.

21. Schumpeter, *History of Economic Analysis*, pp. 931–32.

22. Eugen von Böhm-Bawerk, *History and Critique of Interest Theories*, vol. 1, *Capital and Interest*, trans. George D. Huncke and Hans F. Sennholz (South Holland, Ill.: Libertarian Press, 1959), p. 482, note 112.

23. Ibid., p. 476, note 14.

24. Ibid., pp. 14, 32.

25. Carl Menger, "Zur Theorie des Kapitals," (Conrad's) *Jahrbucher für Nationalökonomie und Statistik* (Jena: Gustav Fischer Verlag, 1888), p. 17.

26. Friedrich A. Hayek, "Carl Menger," in *Grundsätze der Volkswirtschaftslehre*, Scarce Tracts in Economic and Political Science (London: London School of Economics and Political Science, 1934), p. xxvi.

27. Mises, *Socialism*, pp. 123, 142.

28. Hayek, "Carl Menger," p. xxvi.

29. Hayek, *Pure Theory of Capital*, p. 89.

30. Mises, *Human Action*, p. 263.

31. More precisely Lachmann suggested that Menger was objecting to the notion of the homogenization of capital (Ludwig M. Lachmann, "Sir John Hicks as a Neo-Austrian," *South African Journal of Economics* 41 [September 1973]: 205).

32. Mises, *Human Action*, p. 515.

33. Ibid., p. 262.

34. Ludwig von Mises, *Human Action: A Treatise on Economics*, 2d ed. rev. (New Haven: Yale University Press, 1963), p. 515.

35. For a listing of writers who have ascribed "mysticism" or "mythology" to the Clark-Knight concept of capital, see Kirzner, *Essay on Capital*, p. 59.

36. Mises, *Human Action*, p. 515.

37. As Knight did in his well-known "Crusonia Plant" example (Frank H. Knight, "Diminishing Returns from Investment," *Journal of Political Economy* 52 [March 1944]: 29).

38. Mises, *Human Action*, p. 844.

39. See John R. Hicks, "Capital Controversies: Ancient and Modern," *American Economic Review* 64 (May 1974): 308–10. According to Hicks, "fundists" are those who see capital as something apart from the physical goods of which it happens to consist at a particular time. The "materialists" are those who refuse to see capital in any sense other than the physical goods

that make it up. Hicks's terminology here is quite unfortunate and may lead to a misunderstanding of his own thesis. From what has been said in the text, it would seem that Clark and Knight are what Hicks meant when he spoke of "fundists." It turns out, however, that Hicks classified them as "materialists"! The Austrian school (which is vehemently opposed to the Clark-Knight notion of capital as a self-perpetuating fund) turns out, in Hicks's classification, to be "fundist" because it viewed the stock of capital goods in terms of the multiperiod future plans in which they enter. The Clark-Knight notion of capital as a fund is therefore quite different from the Austrian notion of a fund. Clearly, in the Clark-Knight view, capital goods are not the representatives of *plans* for future production processes but rather permanent sources of automatic income flow.

40. See note 37 above.

41. Mises, *Human Action*, p. 263.

42. Ibid., p. 260.

43. Ibid., p. 94.

44. Ibid.

45. Ibid., pp. 263–64.

46. Ibid., p. 525.

47. Frank H. Knight, "Introduction," in Carl Menger, *Principles of Economics*, trans. James Dingwall and Bert F. Hoselitz (Glencoe, Ill.: Free Press, 1950), p. 25.

48. Mises, *Human Action*, p. 253.

49. Ibid., p. 536.

CHAPTER SIX

1. K. Lancaster, "The Dynamic Inefficiency of Capitalism," *Journal of Political Economy* 81 (September/October 1973): 1092.

2. "Absolute capital requirements may be so large that relatively few individuals or groups could secure the needed capital, or that entrants could secure it only at interest rates and other terms which placed them at a net cost disadvantage to established sellers" (J. S. Bain, *Barriers to New Competition* [Cambridge: Harvard University Press, 1956], p. 55).

3. For references to the literature on this see G. J. Stigler, "Imperfections in the Capital Market," *Journal of Political Economy* 75 (June 1967): 287–88.

4. E. S. Mason, *Economic Concentration and the Monopoly Problem* (Cambridge: Harvard University Press, 1967), p. 348.

5. See Bain, *Barriers to New Competition*, chap. 3.

6. See, e.g., A. A. Alchian, "Corporate Management and Property Rights," in *Economic Policy and the Regulation of Corporate Securities*, ed. H. G. Manne (Washington, D.C.: American Enterprise Institute, 1969), pp. 342–43.

7. On this see my *Competition and Entrepreneurship* (Chicago: University of Chicago Press, 1973), pp. 85 ff.

8. L. Mises, "Profit and Loss," in *Planning for Freedom*, 2d ed. (South Holland, Ill.: Libertarian Press, 1962), p. 109.

9. I. M. Kirzner, *Competition and Entrepreneurship*, p. 49.

10. L. Mises, *Human Action* (New Haven: Yale University Press, 1949), p. 254.

11. Ibid.

12. H. Demsetz, "The Technostructure, Forty-Six Years Later," *Yale Law Journal* 77 (1968): 805.

13. S. R. Shenoy, "The Sources of Monopoly," *New Individualist Review* 4 (Spring 1966): 42.

14. F. H. Knight, *Risk, Uncertainty and Profit* (New York: Houghton Mifflin, 1921), p. 274, note 1; see also D. M. Lamberton, *The Theory of Profit* (New York: A. M. Kelley, 1965), p. 50.

15. G. J. Stigler, "Imperfections in the Capital Market," *Journal of Political Economy* 75 (June 1967): 287–92.

16. Ibid., p. 288.

17. Ibid., p. 291.

18. See Stigler's remarks on Keynes's distinction between borrower's and lender's risk (ibid., p. 291).

19. J. K. Galbraith, *The New Industrial State* (New York: Houghton Mifflin, 1967), chaps. 5 and 6.

20. Shorey Peterson, "Corporate Control and Capitalism," *Quarterly Journal of Economics* 79 (February 1965): 1–24; A. A. Alchian, "Corporate Management."

21. See H. G. Manne, *Insider Trading and the Stock Market* (New York: Free Press, 1966), for a discussion of how corporate executives may be in a position to win pure entrepreneurial profits for themselves.

22. For critical discussion of earlier proposals concerning the allocation of capital in noncapitalist "competitive" systems, see F. A. Hayek, *Individualism and Economic Order* (London: Routledge and Kegan Paul, 1949), pp. 172–76, 200 ff.

CHAPTER SEVEN

1. W. J. Baumol, "Entrepreneurship in Economic Theory," *American Economic Review* 58 (May 1968): 64.

2. H. Leibenstein, "Entrepreneurship and Development," *American Economic Review* 58 (May 1968): 72.

3. For a survey see F. H. Hahn and R. C. O. Matthews, "The Theory of Economic Growth: A Survey," *Economic Journal* 74 (December 1964): 779–902.

4. Even Hicks's *Capital and Growth* (New York: Oxford University Press, 1965), in which the price theoretic implications of formal growth theory are pursued, is not concerned at all with entrepreneurship.

5. For a sampling of this literature see P. T. Bauer and B. S. Yamey, *The Economics of Under-developed Countries* (Chicago: University of Chicago Press, 1957), chap. 8; M. Abramovitz, "Economics of Growth," in *A Survey of Contemporary Economics* (Homewood, Ill.: Irwin, 1953), 2:157–62; H. G. Aubrey, "Industrial Investment Decisions: A Comparative Analysis," *Jour-*

nal of Economic History 15 (December 1955): 335–51; N. Rosenberg, "Capital Formation in Underdeveloped Countries," *American Economic Review* 50 (September 1960): 713–14; G. F. Papanek, "The Development of Entrepreneurship," *American Economic Review*, vol. 52 (May 1962).

6. See J. A. Schumpeter, *The Theory of Economic Development* (Cambridge: Harvard University Press, 1934).

7. See I. M. Kirzner, "Methodological Individualism, Market Equilibrium, and Market Process," *Il Politico* 32 (1967): 787–99.

8. Schumpeter, *Theory of Economic Development*, p. 64.

9. F. A. Hayek, *The Pure Theory of Capital* (London: Routledge and Kegan Paul, 1941), pp. 22 ff.; I. M. Kirzner, *An Essay on Capital* (New York: Augustus Kelly, 1966), p. 30; idem, *Market Theory and the Price System* (New York: Van Nostrand), pp. 311–20.

10. Schumpeter, *Theory of Economic Development*, p. 64.

11. P. A. Samuelson, *Economics*, 7th ed. (New York: McGraw-Hill), p. 725.

12. See H. Leibenstein, "Allocative Efficiency vs. 'X-Efficiency,'" *American Economic Review* 56 (June 1966): 392–415; "Entrepreneurship and Development," *American Economic Review* 58 (May 1968): 72–83.

13. Schumpeter, *Theory of Economic Development*, p. 154.

14. See on this the masterly passage in Hayek, *Individualism and Economic Order* (London: Routledge and Kegan Paul, 1949), pp. 201–3.

15. Schumpeter, *Theory of Economic Development*, pp. 138 ff.

CHAPTER EIGHT

1. F. A. Hayek, "Economics and Knowledge," *Economica*, n.s., 4, no. 13 (February 1937): 33–54.

2. G. J. Stigler, "The Xistence of X-Efficiency," *American Economic Review* 66 (March 1976): 216.

3. L. Mises, *Theory and History* (New Haven: Yale University Press, 1957), p. 268.

4. See Stigler, "Xistence of X-Efficiency," p. 215.

5. B. Croce, "On the Economic Principle," trans. in *International Economic Papers*, no. 3 (London and New York: Macmillan, 1953), p. 177.

6. I. M. Kirzner, *The Economic Point of View* (Princeton: Van Nostrand, 1960), pp. 169–72.

7. G. Tagliacozzo, "Croce and the Nature of Economic Science," *Quarterly Journal of Economics* 59, no. 3 (May 1945): 307–29.

8. L. Mises, *Human Action* (New Haven: Yale University Press, 1949), p. 95.

9. Ibid., pp. 102 ff.

10. Ibid.

11. F. H. Knight, *Risk, Uncertainty and Profit* (New York: Houghton Mifflin, 1921), pp. 225–26.

12. H. Leibenstein, "Allocative Efficiency vs. 'X-Efficiency,'" *American Economic Review* 56 (June 1966): 392–415; "Entrepreneurship and Develop-

ment," *American Economic Review* 58 (May 1969): 72–83; "Competition and X-Efficiency: Reply." (*Journal of Political Economy*) 81, no. 3 (May/June 1973): 765–77; "Aspects of the X-Efficiency Theory of the Firm," *Bell Journal of Economics* 6 (Autumn 1975): 580–606. See also H. Leibenstein, *Beyond Economic Man* (Cambridge: Harvard University Press, 1976).

13. Leibenstein, "Competition and X-Efficiency: Reply," p. 766.

14. Leibenstein, "Allocative Efficiency vs. 'X-Efficiency,'" p. 407.

15. Stigler, "Xistence of X-Efficiency."

16. See above, note 2.

17. Put differently, our perception of the impossibility of error does not depend on any "arbitrary" assumption of utility- or profit-maximizing behavior. Error is impossible because it is inconsistent with the postulate of purposeful action.

18. The possibility for *social* "inefficiency" of any kind, in such an errorless world, would, it must appear, then rest either on the possibility that high transaction costs make the "correction" in fact uneconomic or on the highly dubious notion of an omniscient observer from whose perspective the errorless (but imperfectly omniscient) members of society are overlooking valuable opportunities for improving their positions. On all this see further, I. M. Kirzner, *Competition and Entrepreneurship* (Chicago: University of Chicago Press, 1973), chap. 6. See also the final section of the present chapter.

19. Although the extent to which available opportunities *are* perceived is not at all unrelated to the concept of purposeful action. (See also pp. 28–32.)

20. The other reasons include the circumstances that, were one to discover someone whose superior alertness to profitable opportunities one wishes to hire, we would expect that other "alert one" to have already taken advantage of those opportunities or at least that he will anyway do so very shortly on his own account. (See above, p. 8.)

21. For further discussion of some of the issues raised in this and the following sections, see my *Competition and Entrepreneurship*, chaps. 2 and 3.

22. W. S. Jevons, *The Theory of Political Economy*, 4th ed. (1911; reprinted Pelican Books, 1970), p. 137.

23. On all this, see Hayek's pioneering contribution in his 1937 paper (see above, note 1). See also above, chap. 2.

24. Leibenstein, "Entrepreneurship and Development," and Kirzner, *Competition and Entrepreneurship*, p. 46 n.

25. Leibenstein, "Allocative Efficiency vs. 'X-Efficiency,'" p. 413.

26. L. Robbins, "The Representative Firm," *Economic Journal* 38 (September 1928): 387–404.

27. Ibid., p. 391.

28. See A. Marshall, *Principles of Economics*, 8th ed. (London: Macmillan, 1920), pp. 432 ff.

29. Robbins, "The Representative Firm," p. 393.

30. Stigler, "Xistence of X-Efficiency," pp. 214 ff.

31. Ibid., p. 215.

32. Robbins, "The Representative Firm," pp. 392–96.

33. See, e.g., G. Calabresi, "Transaction Costs, Resource Allocation and Liability Rules: A Comment," *Journal of Law and Economics* 11 (April 1968): 68.

CHAPTER NINE

1. See, e.g., F. A. Hayek, "Economics and Knowledge," and idem, "The Use of Knowledge in Society," *American Economic Review* 35 (September 1945): 519–30, both reprinted in *Individualism and Economic Order* (London: Routledge and Kegan Paul, 1949); D. M. Lamberton, ed., *Economics of Information and Knowledge* (New York: Penguin Books, 1971); J. Hirshleifer, "Where Are We in the Theory of Information?" *American Economic Review* 63 (May 1973): 31–39.

2. F. A. Hayek, *The Counter-revolution of Science* (Glencoe, Ill.: Free Press, 1955), pp. 26–27.

3. Ibid., p. 33.

4. Ibid.

5. Ibid.

6. G. L. S. Shackle, "On the Meaning and Measure of Uncertainty: I," *Metroeconomica* 4 (1952): 87–104, as reprinted in *Uncertainty in Economics and Other Reflections* (Cambridge: Cambridge University Press, 1955), pp. 17–18.

7. K. E. Boulding, "Knowledge as a Commodity," in *Beyond Economics: Essays on Society, Religion and Ethics* (Ann Arbor: University of Michigan Press, 1968), p. 146.

8. Hayek, "Economics and Knowledge."

9. Shackle has suggested that this assumption came from "adopting codes appropriate to the science of *inanimate* events, where the question does not arise how massive bodies come to be aware of their duty to attract each other with a force proportionate to the inverse square of their distance" (G. L. S. Shackle, *Epistemics and Economics* [Cambridge: Cambridge University Press, 1972], p. 53).

10. K. E. Boulding, "The Economics of Knowledge and the Knowledge of Economics," *American Economic Review* 56 (May 1966): 3.

11. M. Hollis and E. J. Nell, *Rational Economic Man* (Cambridge: Cambridge University Press, 1975), p. 228.

12. G. J. Stigler, "The Economics of Information," *Journal of Political Economy* 69 (June 1961): 213–25.

13. G. J. Stigler, "Imperfections in the Capital Market," *Journal of Political Economy* 75 (June 1967): 291; see also G. J. Stigler, "The Xistence of X-Efficiency," *American Economic Review* 66 (March 1976): 213–16.

14. Shackle, *Epistemics and Economics*, p. 156.

15. Ibid., p. 76.

16. See note 8.

17. J. M. Buchanan, "What Should Economists Do?" *Southern Economic Journal* 30 (January 1964): 213–22.

18. See Hayek, "Use of Knowledge in Society."

19. I. M. Kirzner, *Competition and Entrepreneurship* (Chicago: University of Chicago Press, 1973).

CHAPTER TEN

1. See for example F. H. Knight, "Profit," in *Encyclopedia of the Social Sciences* (New York: Macmillan, 1934); J. F. Weston, "Profit as the Payment for the Function of Uncertainty-Bearing," *Journal of Business* 22 (April 1949): 106–18; J. F. Weston, "The Profit Concept and Theory: A Restatement," *Journal of Political Economy* 62 (April 1954): 152–70; M. Bronfenbrenner, "A Reformulation of Naive Profit Theory," *Southern Economic Journal* 26 (April 1960): 300–309. See also I. M. Kirzner, *Competition and Entrepreneurship* (Chicago: University of Chicago Press, 1973), pp. 75 ff.

2. For an important recent treatment of entrepreneurship emphasizing its human capital aspects, see T. W. Schultz, "The Value of the Ability to Deal with Disequilibrium," *Journal of Economic Literature* 13 (September 1975): 827–46.

3. G. L. S. Shackle, *Decision, Order and Time in Human Affairs* (Cambridge: Cambridge University Press, 1969), pp. 252 ff.

4. Kirzner, *Competition and Entrepreneurship*.

5. J. A. Schumpeter, *The Theory of Economic Development* (Cambridge: Harvard University Press, 1934, trans. from German edition, 1911, by R. Opie), p. 160.

6. W. Stanley Jevons, *The Theory of Political Economy* (1871; reprinted Penguin Books, 1970), p. 137.

7. L. Mises, *Human Action*, 1st ed. (New Haven: Yale University Press, 1949), p. 253.

8. See Kirzner, *Competition and Entrepreneurship*, pp. 30–43 for more extended discussion of this; see also later in this chapter.

9. Menger was fully aware of the possibility of error in valuation. See C. Menger, *Principles of Economics*, trans. and ed. J. Dingwall and Bert F. Hoselitz (Glencoe, Ill.: Free Press, 1950), p. 120.

10. L. Mises, "Profit and Loss," in *Planning for Freedom* (South Holland, Ill.: Libertarian Press, 1962), pp. 125 ff.

11. So that we must, it seems, modify our earlier statement that eventually Menger's Law will ensure that the full value of the superior catch comes to be imputed to the physical resources that go into building the boat. Menger's Law, it now appears, will impute the output value to the *entire* resource complex, with Crusoe's new knowledge seen as an integral component of that complex.

12. See further Kirzner, *Competition and Entrepreneurship*, pp. 30 ff.

13. L. Robbins, *An Essay on the Nature and Significance of Economic Science* (London: Macmillan, 1932; 2d ed., 1935).

14. It is true, of course, that within the concept of allocation it is possible to incorporate the deliberate search for and discovery of new information that

may alter the perceived ends-means framework. Such search occurs *within* some accepted (original) framework of ends and means. The assertion in the text refers to spontaneous discovery of error in the framework.

15. It is of some interest that Robbins's own concept owed a good deal to Mises; see *Nature and Significance*, 2d ed., pp. xvi, 16, n. 1.

16. L. Lachmann, "From Mises to Shackle: An Essay," *Journal of Economic Literature* 14 (March 1976): 54–62.

17. Of course, the element of fortune that enters here relates not to the circumstance that external events luckily turn out to fit Crusoe's hunch, but to the circumstance that Crusoe luckily adopted the hunch that correctly envisaged the future.

18. Of course there are well-known special problems in valuing a resource able to be used again and again without wear and tear. See, e.g., Mises, *Human Action*, p. 128.

19. See chap. 2.

20. See chap. 9.

21. For an earlier—albeit incomplete—recognition of this parallelism, see my *Competition and Entrepreneurship*, pp. 31 ff.

22. See Kirzner, *Competition and Entrepreneurship*, chap. 2, for a discussion of this process.

23. If it is argued that our participant *anticipated* a price differential that he proceeded to exploit at the first instant of its occurrence, then the question in the text may need to be reworded to refer to profitable activity in the relevant forward markets.

24. Shackle, *Decision, Order and Time*, pp. 267 ff. I am indebted to Professor S. C. Littlechild for this reference.

25. Schumpeter, *Theory of Economic Development*, p. 143; see also F. Machlup, *The Economics of Sellers' Competition* (Baltimore: Johns Hopkins Press, 1952), pp. 226 ff.

CHAPTER ELEVEN

1. J. S. Mill, *Principles of Political Economy*, ed. William J. Ashley (London, 1923), p. 218.

2. See G. Myrdal, *The Political Element in the Development of Economic Theory* (Cambridge: Harvard University Press, 1954), pp. 71 ff.; R. Schlatter, *Private Property: The History of an Idea* (New Brunswick: Rutgers University Press, 1951), chap. 7; C. B. Macpherson, "The Social Bearing of Locke's Political Theory," *Western Political Quarterly* 7 (1954): 1–22; A. Ryan, "Locke and the Dictatorship of the Bourgeoisie," *Political Studies* 13 (1965): 219–30.

3. Myrdal, *Political Element*. Strictly speaking, Locke did not actually assert that, by mixing his labor with a nature-given resource, he has thereby "produced" the result. However, he has certainly been understood as having implied as much. Thus, commenting on the notion "that, if a man 'makes' something, it is his," Oliver cites Locke as having given expression to this

idea in his labor theory of property rights (H. M. Oliver, *A Critique of Socioeconomic Goals* [Bloomington: Indiana University Press, 1954], p. 27). This is further discussed later in this chapter.

4. M. Friedman, *Price Theory: A Provisional Text* (Chicago: Aldine, 1962), p. 196.

5. M. Friedman, *Capitalism and Freedom* (Chicago: University of Chicago Press, 1962), p. 167. On this see also Oliver, *Critique of Socioeconomic Goals*, p. 37. In an extensive critique of Oliver's discussion, M. N. Rothbard, *Power and Market, Government and the Economy* (Menlo Park, Calif.: Institute for Humane Studies, 1970), p. 183, makes it clear that he supports the same underlying ethic.

6. Friedman, *Price Theory*, p. 196.

7. J. B. Clark, *The Distribution of Wealth* (New York and London: Macmillan, 1899), p. 3.

8. J. Locke, *An Essay concerning the True Original, Extent and End of Civil Government*, paragraph 27.

9. J. A. Schumpeter, *The Theory of Economic Development* (Cambridge: Harvard University Press, 1934), p. 76.

10. On this see, for example, the discussion in F. Machlup, *The Economics of Sellers' Competition* (Baltimore: Johns Hopkins University Press, 1952), pp. 226–28. See also chapter 10 in this book.

11. Schumpeter, *Theory of Economic Development*, p. 143.

12. Ibid.

13. See Schumpeter, *Theory of Economic Development*, p. 153; Machlup, *Economics of Sellers' Competition*, p. 226; Knight, *Risk, Uncertainty and Profit*, p. 271.

14. On all this see my *Competition and Entrepreneurship* (Chicago: University of Chicago Press, 1973), chap. 2.

15. Knight, *Risk, Uncertainty and Profit*, p. 271; emphasis on the central clause supplied. Similar statements are to be found in F. Hawley, *Enterprise and the Productive Process* (New York: Putnam, 1907), pp. 85, 102, 112, 127.

16. J. P. Day, "Locke on Property," *Philosophical Quarterly* 16 (1966): 207–20, reprinted in *Life, Liberty, and Property: Essays on Locke's Political Ideas*, ed. G. J. Schochet (Belmont, Calif.: Wadsworth, 1971), p. 109. All page references will be to this reprint.

17. See Day, "Locke on Property," pp. 109–10; and see note 3 above.

18. Locke, *Essay*, paragraph 33.

19. Ibid., paragraph 28.

20. Day, "Locke on Property," pp. 113 ff.

21. On all this, see ibid.

22. Myrdal, *Political Element*, p. 74. It should be noted, however, that just as the later classical economists used expressions like "trouble," "sacrifice," and "pain" synonymously with "labor"—and are for this reason described by Myrdal as having viewed labor strictly as the "trouble caused by effort" (ibid.)—so too does Locke occasionally (see paragraphs 30, 34) seem to iden-

tify the justification for ownership of the product of one's labor as resting on one's having been he "who takes pains about it."

23. See the reference in E. Halévy, *The Growth of Philosophic Radicalism* (Boston: Beacon Press, 1955), p. 45, to Hume's view that "we are the proprietors of the fruits of our garden, and of the dung of our flock by virtue of the normal operation of the laws of association."

24. See Oliver, *A Critique of Socioeconomic Goals* (Bloomington: Indiana University Press, 1954), p. 33; see also the sources referred to above in notes 4 and 7.

25. See A. C. Cutler, "Some Concepts of Human Rights and Obligations in Classical Protestantism," in *Natural Law and Natural Rights,* ed. A. L. Harding (Dallas: Southern Methodist University Press, 1955), p. 16.

26. I. Kant, *Philosophy of Law*, ed. Hastie (Edinburgh, 1887), p. 92.

27. Schlatter, *Private Property*, p. 256.

28. Ibid.

29. On the question of the influence of Locke's labor theory of property on the later classical labor theory of value, there has been controversy. Myrdal, *Political Element*, pp. 71 ff.; Halévy, *Growth of Philosophic Radicalism*, p. 44; and W. A. Weisskopf, *The Psychology of Economics* (Chicago: University of Chicago Press, 1955), pp. 22 ff., 145, all assert a direct influence. See however, J. A. Schumpeter, *History of Economic Analysis* (London: Oxford University Press, 1954), pp. 120, 310–11; see also I. M. Kirzner, *The Economic Point of View* (Princeton: Van Nostrand, 1960), pp. 25, 190, nn. 8, 9.

30. Myrdal, *Political Element*, p. 72; see especially Myrdal's reference to Rodbertus.

31. Weisskopf, *Psychology of Economics*, pp. 25, 145.

32. For further discussion of the entrepreneurial element in the decisions of factor owners, see below, pp. 197–99.

33. Oliver, *Critique of Socioeconomic Goals*, p. 37.

34. Ibid., p. 42.

35. Samuelson's discussion is in his "Intertemporal Price Equilibrium: A Prologue to the Theory of Speculation," *Weltwirtschaftliches Archiv* 79 (December 1957): 209. For further comment, see Kirzner, *Competition and Entrepreneurship*, chap. 6.

36. See Schlatter, *Private Property*, p. 191, n. 2, for references to use made of Locke's labor theory to condemn the ethical status of entrepreneurial profit.

37. See further Kirzner, *Competition and Entrepreneurship*, chap. 2.

CHAPTER TWELVE

1. R. Nozick, *Anarchy, State, and Utopia* (New York: Basic Books, 1974), pp. 178–82.

2. Ibid., p. 153.

3. Ibid., pp. 160–64. See also Nozick's extensive discussion of the voluntariness of market transactions, pp. 262–65.

4. See the discussion of this point in J. S. Mill, *Principles of Political Economy*, Ashley ed. (London: Longmans, Green, 1909), pp. 796 ff.; M. N. Rothbard, *Power and Market* (Menlo Park: Institute for Humane Studies, 1970), p. 34; H. B. Acton, *The Morals of Markets* (London: Longmans, 1971), p. 4; Nozick, ibid., p. 152. See also the discussion in G. Tullock, *The Social Dilemma* (Blacksburg: University Publications, 1974), p. 11.

5. F. A. Hayek, "Economics and Knowledge," *Economica* 4 (1937), in *Individualism and Economic Order* (London: Routledge and Kegan Paul, 1949), p. 42.

6. L. Mises, *Human Action* (New Haven: Yale University Press, 1949), p. 249. See also F. H. Hahn, *On the Notion of Equilibrium in Economics* (Cambridge: Cambridge University Press, 1973), pp. 7 ff.

7. It ought perhaps to be emphasized that it is not only a relatively small class of business entrepreneurs the justice of whose acquisitions are being questioned. As Mises pointed out (*Human Action*, p. 253), every acting individual displays entrepreneurial characteristics. Since almost all market transactions involve less than perfect omniscience, the errors they reflect might seem to cast a shadow over the justice of *all* market transfers. Pure entrepreneurial profit may be present, to some extent, in any sale and in any purchase.

8. For some discussion of the morality of profits, and of the arguments of its critics, see H. B. Acton, *The Morals of Markets* (London: Longmans, 1971), chap. 2.

9. See Mises, "Profit and Loss," in *Planning for Freedom* (South Holland, Ill.: Libertarian Press, 1952), pp. 108 ff.; see also I. M. Kirzner, *Competition and Entrepreneurship* (Chicago: University of Chicago Press, 1973), pp. 85 ff.

10. To do this is again to deliberately accept an uncertainty—namely, the possibility that, *without expenditure of the resources needed to remove the possibility of error*, error may occur—concerning which accurate knowledge is simply unavailable. There is no way, without expenditure of those resources, to know whether error will or will not occur.

11. We prefer, for present purposes, not to press this position in even more uncompromising form, which might maintain that one who has been deceived has, again, merely refrained deliberately from spending the resources necessary to ensure against deception.

12. See chapter 8. The view denying scope for error within economic analysis has been stated by G. J. Stigler, "The Xistence of X-Efficiency," *American Economic Review* 66 (March 1976): 216.

13. Despite our insistence on the prevalence of genuine error, we must of course readily grant that many cases in which an entrepreneur appears to be exploiting the ignorance of others *do* result merely from the deliberate judgment of others, in the face possibly of the very same information available to

entrepreneurs, concerning a future that, they are well aware, is highly uncertain.

14. G. S. Bower and A. K. Turner, *The Law of Actionable Misrepresentation* (London: Butterworths, 1974), p. 104.

15. S. E. Williams, *Kerr on Fraud and Mistake*, 6th ed. (London: Sweet and Maxwell, 1929), p. 76.

16. For a fascinating pioneer discussion of both the morality and the law surrounding exchanges made on the basis of incomplete or faulty information, see Gulian G. Verplanck, *An Essay on the Doctrine of Contracts: Being an Inquiry How Contracts Are Affected in Law and Morals by Concealment, Error, or Inadequate Price* (New York, 1825). Verplanck showed remarkable awareness of the element of pure (entrepreneurial) profit in all exchanges and of how this implies the impracticality of a legal system that insists on "full disclosure" in all exchanges.

17. Bower and Turner, *Law of Actionable Misrepresentation*, p. 106.

18. Williams, *Kerr on Fraud and Mistake*, p. 76. An oft-cited opinion of Cardozo does, however, appear to argue that the law simply reflects the "morals of the market place"; so that where, as in the case of partners, morality calls for loyalty to one another, or where, as in the case of trustees, morality call for not "honesty alone, but the punctilio of an honor the most sensitive," this should and will find expression in the law. See the quote in H. Manne, *Insider Trading and the Stock Market* (New York: Free Press, 1966), pp. 20–21.

19. See Mises, *Human Action*, p. 147. For a recent plea not to reach conclusions concerning the morality of particular economic practices (specifically, insider trading) before thoroughly exploring the welfare consequences of these practices, see Manne, *Insider Trading*, p. 15.

20. See, e.g., Manne, *Insider Trading*, p. 18.

21. W. J. Ashley on the "Just Price" in *Dictionary of Political Economy*, ed. R. H. I. Palgrave (London: Macmillan, 1896), 2:500.

22. Nozick, *Anarchy, State, and Utopia*, p. 262 (italics in original).

23. Ibid., p. 161.

24. B. W. Dempsey, "Just Price in a Functional Economy," *American Economic Review* 25 (September 1935): 471–86, reprinted in *Economic Thought: A Historical Anthology*, ed. J. A. Gherity (New York: Random House, 1965); R. de Roover, "The Concept of the Just Price: Theory and Economic Policy," *Journal of Economic History* 18 (December 1958): 418–34, reprinted in ibid.; J. A. Schumpeter, *History of Economic Analysis* (New York: Oxford University Press, 1954), part 2, chap. 2; J. T. Noonan, *The Scholastic Analysis of Usury* (Cambridge: Harvard University Press, 1957); S. Hollander, "On the Interpretation of the Just Price," *Kyklos* 18 (1965): 4; M. N. Rothbard, "New Light on the Prehistory of the Austrian School," in *The Foundations of Modern Austrian Economics*, ed. E. Dolan (Kansas City: Sheed and Ward, 1976).

25. See, e.g., the view of Cajetan, cited in de Roover, "Concept of the Just Price," p. 29.

26. Hollander, "On the Interpretation of the Just Price," p. 625.

27. See de Roover, "Concept of the Just Price," p. 28; Hollander, "On the Interpretation of the Just Price," p. 624.

28. See Hollander, "On the Interpretation of the Just Price," p. 624.

29. H. M. Oliver, *A Critique of Socioeconomic Goals* (Bloomington: Indiana University Press, 1954), p. 42.

30. See above chapter 11, and the discussion there of the views of Oliver.

31. It seems particularly important to distinguish the finders-keepers ethic from the ethic of "first come, first served" that Vickrey, for one, has described as of dubious quality. W. Vickrey, "An Exchange of Questions between Economics and Philosophy" (1953), reprinted in *Economic Justice*, ed. E. S. Phelps (Penguin Books, 1973), p. 58.

32. The notion of the discoverer as creator should, of course, be linked with the view of F. H. Knight, that it is not the factors of production that produce the output, but the entrepreneur who decides to enlist the services of these factors (F. H. Knight, *Risk, Uncertainty and Profit* [New York: Houghton Mifflin, 1921], p. 271). See also F. B. Hawley, *Enterprise and the Productive Process* (New York: Putnam, 1907), pp. 85, 102, 112, 127.

33. See below, p. 220 for a discussion of the (very limited) recognition of the ethical significance of *discovery* in Nozick's system.

34. It was Schumpeter (*Theory of Economic Development* [Cambridge: Harvard University Press, 1934], translated from the German work published in 1911) who emphasized the *creative* role of the entrepreneur. It should perhaps be noted that the writer has elsewhere demurred from Schumpeter's view of the entrepreneur as *disrupting* earlier states of repose (I. M. Kirzner, *Competition and Entrepreneurship* [Chicago: University of Chicago Press, 1973], pp. 72 ff.). See also above, chapter 7. The position taken here in the text is not, I believe, inconsistent with my earlier insistence on the *equilibrating* role of the entrepreneur, seen as responding to the existence of as yet unexpected opportunities. For individuals in a society, of whom none has as yet perceived the existence of a profitable opportunity, this opportunity may properly be said not yet to exist: its first discoverer may be properly seen as its creator. Nonetheless, the theorist analyzing the social role of entrepreneurial discovery is surely entitled to point out that, before the discovery of a productive opportunity, its existence did mean that society has failed in some sense to achieve its greatest possible level of output. It is not improper, at *this* level of discourse, to insist on the entrepreneur as *responding* to the opportunities "out there," of which he becomes aware.

35. See note 9.

36. See Kirzner, *Competition and Entrepreneurship*, chaps. 1 and 2.

37. P. A. Samuelson has derided the social utility of the vast speculators' profits won by entrepreneurs several seconds more nimble than their fellows in assessing new information (*Weltwirtschaftliches Archiv* 79 [December

1957]: 209). One may question the validity of Samuelson's argument at the utilitarian level (see, e.g., Kirzner, *Competition and Entrepreneurship*, pp. 224; also above pp. 196–97), while recognizing the possibility that one may *not* choose to extend one's finders-keepers ethic (if, indeed, one subscribes to it at all) to defend the morality of the case discussed by Samuelson.

38. To put the point somewhat differently, the discussion in the text *has* sought to show that *all* market transactions can be seen as in no way involving imperfect consent. This was done on the basis of the insight that all entrepreneurial gain reflects not exploitation of error, but creation (i.e., finding) of new value. At the same time this may *not*, of itself, be seen as *justifying* all cases of such gain, since one may not wish to recognize the justice of *every* finder, under *all* conceivable circumstances, becoming a keeper.

39. Nozick, *Anarchy, State, and Utopia*, pp. 150–55.

40. Ibid., p. 151.

41. See in the following section for a discussion of the limited degree to which Nozick appears ready to recognize an ethical role for pure discovery.

42. For the biblical version of an entitlement theory based on *divine* Creation, see Psalms 24:1, 2; 115:16.

43. It may be objected, both to the argument of the text itself and to its application of the finders-keepers ethic, that if I discover new, hitherto unnoticed value in my neighbor's property, that the additional value ought, according to the finders-keepers ethic, be mine *without* any transfer of the property at all. To the extent that the new value can be consumed without violating the rights of the neighbor, this seems not unreasonable. (One thinks of the legal questions raised when it was discovered, through the invention of flying, that air rights over land were more valuable than hitherto realized.) In general, where the newly discovered value cannot be consumed without violating existing rights, it will be in the interest of the discoverer to buy up *those* rights, in order to enjoy the new values *he* has discovered.

44. John Locke, *An Essay concerning the True Original, Extent and End of Civil Government*, chap. 5, sec. 27.

45. Nozick, *Anarchy, State, and Utopia*, p. 175.

46. Ibid., p. 178.

47. Ibid., pp. 179–80 and the footnote on p. 179.

48. Nozick's position on this point has potentially far-reaching implications for the justice of monopoly positions in production obtained through sole acquisition of needed resources. For a discussion *not* involving the issue of the justice of such monopoly cases, but from the perspective of their alleged harm to society, see Kirzner, *Competition and Entrepreneurship*, pp. 236–42, where a variety of considerations are weighed against one another. The discussion in the subsequent paragraphs in the text, questioning Nozick's views, points not to any vindication of monopoly producers from possible charges that their activity in some sense harms society, but to a defense of the moral legitimacy of monopoly resource ownership even were it to be

shown that the rest of society would, in some sense, be better off were such monopoly not present.

49. Nozick, *Anarchy, State, and Utopia*, p. 182.

50. Ibid., p. 181.

CHAPTER THIRTEEN

1. G. J. Stigler, "Reflections on Liberty," in *The Citizen and the State* (Chicago: University of Chicago Press, 1975), p. 14.

2. This was very clearly recognized in the earliest writings in which the economist's view of choice was spelled out. See L. Robbins, *The Nature and Significance of Economic Science*, 2d ed. (London: Macmillan, 1935), pp. 12, 24, 33, 46; F. H. Knight, "The Nature of Economic Science in Some Recent Discussion," *American Economic Review* 24 (June 1934): 229.

3. See, on this, I. M. Kirzner, *The Economic Point of View* (Princeton: Van Nostrand, 1960), pp. 161 ff.; idem, *Competition and Entrepreneurship* (Chicago: University of Chicago Press, 1973), pp. 33 ff.

4. See, e.g., G. L. S. Shackle, *Epistemics and Economics: A Critique of Economic Doctrines* (Cambridge: Cambridge University Press, 1972), for countless observations on this matter (many of them indexed under "choice").

5. L. M. Lachmann, "From Mises to Shackle: An Essay on Austrian Economics and the Kaleidic Society," *Journal of Economic Literature* 14 (March 1976): 54–62.

6. It is true that the given framework of ends and means is seen as that of the decision maker himself—the goal referred to in the text is the agent's "own" goal—but freedom is not, in the narrow view, referred back to the choice process by which that framework came to have been adopted as the relevant one.

7. See Kirzner, *Competition and Entrepreneurship*, pp. 33 ff.

8. The distinction drawn here between the narrow economist's view on freedom, and the broader entrepreneurial view has not, to my knowledge, been made in the literature. In the philosophical literature, it seems rather clear, many writers had the broader view in mind, apparently without dreaming of the possibility of the narrower view. Many of the writers cited by Mortimer J. Adler in chapter 24 of his *Idea of Freedom* (Garden City, N.Y.: Doubleday, 1958), "Creativity through Choice as an Element in the Meaning of Self-Determination," appear to fall into this class. Among economists, F. H. Knight, whose writings on freedom have been the most voluminous, complex, and difficult, appeared possibly to have at least glimpsed the broader view in a number of passages. "In economic discussion liberty means the right of the individual to choose his own ends and the means or procedure most effective for realizing them" (F. H. Knight, *Freedom and Reform* [New York: Harper, 1947], p. 377). "In practical application, the doctrine of maximum individual freedom necessitates . . . that the individual is the final judge of the *means* to his own happiness, as well as of the result" (ibid., p. 2). Isaiah Berlin has explored J. S. Mill's views on human freedom in terms that

perhaps suggest the importance of the distinction argued in this paper. Berlin attributes to Mill a view of freedom that sees man as "The seeker of ends, . . . with the corollary that . . . the larger the field of interplay between individuals, the greater the opportunities of the new and the unexpected; the more numerous the possibilities for altering his own character in some fresh or unexplored direction" (I. Berlin, "John Stuart Mill and the Ends of Life," in *Four Essays on Liberty* [New York: Oxford University Press, 1969], p. 178). "Mill believes," Berlin maintains, "that man is spontaneous, that he has freedom of choice, that he moulds his own character . . . Mill's entire view of human nature turns out to rest not on the notion of the repetition of an identical pattern, but on his perception of human lives as subject to perpetual incompleteness, self-transformation, and novelty" (ibid., p. 189).

9. A clear example is that offered by T. G. Moore's interesting suggestion for measuring the degree of freedom in a society. Moore's thesis is "that freedom can be defined in terms of welfare. A change in the cost of action . . . can be considered to be a movement toward freedom if it increases welfare. . . . If the cost to the individual of performing some action is lowered without affecting the cost to others, then we will consider that a movement toward a freer society" (T. G. Moore, "An Economic Analysis of the Concept of Freedom," *Journal of Political Economy* 77 [July/August 1969], pp. 532 ff.).

10. F. A. Hayek, *The Constitution of Liberty* (Chicago: University of Chicago Press, 1960), pp. 16 ff.

11. F. Machlup, "Liberalism and the Choice of Freedoms," in *Roads to Freedom: Essays in Honor of Friedrich A. von Hayek*, ed. E. Streissler (London: Routledge and Kegan Paul, 1969), pp. 124 ff.

12. On some of the difficulties in Knight's discussions of freedom, see Machlup, ibid., pp. 129 ff.; Hayek, *Constitution of Liberty*, p. 422, n. 7.

13. J. Locke, *Essay concerning Human Understanding*, vol. 1, book 2, chap. 21, sec. 8. See the discussion of Locke's view in M. J. Adler, *The Idea of Freedom*, pp. 115 ff.

14. F. H. Knight, "The Meaning of Freedom," in *The Philosophy of American Democracy*, ed. C. M. Perry (Chicago: University of Chicago Press, 1943), p. 65.

15. Machlup, "Liberalism and the Choice of Freedoms," p. 130.

16. Stigler, "Reflections on Liberty."

17. R. M. Hare, *Freedom and Reason* (Oxford: Clarendon Press, 1963), p. 3.

18. B. Blanshard, *Reason and Analysis* (LaSalle, Ill.: Open Court, 1973), p. 493.

19. F. A. Hayek, "The Use of Knowledge in Society," *American Economic Review* 35 (September 1945): 519–30.

20. Hayek, *Constitution of Liberty*, p. 29.

21. Ibid., p. 31.

Index

DATE DUE